THE INDIVIDUATED SELF

THE INDIVIDUATED SELF

Cervantes and the
Emergence of the Individual

by

John G. Weiger

Ohio University Press
Athens, Ohio

Library of Congress Cataloging in Publication Data

Weiger, John G
    The individuated self.

    1. Cervantes Saavedra, Miguel de, 1547-1616—
Knowledge—Psychology. 2. Cervantes Saavedra, Miguel
de, 1547-1616—Characters. I. Title.
PQ6358.P7W4   863'.3   78-13019
ISBN 0-8214-0396-6

For MARK
my son,
but as well
hijo de sus obras

Cervantes, the greatest poet of the imaginary knowledge of man

—Jacques Maritain

CONTENTS

Preface

During a recent stay in Spain I was advised to be prepared for *el día del libro*, the day of the book. On this day each year, booksellers throughout much of Spain display their volumes in front of their establishments, in malls, in parks, beside vendors of lottery tickets and at the entrances to movie theaters. The date of this annual homage to literature is the twenty-third of April. I remarked casually that I presumed the event to be in commemoration of the death of Cervantes who, as did Shakespeare (although the difference in calendars in reality separates the occasions by ten days), died on April 23 in 1616. My Spanish companions were amazed. Hardly any Spaniard would know that fact, I was told. The judgment may be harsh, for the well-educated Spaniard does indeed carry this datum in his head. (Upon reflection, how many Americans can give us a similar piece of information about, say, Melville or Whitman, not to mention O'Neill or Hemingway, much less Shakespeare or Shaw?) I would have dismissed the incident as not worthy of recollection had I not been presented with the other side of the coin a few months later.

The occasion was a more boisterous one and, mindful of the previous experience, I was moved to boast (with much exaggeration) that I could recite *Don Quixote* by heart. Encouraged to do so, I began, "*En un lugar de la Mancha, de cuyo nombre no quiero acordarme, no ha mucho tiempo que vivía, un hidalgo. . . .*" My friends, none of whom had a university education, roared in amusement at my recitation of the opening words of Cervantes' masterpiece. "Ah, that we all know by heart too!"

No doubt they did. And the contrast between the two incidents reflects more, I think, than the difference between a dry piece of history and a line which they may have had to memorize in primary school. What had remained fixed in the minds of my Spanish friends was perhaps the most familiar, but more importantly, the most mysterious sentence in Cervantes' long novel. It has been explicated by many scholars, and in the present book we, too, shall have a go at it: "In a place of La Mancha whose name I don't care to recall, there lived not long ago, a gentleman. . . ." The sentence which, my friends assure me, is unforgettable, initiates the story of "a gentleman" from "a place," and the author himself doesn't wish to remember the name of the place. As for the gentleman, we learn very quickly that the author doesn't know that name either, and that it matters little. Surely one of the reasons *Don Quixote* is the masterpiece it is has to do with this beginning: not the chronicle of a great king, nor the saga of an epic hero. Satire and parody aside, we are embarking upon the reading of the story of "a gentleman," *a person*. An individual? There lay the challenge to the ordinary reader: if the protagonist is not to be endowed with superior characteristics, and if it is equally clear that he is not of a base class worthy only of contemptuous ridicule, what will distinguish him from other gentlemen? In a word, who is he? More intriguing is the possibility that we will witness his individuation.

Herman Wouk has written that Cervantes "moved the art [of narrative] away from high life and the beautiful people to all life and to all people. . . . [Cervantes] looked to ordinary life rather than to high life for his substance. In this—only in this—he surpassed the greatest of secular writers, Shakespeare. . . . The common man is there in Shakespeare, and brilliantly there in Bottom, in Feste the Jester, in the Gravedigger, the Porter, even, we may say, in Malvolio, but he is comic relief out of a lower order. Shakespeare knew that tiresome open commercial literary secret, that the groundlings love a lord. In this Cervantes was more nearly modern. . . ."[1] As we shall see from several vantage points, Cervantes appears more modern in a variety of ways. A recent work concerned with literature and the individual suggests that the prose of Swift and Smollett "marks, in a premonition of Romanticism, the isolation and the journey into solitude which attends upon the intensification of the individual sensibility."[2] Leaving aside the reference to a nineteenth-century movement, we shall note that Cervantes not only has understood the enduring metaphor of the journey in his probing of the individual—in this Homer and Dante are of deeper influence than the more frequently mentioned books of chivalry—but he has as well intuitively perceived the psychological effects upon the individual sensibility which isolation may produce.

"Loneliness, far from being a rare and curious phenomenon . . . is the central and inevitable fact of human existence," Thomas Wolfe has written.[3] Although we may dispute the absolute nature of the assertion, we cannot quarrel with the basic perception, namely, how integral the fact of being alone is to human existence generally. Cervantes long ago grasped this fundamental characteristic of the individual and examined it from a number of perspectives, as we shall discuss in our chapter on this phenomenon.

To write another book on Cervantes is equivalent to a similar undertaking about Shakespeare. The question to be raised is not why, for the answer lies not in this volume but in the greatness of the artist who still today engages the mind of his most recent readers. And therein lies the challenge: how shall I respond to this great artistry? Mark Van Doren has put it so well: *Don Quixote*, he declares, "is both simple and mysterious. The sign of its simplicity is that it can be summarized in a few sentences. The sign of its mysteriousness is that it can be talked about forever."[4] Indeed, if nothing else, the present volume justifies Van Doren's observation for, leaving to one side the ultimate merits of my own contribution, the continuing mystery of Cervantes' kaleidoscopic vision and representation of humanity are the real reason why someone has been moved to write "another" book on Cervantes. And it will hardly be the last book on Cervantes, much less the last word. As Van Doren so clearly observes, "a strange thing happens to [*Don Quixote's*] readers. They do not read the same book. Or if they do, they have different theories about it. . . . Yet it survives them all, as any masterpiece must do. . . ."[5]

Accordingly, there is interest for us, as we prepare to examine the nature of the individual in Cervantes' works, in the following assessment by the renowned contemporary Argentine writer, Jorge Luis Borges: "The adventures of the *Quixote* are not so well planned, the slow and antithetical dialogues . . . offend us by their improbability, but there is no doubt that Cervantes knew Don Quixote well and could believe in him. Our belief in the novelist's belief makes up for any negligence or defect in the work. What does it matter if the episodes are unbelievable or awkward when we realize that the author planned them, not to challenge our credibility, but *to define his characters*?"[6] As will become plain in my second chapter, I do not share Borges' evaluation of Cervantes' alleged awkwardness, but my purpose in citing this opinion is to bring out that even from this perspective a recognition of the importance of character definition stands out. On another occasion, Borges suggested that "Cervantes was no stylist (at least in the modern acoustic-decorative sense of the word) and he was *too interested by the destinies* of Quixote and Sancho to allow himself to be distracted by his own voice."[7] Once again, repeated passages of the present volume will reveal my disagreement with the notion that Cervantes was not concerned with such matters as the acoustic effect of his language. (Cervantes himself, with his accustomed irony, reveals his awareness of the matter in, among other places, the concluding sentence of the initial chapter as he relates Don Quixote's reaction to the names he has bestowed upon himself, his nag, and his lady: "A musical name to his ears, out of the ordinary and significant, like the others he had chosen for himself and his things.")[8] Nonetheless, it is again of interest that it is the destinies—significantly plural—of the characters that stand out in relief. Significant as well, therefore, is Borges' complaint that Spanish scholarship has tended to stress Cervantes' stylistic gifts instead of *Don Quixote's* "greater (and perhaps the only unimpeachable) value," namely the psychological one.[9] Here, too, we shall come upon these matters in several chapters in the present volume as we seek the processes of individuation, not only in *Don Quixote* but in a number of other works by Miguel de Cervantes.

Don Quixote himself will remain a frequent point of reference, primarily because he is our most familiar personage. To say that he is as well Cervantes' greatest creation as a character may seem a redundant asseveration. However, if we ponder the best known episode of all of Spanish literature, we may wish to reconsider—though not necessarily reject—this assessment. There is a rational consistency in having Don Quixote see giants where we may see windmills, and it can scarcely be related to any notions about his idealism. Is it not reasonable to appreciate the response of someone whose understanding of the world had been informed by what his readings—in particular, the romances of chivalry—had impressed upon his memory? Since windmills did not form a part of that world, is it not consistent with his education to apply to the strange shapes, whose appendages moved about seemingly of their own accord, the concept of gigantic beings? (Would we today see flying saucers had we not read of their "existence" earlier?) Don Quixote himself makes us aware of the consistency of his interpretations in the adventure of the fulling mills (I, 20) in response to Sancho's mockery of his master's inability to recognize these new mills for what they are: "Am I obliged, being a knight as I am, to recognize and distinguish sounds and know whether they come from fulling hammers or not? Especially when I may never before have laid eyes on such things, as happens to be the case, whereas you, rude peasant that you are, were born and brought up among them." What is perhaps more intriguing—in addition to the evident humor—is that it is Sancho who, instead of rejecting his master as a madman, rejects the voice of common sense that he himself projects, and so continues to follow Don Quixote in search of an ideal (his island) nonetheless. It is because of such instances that we must see the process of individuation from a number of varied, though overlapping, perspectives.

On a number of occasions I shall insist on the nothingness of Don Quixote's first fifty years of life. By this is meant not an absence of a formative period—I have just referred to his education—but a lack of accomplishment. Ruth El Saffar refers to the protagonist's "prehistory as bored country squire."[10] As the following chapters attempt to show, this assessment is accurate but understated. More than boredom, frustration following upon his recognition of not having achieved individual status is what moves the protagonist to insist on emulating the prowess of his bookish heroes. His prehistory—which is to say, his vicarious experience in the literary world of knight-errantry—is a vital force in his attempt to break with his past status as a nonentity. Closer to my own perspective is El Saffar's subsequent observation about Don Quixote in Part II: "He therefore appears to retire within himself, and to show signs of boredom, irritation, weariness, and melancholy. All impulse to self-creation has disappeared, leaving in its place the necessity for self-discovery."[11] I shall devote an entire chapter to the effects of his retiring within himself, but once again, boredom is not what I perceive in Don Quixote. Depression and melancholy, yes; boredom, no. (Boredom, as we shall note at the close of Chapter 4, is more appropriately applied to the young gentlemen of *The Illustrious Kitchenmaid*, who leave home in quite a different psychological state of mind.) As El Saffar very convincingly concludes, "Don Quixote escapes from fiction at the end of Part II as from a bad dream. His renunciation of his self-created image corresponds with his acceptance of death and the reality of a truth that transcends human understanding."[12] (I would qualify this observation only by speaking of *one* of his self-created images: that of the knight-errant.) Finally, as El Saffar accurately points out, "the ending is not defeat, as so many have interpreted Don Quixote's death, but victory."[13] Precisely because I share her point of view, I cannot consider boredom as a characteristic of someone whose existence travels along such a trajectory. It is, therefore, this path of self-discovery, or the process of individuation, that I shall seek to explore in the chapters that follow.

I should clarify that the present book in no way pretends to provide an exhaustive study of the use of names in Cervantes' works. The continuing interest in these matters is reflected not only by the growing bibliography on the subject but the inevitable paper on some aspect of names at nearly every scholarly convention that deals with Cervantes. But it is not volume alone that turns me from the task of analyzing names in the works of Cervantes to a larger extent, despite the repeated use I make of the phenomenon throughout the chapters in the present book. My criterion has been to relate these matters to the focus of the book, namely, the process of individuation. Intriguing as so many other aspects of the names are, I have stressed only those facets which appear to me related to the individual's emergence from the collective mass. With respect to the meat that still remains to be enjoyed on the bone of nomenclature, as Cervantes might have said, let some other dog chew on that bone. As a matter of fact, he *did* say it.

✻ ✻ ✻ ✻ ✻

I should like to thank Barbara K. Manchester, who typed two early drafts of portions of the manuscript in 1975 and 1976. Thanks to a sabbatical leave granted me by the University of Vermont during the 1976-77 academic year, I was able to spend half a year in Spain and the remainder of that time divided between my study at home and libraries in Cambridge and New York. My thanks go to Mrs. Helen Paddock of Harvard University's Widener Library for facilitating several visits which were of benefit to me for this and related undertakings. The encouragement of the Ohio University Press to bring my work to completion provided no little stimulus in the fulfillment of my plan to have the manuscript ready by the summer of 1977. To my wife Leslie goes the credit for having helped put the manuscript in its final form. Finally, I cannot overstate the personal gratification afforded me by all the members of the faculty of Romance Languages at the University of Vermont in their having welcomed me back home after an excursion to the administrative world. Their warm reception helped reaffirm that among books, ideas, and students, *estamos en casa*.

JOHN G. WEIGER

Badalona, Spain and *Shelburne, Vermont*

xvi

Chapter 1

Introduction:

Individuation, Not Individualism

I NO WINDMILLS

This is not a book about Don Quixote tilting at windmills. What is meant by this unconventional opening sentence is precisely what it states: I am not going to present another explication of *Don Quixote* (although the last word on this masterpiece will not have been said for generations to come, if ever), nor am I going to re-examine all the episodes and present them all in a new light. If Don Quixote sees giants where others see windmills, let him. I shall not play his Sancho and tell him what they "really" are.

What is central to my topic are the various ways in which individual human beings are portrayed by Cervantes as they become aware of themselves, or, if you will pardon an apparent grammatical incongruency, how they become aware of their selves. While I am on the subject of grammar and congruence, let me point out that while teachers of the English language still debate the "correctness" of "it is I" or "it is me," the Spanish language makes it very simple and congruent: *soy yo*, "I am I."[1] Don Quixote takes it a step further in two famous sentences which, with slight variation, are repeatedly pronounced in Cervantes' works: "I know who I am and who I may be, if I choose," and "each person is the child of his own works." I need not elaborate on

1

the first sentence. Clearly the protagonist is proclaiming not only his self-awareness, but more importantly, a knowledge of the potentialities that lie within the grasp of his personality.

On the other hand, for the reader who is not familiar with the Spanish language or the tradition within which Cervantes wrote, a brief explanation of the apparently trite "each person is the child of his own works" is in order. The Spanish for this well-known line is *cada uno es hijo de sus obras.* Translated literally, it means "each one is the son [or child] of his works." It seems to have no profound meaning. However, to the Spanish ear, *hijo de sus obras* cannot fail to invite comparison with *hijo de algo,* literally "son of something" and more appropriately translated as "son of somebody." *Hijo de algo* was subsequently shortened to *hi de algo* and eventually to *hidalgo,* meaning "gentleman."[2] Since *hijo de algo* or *hidalgo* explained one's status as deriving from one's ancestors, the countering assertion that each one is *hijo de sus obras,* that is, each one's worth is the result of what *he* does rather than what his forebears did (or were reputed to have done), is an expression of more than idle observation in an age which antedates the great social revolutions by nearly two centuries.

I have said that I would not deal with windmills. By this I meant to convey that I shall not concentrate on what is often called Don Quixote's idealism. (I may have reason to mention windmills or a barber's basin and why they seem to be giants or a helmet, but the point of departure will be the individual's perspective, not his supposed idealism.) I shall instead try to focus on Don Quixote's reality, upon his humanity, upon his personality, or, put even more simply, upon him as a person. This same interest in him as an individual motivates my assessment of the variegated characters in this and other works of Cervantes.

There will be little talk of windmills for another reason, namely, that my purpose in writing of Cervantes' artistry with respect to the individual is at the same time an attempt to show how that artistic conception was a literary manifestation of his observations on the manifold aspects of the process of becoming conscious of one's self. These observations deal with humanity and therefore go beyond the purely literary. We can recognize their manifestations in circumstances which antedate Cervantes as well as in those which have occurred in the more than three centuries since his death.

2

II IDENTITY

My title for this chapter contains another indication of what I do not propose to do. Individualism is a phenomenon which does make its appearance in Cervantes' works, but it is not the central concern of my study. The process of *becoming* an individual, on the other hand, is something quite apart from, although ultimately related to, the concept called individualism. The latter connotes a rebellious attitude toward established conventions and reaches its apogee in the late eighteenth century (particularly in the French and American revolutions) and is reflected in the Romanticism of the various arts in the nineteenth century. It was in such a context, of course, that Don Quixote was viewed as an idealistic, individualistic precursor of Romanticism.[3] Moreover, one need hardly be a literary scholar, much less a sociologist, to explain the success of Wasserman's *Man of La Mancha* in the late 1960s.

It is curious to note, then, that Barzun overlooks Cervantes when he concludes that it "may indeed be said that the great artistic innovation in *Faust* is its willing vulgarity. For the first time since Shakespeare, a work of high intention took account of the low and small and commonplace."[4] Barzun's qualifying remark in the next paragraph that he had in mind not those who dealt exclusively with society but those who concerned themselves with the universe may explain why the picaresque novel is not included in his comment, but *Don Quixote* assuredly treats of universal concerns.[5] Perhaps it is both his commonness and his universality that have given to Don Quixote the unique quality of being a fictional character whose "likeness" most people readily recognize.

Take away the requisite props and most figures of world literature become unrecognizable. Yet even without his nag or his windmills or his chubby companion, Don Quixote is readily identified in sculptures, paintings, carvings, etchings and drawings. Could the same be said of Hamlet, Siegfried, Beowulf or even the ubiquitous Don Juan? Cervantes himself, who correctly predicted the popularity of his book, may not have anticipated fully this phenomenon when he had Don Quixote insist upon the historical existence of Guinevere and Launcelot because "there are persons who can recall having seen Dame Quintañona [Guinevere's lady-in-waiting] . . . . So true is this that I can remember how my grandmother . . . used to say to me, when she saw a

3

lady in a venerable hood, 'That one, my grandson, looks just like Dame Quintañona.' From which I infer that she must have known her or at least have seen some portrait of her" (I, 49). It would be inaccurate, however, to assume that Cervantes was not aware of some of the impact which his creations had already had upon his readers, for in II, 3; on discussing the reception of Part I of *Don Quixote*, Sansón Carrasco remarks that "no sooner do folks see some skinny nag than they at once cry, 'There goes Rocinante!'"

What Cervantes has achieved as an artist, then, is to pluck from the ranks of the unimposing, a country gentleman and convert him into one of the handful of figures of world literature. What is more, his literary creation is one—perhaps the only one—of that select group of fictional personages to have become so individualized that his "mournful countenance" is uniquely identifiable.[6]

"Trite as it seems to us, the logical statement of identity—'I am I'—the fundamental statement of consciousness is in reality a tremendous achievement."[7] To a large extent, the story of Don Quixote is the recounting of just such a tremendous achievement. What makes it truly "tremendous" is the wealth of nuances inherent in Don Quixote's assertion, "I know who I am and who I may be, if I choose." Shakespeare's characters can also assert their identity and thus we are not startled to hear Antony affirm, "I am Antony yet" (*Antony and Cleopatra*, III); or even Hamlet, who so often is plagued by doubt, assert that "this is I, / Hamlet the Dane" (*Hamlet*, V). Theodore Spencer repeatedly insists that Shakespeare's individualists are the villains in the plays.[8] I am not convinced that "individualist" is the appropriate term to differentiate Iago, Edmund, Goneril and others from those of more virtuous character, simply because the former disrupt and the latter preserve the order of things. Individualism is not, in my opinion, "one of the attributes of villainy,"[9] if by this Spencer means, as his context confirms, that individualism is a clear symptom of villainy, rather than one trait which villains may share with heroes.

To wander into a debate about Shakespeare would be to stray from my purpose. Nonetheless, a few words about Cervantes' great contemporary will help to provide a fuller context for my observations on the "tremendous achievement" of Cervantes' most famous protagonist. Two examples will suffice. In Act III of *King Lear*, Shakespeare has his protagonist discover man's essential nature. In the famous mad scene on the heath, King Lear, against the background of the storm, begins to tear off his clothes as he asks, "Is man no more than this?" He answers his own question: ". . . unaccommodated man is no more but such a poor, bare, forked animal as thou art." Spencer (p. 149) quite accurately comments that "Lear finds out what man is really like," and then concludes: "We see him reduced to relying on the lowest dregs of human nature, his mind in pieces, trying to get to reality by stripping off his clothes" (p. 151). Of course, Spencer is correct, but I can see the emphasis easily placed not so much on Lear's lowliness as on his essence. Or, to use Spencer's own word, is not the significant word "reality"? Better still, let us use Shakespeare's words: has not Lear found the "unaccommodated," that is, unadorned man, and is this not the individual?[10] In short, I see individualism where Spencer does not, because the self-awareness symbolized by Lear's nakedness is to me what makes Lear see himself as an individual. There is no need to stand out in rebellion in order to pass through the process of individuation, unless we wish to see with only the eyes of the Romantics.

My second example comes closer to Don Quixote: it is the speech on virtue by Iago in the first act of *Othello*: "Virtue! 'tis in ourselves that we are thus or thus. Our bodies are gardens, to the which our wills are gardeners; . . . why, the power and corrigible authority of this lies in our wills. . . . [And] we have reason to cool our raging motions, our carnal stings, our unbitted lusts. . . ." Because Iago is so rational that he has total control of his passions (Spencer calls him "an emotional eunuch"), he is defined as "an unscrupulous individualist" (Spencer, p. 132) and his speech is viewed by Spencer as "a clear indication of villainy" (p. 147). As I have said, it is not my purpose here to engage in a polemic about the works of Shakespeare. In fact, I have no quarrel with the essential aspects of Spencer's observations. My purpose in bringing this example to the fore is to dispute the almost conditioned response to a word like "unscrupulous" by following it with "individualist," as though the latter connoted something pejorative.

Whether Iago is a villain or not—and of course he is—is secondary to my own study, for which the speech on virtue stands out as an example of an affirmation that the individual has the opportunity to act virtuously if he wills it. (This principle is also articulated in a crucial passage of Cervantes' last great novel, the *Persiles*.) Iago has chosen to act viciously and while it is true that in so doing he has upset the order of things, it is equally true that he had the choice *not* to behave in such a manner. It is in this sense that he approaches Don Quixote, who elected to behave in a virtuous manner, not to mention a certain kinship with regard to asexual responses in both men's lives.[11] But what links them in the context of individualism is Iago's insistence on our will as the determining factor in our behavior. The image of the body as a garden and the will as its gardener suggests man as a *tabula rasa*, ready for the imprint of his own volition.

Don Quixote's affirmation is analogous: he knows who he may be if he chooses. Yet, it seems to me, he has a firmer grasp of the inherent possibilities and his life reveals a firmer belief in a deeper meaning. Iago does not carry the concept beyond that of saying that each individual, through the exercise of his will, determines the kind of person he will be. On another occasion, Don Quixote proclaims that "each man is the architect of his own fortune" (II, 66), a statement also found in the "Speech on the State," believed to have been composed by Sallust in 46 B.C.: "But experience has shown that to be true which Appius says in his verses, that every man is the architect of his own fortune."[12] A similar view is held by Periandro in Cervantes' *Persiles*, in which the hero maintains that "we ourselves make our own fortune and there is not a soul who lacks the capacity to raise himself to his proper place" (II, 13).[13] Aristotle had earlier stated that "a man is the origin of his actions, and that the province of deliberation is to discover actions within one's power to perform."[14]

By going back to Aristotle (although Plato touches upon the concept as well, for example, in *Republic*, 10:617e), we have really come full circle. Both Iago and Don Quixote agree that an individual designs his own fortune, and Sallust and Aristotle, among others, agree. But only Aristotle and Don Quixote—which is to say, Aristotle and Cervantes—insist on tying this concept to self-knowledge. (It is significant that the first piece of advice given by Don Quixote to Sancho as the latter is preparing for his governorship, is to fear God, followed by the admonition "to bear in mind *who you are* and seek to know yourself, which is the most difficult knowledge to acquire that can be imagined" [II, 42; italics mine].) Predmore has perceived the connection between the "architect of his own fortune" statement of Don Quixote at the end of the book following his physical defeat by the Knight of the White Moon (Sansón Carrasco), and the assertion toward the beginning that he knows who he may be if he chooses: "Despite the oft-recognized ambiguity of part of [Don Quixote's] speech, there is not the slightest doubt that he is assuming full responsibility for his crucial defeat. And this becomes him, for he has amply demonstrated that he belongs to the small and heroic company of those who are not content to be creatures of circumstance, but who dare to try to be what they have chosen to be."[15]

III INDIVIDUATION

Referring to Shakespeare, it was Goethe who said, "The highest achievement possible to man is the full consciousness of his own feelings and thoughts, for this gives him the means of knowing intimately the heart of others."[16] Barzun adds: "Every part of this maxim could be the subject of an extended commentary showing the ramifications of the quest for two-fold knowledge. It would be filled with such terms and phrases as Individualism, Experience, and the Eternal Feminine. . . . Taken from *Faust* or its interpreters, these are by now established names for principles or realities that Goethe found emergent in his world. But if one had to choose a single characteristic with which to define modern man without further qualification one would almost infallibly say: self-consciousness."

Auerbach makes a similar observation on Montaigne: "For he conceives of an *ignorance forte et généreuse* . . . and values it more highly than all factual knowledge because its acquisition requires greater wisdom than the acquisition of scientific knowledge. It is not only a means of clearing the way for him to the kind of knowledge which matters to him, that is, self-knowledge, but it also represents a direct way of reaching what is the ultimate goal of his quest, namely, right living: *le grand et glorieux chef d'oeuvre de l'homme, c'est vivre à propos.*"[17] Auerbach further comments upon Montaigne's famous sentence upon *l'humaine condition*: "If every man affords material and occasion enough for the development of the complete moral philosophy, then a precise and sincere self-analysis of any random individual is directly justified" (p. 297). And with respect to *Don Quixote* itself, Levin concludes that "it would be a mistake to believe that the quixotic principle is a negative one simply because it operates through disillusionment. Rather, it is a register of development, an index of maturation. Its incidental mishaps can be looked back upon as milestones on the way to self-awareness."[18]

From Cervantes' point of view, then, it is essential to know one's strengths and weaknesses, in order to be an individual in the sense in which I have been employing this term, namely to realize one's full potential as a person. For this reason, it is so critical to focus on both parts of Don Quixote's statement: Self-knowledge is the meaning of "I know who I am," but the second part embraces more than an extension of the first, for it includes the awareness that within the limitations revealed by his particular self-knowledge, he can be other things as well: "and who I may be if I choose."

Cervantes makes use of several devices to reinforce the concept of an individual's ability to become something by making use of his particular attributes. One statement that recurs in his works is enunciated by the Duchess in II, 33, to the effect that "bishops are made out of men," an observation also made by the protagonist of *The Glass Graduate*, who will not reveal the name of his birthplace nor that of his parents until he can honor them through the fame achieved by his studies, because "I have heard that even bishops start off as men" (p. 121). That each man has his own peculiar set of attributes with which to shape his destiny is emphasized in Don Quixote's refusal to accept the validity of the spurious work allegedly about him: "There is no other I in the world" (II, 70).[19]

Similarly, Sancho explains his having abandoned the governorship of his island as the result of his having received "the knowledge that I am not fit to govern anything, unless it be a herd of cattle" (II, 54). I am aware that Sancho's words may be turned against my argument, namely that he ought to stay in his assigned place (a phrase he himself uses on occasion), not follow idealistic madmen around the world nor dream of a peasant being converted into a governor. The point, however, is not that this argument is in contradistinction to mine; my own thesis is quite simple: Sancho (or any other individual) must first learn this by getting to know his particular limitations, i.e., self-knowledge. In short, the individual must experience and observe, as Don Quixote did, what the potentialities of life are for him. As Sir Alfred Ayer has written, if a system is "logically rigorous, we can be assured that if any objects satisfy its premises, they also satisfy its conclusions; but that there are objects which do satisfy the premises is something that cannot be known *a priori*: it has in the end to be discovered by observation."[20] I shall return briefly to the manner of Sancho's discovery in the chapter on isolation and desolation.

Aubrey Bell, in his chapter "The Popular Vein," explains the thinking of a Sancho in greater detail. Among other matters, he notes that the Spanish peasantry is "too close to the tragic realities of life to indulge in such irrelevancies [as when governments make war]. . . . It can afford to be indifferent to politics and to the accidental distinctions of rank and wealth. . . . Cervantes gives us many instances of this proud independence. 'I in my station,' says the peasant Dorotea to the duke's son Don Fernando, 'am worth as much as you in yours.'" Bell goes on to clarify that it would be "unwise to infer from these and similar remarks that Cervantes advocated the external equality of all men. . . . Cervantes did not indulge in the modern cult of external equality. Like Plato, he would have each man keep to his own work . . . and in so doing by diligence and intelligence without injuring any he might rise to the highest office. . . ."[21]

So it is that the concept contained in Iago's speech on virtue is more limited than Don Quixote's statement that he knows who he is and who he may be if he chooses. Iago agrees that one's will determines one's character and proceeds to spend his life in unidimensional fashion, that of the villain. Don Quixote insists first on knowing himself, whereupon he may be free to choose other roles dependent upon that self-knowledge. This helps to explain the niece's remark in I, 6, that "I shouldn't wonder at all if my uncle, after he has been cured of this chivalry sickness, reading one of these [pastoral] books, should take it into his head to become a shepherd and go wandering through the woods and meadows singing and piping, or, what is worse, become a poet. . . ." Leaving aside Cervantes' tongue-in-cheek comment about poets, this passage not only prefigures precisely what Don Quixote will essay later in his career, but more importantly, forms part of that *leitmotiv* which I have been describing, namely, the ability to play many roles. I shall expand on this theme from another perspective in Chapter 5.

IV INDIVIDUATION THROUGH VARIEGATION

What is fundamental to all of the foregoing is the ability to take advantage of the inequities of life. The picaresque novel was one of a number of genres which had bitterly pointed out some of these inequities, but only with sarcasm and hence to a large extent, with grudging acceptance. One scholar has tried to compare Don Quixote's reaction to the troupe of players with that of Quevedo's picaresque protagonist in the latter's *Buscon*. His conclusion is that in the picaresque tale, there is "no speculation about the kinds of reality an actor portrays, nor is there any questioning of the nature of life and its mirror image, death. The narrative line is uncluttered; acting is at the same level as gaming."[22] Cervantes, on the other hand, never ceases to encourage the grasping of the opportunities presented by the richness and variety of life. In order to do so, of course, one must be free to make such choices: "Much human history bears witness to the numinous and charismatic power which may be exercised on human beings by the beneficent and saintly individual who has undergone a process of spiritual and moral self-discipline. . . . Creativity, whether in the arts or in the sciences, cannot be imposed from without, and requires freedom as a necessary condition. It resembles the mystical experience of religion in that it is felt as coming from the deeper levels of the human psyche. The creative individual does not produce innovations by an effort of the will. On the contrary, new creations present themselves to his consciousness with a compulsiveness which was formerly ascribed to divine inspiration. Modern man no longer attributes inventive genius to external spiritual powers; but the experience of creativity remains the same, although interpretations have become psychological rather than theological."[23]

This viewpoint, namely that one cannot achieve self-knowledge and realize one's potential except in freedom, underlies much of Cervantes' writings and, as we shall see, is a major motivating force which propels Don Quixote. In addition to some of the adventures already alluded to, we need only think of Don Quixote's intentions in episodes such as the attempt to free Andres, the liberating of the galley slaves, and his desire to liberate the kingdom of Micomicon (not to mention his dream of disenchanting Dulcinea). These and numerous other examples are not merely a reflection of Cervantes' own experiences of captivity (in Algiers and in jail), but on a grander scale serve to illustrate the precondition for individuation. Nowhere is this more clearly stated than in the famous passage from II, 58, in which Don Quixote defines liberty as "one of the most precious gifts that the heavens have bestowed on men; with it the treasures locked in the earth or hidden in the depths of the sea are not to be compared; for the sake of freedom, as for the sake of honor, one may and should risk one's life, and captivity, on the other hand, is the greatest evil that can befall a human being."

A number of episodes in *Don Quixote* which deal with this theme have been commented upon extensively by many observers and I shall not restate what has already been written. I do, however, wish to stress those aspects which bear upon the emergence of the individual. On the purely literary level, for example, there is scarcely a commentator who can pass by the phenomenon of having the characters in Part II discuss, as though they were external to the book as we are, their own adventures as related in Part I. The usual reaction is to dwell on the relationship of life to literature or of reality to art. With regard to the matter at hand, I find of special interest an observation that as Don Quixote and Sancho converse and comment on Part I, they take part in a form of liberation.[24] The importance of this for the protagonist's development and his subsequent ability to perceive life as a variety of possibilities is evident: his liberation from the pages of a book about knight-errantry liberates him from the conventions of that literary genre and prepares the way for self-knowledge and his ultimate emergence as the individual, Alonso Quijano.

Another episode which has received much attention is that of the freeing of the galley slaves. Again, I need not repeat what has already been written about so many facets of this adventure, including the aspect of Don Quixote's views on liberty. What is of significance to my own perspective is that Don Quixote does not abstractly defend the principle of freedom: he insists that he be able "to inquire of *each one of them, individually,* the cause of his misfortune" (I, 22; italics mine).

Don Quixote's insistence on dealing with the prisoners individually has several implications. Riquer justly dismisses as arbitrary the interpretation of the Romantics, according to which Don Quixote is viewed as a paladin of liberty and valiant adversary of tyranny. On the other hand, I am not so ready to accept Riquer's alternative, which labels this adventure as one of the greatest *quijotadas* of Don Quixote, Riquer himself emphasizing that he is giving this word the sense it has acquired in Spanish (which is akin to our everyday use of the word "quixotic" when we speak of foolish idealism).[25] That it is quixotic in the sense that it is typical of Don Quixote I do not deny (even to the point that his actions more often than not invite ludicrous and nearly catastrophic reactions). Yet it is also consistent with the theme I have been developing and that, more than a mere dismissal, negates the Romantic point of view.

Romanticism, despite its own egocentric version of individualism, would have focused on the liberation of common men from the shackles of monarchical power. One can easily hear, in such a context, the Prisoners' Chorus from Beethoven's *Fidelio*. Yet a reading of the galley slaves adventure in *Don Quixote* evokes no such music in one's ears. Not only is the background picaresque, bitter and sarcastic, but the outcome, as the freed prisoners hurl stones at their liberator,

11

forbids a Romantic interpretation. Aside from the abstract theme of freedom and liberation which, if alone, could prefigure a Romantic point of view, what stands out is Don Quixote's way of handling this group: not as a class but as individuals. He asks them one at a time about themselves and how it came about that each of them finds himself in his current predicament. In short, not only does he wish to learn about others by viewing them as individuals from his own vantage point; by insisting on a dialogue with each one he is forcing *them* to see themselves as individuals. I shall return to this fundamental point.

As readers of *Don Quixote* know, this adventure introduces us to one of the more interesting minor personalities of the novel. All of the other prisoners are hurriedly described in one or two lines prior to Don Quixote's interrogations, and none of them is called by name, other than to be given an ordinal number (e.g., "a fourth prisoner") or simply called "another," although each is singled out with respect to what he has done to warrant such a fate. One of the prisoners, however, is given singular treatment by Cervantes: it requires some thirty lines, which include his age, appearance, manner of being shackled and number of criminal charges against him, before we are finally told his name. It turns out that this individual's name is Ginés de Pasamonte, otherwise known as Ginesillo de Parapilla.

I shall come back to Ginés' name, particularly since Ginés himself has something to say about this matter. Ginés is an individual and the variation of his name implies his ability to form his character. Among other things, we learn that he is writing a book entitled *The Life of Ginés de Pasamonte*, a book which he claims will put *Lazarillo de Tormes* to shame. (Thus we learn that Ginés is a *pícaro* or rogue.) A remark he makes has been commented on repeatedly, but it bears mentioning because it emphasizes once again the individual's ability to influence his life: asked whether the book has been finished, Ginés responds, "How could it be finished . . . when my life is not finished as yet?"

Being a *pícaro*, Ginés naturally has a more narrow understanding of man's potentialities than does Don Quixote, but he is not oblivious to the fact that such potentialities exist. This explains one of his statements about his name: "Man goes as God pleases, that is plain to be seen, . . . but someday someone will know whether my name is Ginesillo de Parapilla or not." Ginés accepts the limitations placed on a man's maneuverability by his Creator, but he recognizes that within the parameters set by God, he has the capacity to become what he wants and this will be symbolized by the acceptance of his name. Different as they are in so many respects, Ginés and Alonso Quijano have this much in common. What basically differentiates them is similar to the distinction noted earlier between Don Quixote and Iago. Casalduero (*Sentido y forma del Quijote*, p. 113) calls Ginés a deceiver and uses the Spanish word *burlador*, which is the word used by Cervantes' contemporary, Tirso de Molina, to describe the legendary Don Juan in the latter's play, *El burlador de Sevilla*. Although he confesses that there is no way to prove it, Casalduero believes that in the adventure of the galley slaves, Cervantes intended to have the two great myths of Spanish culture confront each other. While I see some problems with chronology here (which may be dismissed if we bear in mind that both Don Quixote and Don Juan have their antecedents), it is not difficult for me to accept the confrontation of two typological personalities, each in his own way seeking to find the range of possibilities open to him in this life, Ginés using roguery and deception in order to "make it" through this world, and Don Quixote trying to uncover the deceptions of this life in order to seek the greater truths of eternity.

That Ginés is not only a forerunner of what we would today call a "con man" but is at the same time aware of the matters I have been discussing is revealed by Cervantes in Part II when he has Cid Hamete Benengeli tell the reader that Master Pedro really is Ginés de Pasamonte. Now this has several implications for this study. In the first place, it is obvious that he has changed not only his name but his trade as well. Secondly, he has adopted that very profession which has been described as possessing the varieties of human actions, namely the theater.[26] (Another charlatan is the leading character of Cervantes' short play, *El retablo de las maravillas*, which purports to present a series of dramatic scenes that are merely figments of the imagination and that, for reasons I will return to at a later stage, the audience pretends to see.) This latest role of Ginés, then, is in accord with the individual's self-knowledge, and the resultant ability to play many parts. I therefore cannot agree with Karl's view of Ginés "suspending his own being while he becomes Master [Pedro]. . . ."[27] I think it more in accordance with Cervantes' view to say that Ginés has evolved into yet another aspect consistent with his own character, namely that of a deceiver in a milieu which by definition is make-believe.

I venture to say that Don Quixote recognized Master Pedro as Ginés de Pasamonte. This is consistent with Don Quixote's role as the seeker of truths and adds a new dimension to his bursting onto the stage and slashing away at Master Pedro's puppets. When Ginés' identity was first called into question in I, 22, his anger about his name caused him to admit that people do call him Ginesillo de Parapilla, adding, "but I'll put a stop to it, or else I'll skin their you-know-what." Now this man has succeeded in putting a stop to it, for he is currently called Master Pedro. This same fellow, who spoke in this way about his identity and subsequently thanked his liberator by throwing stones at him, is now in II, 26, once again presenting a deception.

When Don Quixote begins his slaughter of the puppets, thereby ruining Master Pedro's appurtenances, he first thinks that "it would be a good thing for him to aid the fugitives" and orders the pursuing puppets to "cease your pursuit and persecution." Once more, then, Don Quixote is involved in an attempt at liberation, this time causing the damage to be inflicted upon the very person who had treated him so badly earlier. What is more, Cervantes tells us that "among the many blows he dealt was one downward stroke that, if Master Pedro had not ducked and crouched, would have sliced off his head more easily than if it had been made of almond paste." Significantly, in II, 27, when Master Pedro's identity is revealed to the reader, Cervantes' final words about him are: "But it would have cost him dearly had the knight dropped his hand a little more that time he cut off King Marsilio's head and destroyed all his cavalry, as told in the preceding chapter." We may ask first, why tell it again? Secondly, is the reference in each case to a downward blow—especially after the identity revelation brings to mind the galley slaves episode[28]—an attempt by Cervantes to relate Don Quixote's gesture to Ginés' threat to "skin their you-know-what"?

Since the adventure of Master Pedro's puppet show follows immediately that of the Cave of Montesinos and is followed in turn by Don Quixote's refusal to participate in the battle of the braying towns, and since in the Master Pedro episode itself the so-called divining ape refuses to pronounce as true Don Quixote's experience in the Cave, the context would seem to argue that Don Quixote has good reason not to take part in the nonsensical dispute between the braying towns, while he may have two excellent reasons for attacking the puppets and nearly killing Pedro-Ginés: one, his anger at not having his adventure in the Cave believed, and, two, the possibility that he has recognized Pedro as Ginés and wishes to settle an old score.

But there is more. The Ginés of the galley slaves adventure is cross-eyed; Master Pedro is described similarly. In point of fact, our attention is dramatically drawn to his bandaged eye and side of the face by a sudden intrusion on the part of the narrator: "I neglected to say that this Master Pedro had his left eye and almost half his cheek covered with a green taffeta patch" (II, 25). Don Quixote's first words to Master Pedro are in Italian: *Che pesce pigliamo?* As is customary in such situations, Cervantes attempts a transliteration: ¿*qué peje pillamo?* The expression (which literally means "which fish are we going to catch?" and is used to convey the thought "how are we going to make out?") echoes the name which Ginés had not wanted anyone to call him: *Parapilla.* Given the fact that *pillar* is a common Spanish word meaning "plunder," as well as the common construction with the prefix *para* (as in *parapoco*, "good for nothing"), the name Parapilla would— if it signifies anything—be an expression quite appropriate for our Ginés-Pedro: "fit for plunder." Accordingly, the fact that Cervantes has Don Quixote choose, from among all the possible Italian expressions he might have used, a construction which includes the form *pillamo*, suggests that Don Quixote did indeed recognize the former galley slave and has used the puppet presentation to settle an old score.

If my argument is cogent, then Don Quixote's actions with the puppets and the braying towns also reveal the sanity and consistency of character at this stage of his life. My suggestion that Don Quixote's rational behavior is perceptible in the adventure of the puppets—an instance which is sometimes represented as evidence of his lingering inability to cope with reality—is given further weight by his willingness to pay for the damage he has done to Pedro's puppets. To put it in the context of one sociologist, "where one moves among strangers it becomes increasingly important to have other mechanisms for handling aggression. In situations of high mobility and flux the individual must have a built-in readiness to feel himself responsible when things go wrong."[29]

I said earlier that I would return to what I described as a fundamental point, namely that by forcing each of the galley slaves to tell his own story, one at a time, Don Quixote makes these people behave as individuals. This, in some senses, is a facet of Don Quixote's character that has not gone unobserved. I call it fundamental not only because it is clear to all readers—regardless of their interpretation of the character or of the novel—that Don Quixote has an ineluctable impact upon all those with whom he comes in contact, but because so many of the people he meets are, so to speak, set in their own individual orbit after having crossed Don Quixote's path. To put it another way, not only is *Don Quixote* the story of a person who succeeds in finding his own individuality, but a novel on a grand scale which shows Cervantes, often through the actions of his protagonist, causing an entire parade of types to emerge from their typological shells into greater or lesser degrees of acknowledgment that they are individuals.

This process of individuation which we have seen operating upon the protagonist has its effects, then, on others as well. The influence of Don Quixote upon Sancho Panza is so well known that I need not comment upon it. Only slightly less familiar is the influence of Sancho on Don Quixote, but it, too, is frequently commented upon.[30] To a somewhat lesser extent, various critics have observed similar effects— today we would call it "consciousness raising"—upon other characters who populate the novel, ranging from the prostitutes at the inn whom Don Quixote insists on calling maidens and ends up by renaming (including the addition of the title "Doña"), through the spectacle of the curate's attempt to disguise himself in women's clothing in order to induce Don Quixote to return home, to the most dramatically interesting of all: Sansón Carrasco. This know-it-all recent college graduate insists that his rational approach will bring the allegedly insane Don Quixote back to his senses; yet as he progresses from the Knight of the Mirrors to the Knight of the White Moon, his motivation changes from his original desire to restore to sanity someone who believes himself to be a knight, to his own knightly response to his first defeat by pursuing Don Quixote expressly in order to exact vengeance. What this all can be reduced to, then, is that the reader of Cervantes will find for himself numerous instances of people who at first blush appear to be types or characters of no importance but who, on closer inspection, are examples in varying degrees of those who see some of their own potentialities and strive—often without realizing it—to assert their existence as themselves, that is, as individuals.

V   DEVIATION AS A MEANS TO INDIVIDUATION

But it is not only in *Don Quixote* that Cervantes reveals the individual. I shall describe other aspects of the process of individuation in the chapters to follow; for the moment, I should like to single out some instances from other works of Cervantes, beginning with the *Novelas ejemplares*. I do not need to become embroiled in the age-old polemic concerning the meaning of the word "exemplary" for these tales, a discussion which usually revolves around the question of whether these stories are meant to reveal models of virtue or their opposite. For the purposes of my study, I shall simply accept Cervantes' word as it is most easily defined, namely that these short novels are intended to portray examples, without the necessity of affixing value judgments *a priori* to the entire collection.

I have already alluded to *El Licenciado Vidriera*, which Jones translates as *The Glass Graduate* and Starkie as *The Man of Glass*. (I would prefer *Graduate Glass*, which not only is closer to the original but conforms with Jones' appropriate decision to use Glass as the protagonist's name.) Graduate Glass has much in common with Don Quixote, for he too is considered to be insane, and thus I shall deal with him first. Before his illness, however, certain events occur which reinforce the theme of individuation that runs throughout Cervantes' works. (I shall also deal with Graduate Glass in subsequent chapters, as will be the case with so many of Cervantes' characters; I mention it here to avoid the cumbersome repetition in each case that I will return to such and such a personage in some future chapter.)

When we first come upon the protagonist he is symbolically asleep beneath a tree.[31] We are informed that he is about eleven years old (impressionable) and in peasant dress (at the bottom of the social scale). He is on his way to the university city of Salamanca and is in search of a master who would provide him, in exchange for his services, the opportunity to study. He is found by two gentleman students and, as I cited earlier in another context, the lad tells them that "no one shall know the name of my country or my parents until I can bring honour to them both." It is at this point that he explains his reasoning as the result of having heard that "even bishops start off as men." After the two gentlemen decide to take him into their service and give him a chance to study, the lad reveals that his name is Thomas Rodaja, which in Spanish means Thomas Littlewheel. With a few strokes of his pen, then (I am still on the first page of the edition I am using), Cervantes has drawn for us the portrait of a youth, emerging from his sleep and from his social class, eager to open his mind's eye through learning, and aware that he, like the bishop prior to becoming a bishop, must start off as all men must, conscious of his potentialities as a man in order to attain self-realization, ultimately worthy because of his own achievements: in a word, an individual.

It does not take Rodaja long to raise himself. Cervantes tells us that he "never failed in any way to pursue his studies" while serving his

17

masters so well that he "became his masters' companion, and no longer their servant." After eight years, the young man takes leave of the gentleman students and the first person to come his way is a nobleman who is also an infantry captain in the King's Guard. Rodaja has apparently fallen in with someone of higher rank and especially one who can open up wider possibilities for his life. As Cervantes carefully points out, the captain praised the life of a soldier, "but he said nothing to him about the cold of sentry duty, the danger of attacks, the horror of battles, the hunger of sieges, the destruction of mines, and other things of this kind, which some consider to be the extra burdens of a soldier's life, when in fact they are the main part of it" (p. 122).

There is a certain parallel here between the captain who can praise warfare from an idealistic point of view (and therefore not from the point of view of the soldier in the field) and the Knight of the Green-Colored Greatcoat in *Don Quixote* who speaks about the niceties of knightly life without being able to represent the view of the knight who becomes involved in battle. It is interesting to note that although their surnames differ, Cervantes has named each of them Don Diego.[32]

As we shall see shortly, however, there are, despite some marked resemblances, some significant differences between Thomas and Don Quixote. The latter was anxious to take Don Diego's implicit challenge literally and therefore saw in the lions an opportunity to demonstrate his manliness (of whatever kind).[33] Thomas Rodaja nearly has an analogous reaction, for his judgment "began to waver, and his will [began] to be set on that [soldierly] way of life, where death is always so near at hand" (pp. 122-23). But the Don Diego of this tale does not bring out the quixotic response in his newly found companion, for Thomas in his late teens is not so defensive about his manhood as was Don Quixote in his late forties. He may even have been intuitively aware of what a twentieth-century social scientist has recently observed: "Most men join the Marines at least in part as a virility rite, with women assumed as a reward. . . . But they early discover that there are no women to be had . . . [unless the soldier is willing to] pay to see it, pay for every inch he touches of it. . . . He learns to fear and distrust women. . . . Throughout human history, war and killing have been significant ways of disposing of single men. Even in troops of baboons the lowest-ranking males are the ones in the vanguard or on the flanks, the ones who face the leopard or the lion. . . . It is a terrible combination when they lose their sense of ever reaching the dominant class; when they despair of being wanted by women and needed by society; when they feel they cannot meet the test and make it as men; when, indeed, they cannot even find the testing ground. Then their talent for death can be turned against themselves. And they are brilliant at it."[34]

Thomas Rodaja, then, still at an age and stage in his life when many possibilities are open to him, prefers not to commit himself to a military career at this time, despite the captain's offer of a commission as an ensign. He is interested in travel, however, and agrees to join the captain on his way to Italy, "but only on condition that he need not take any commission or enlist as a soldier, for he did not want to be obliged to follow the flag." When the captain reminds Thomas of the wages and the opportunity to have leave whenever he wished, Thomas replies, "That would be going against my conscience and against yours, captain; and so I would rather go as a free agent than be under such an obligation." The captain agrees but cannot help observing that "such a scrupulous conscience . . . is more becoming to a monk than a soldier" (p. 123).

As they head for Italy, Thomas is somewhat disappointed by the speed with which they travel "because life in lodgings is easy and has plenty of variety, and every day one comes across new and pleasant things" (p. 124). I tend to agree with Casalduero when he calls this part of the novel the "'Voyage to Italy,' the modern cultural voyage" (*Sentido de las Novelas*, pp. 142-47), something which Casalduero justly observes is not dependent on the originality of the thoughts expressed—for they are not original—but which sustains "the rhythm of a vital experience" (*ibid.*, p. 147). On the other hand, Casalduero overemphasizes the opposition of the secular to the ecclesiastical. More consistent with Cervantes' writings in general and with Thomas' character in particular (as revealed by the final words of the novel) is, I think, the more limited, mundane view of Thomas Rodaja (as opposed to a Don Quixote, for example), whose voyage through the center of Renaissance culture is largely restricted to the admiration of human (or humanistic) creations such as architecture, painting and sculpture, rather than to devotion to the center of the Catholic religion. In short, what I perceive is not a novel or an author dealing with an anti-Church position, but rather a young man who, in his attempt to attain knowledge and self-knowledge which are the gateway to individualism as I have been using this term, focuses on the potentialities of this world and who, unlike some other personages of Cervantes' works, concentrates on life, the possibilities which for him inhere in life, and the fame that may result therefrom.

Such an interpretation is consistent from the first page ("'By the fame I win through my studies,' replied the boy, 'because I have heard that even bishops start off as men'") to the last page ("he added eternal fame by deeds of arms to that which he had begun to acquire by learning, leaving behind him after his death a reputation as a prudent and most valiant soldier"). It is in this context that I read the final sentence of a paragraph which Cervantes introduces with the words, "From there," which in turn is followed by another paragraph that begins with the same words, "From there." This phrase (which is repeated a number of other times during this portion of the novel) provides the emphasis required for Cervantes' obvious insistence on the rapidity with which Thomas is conducting his "Grand Tour." Seen in this light, the sentence I referred to earlier reinforces the worldly aspect of Thomas Rodaja's progress in his learning: "He saw the very room and spot which witnessed the most exalted and important charge ever witnessed [the Annunciation], though not comprehended, by the heavens, the angels, and all the dwellers of eternity" (p. 126). The very next sentence begins, as I have indicated, "From there," and proceeds to tell us where he went next. I find it difficult to avoid asking why Cervantes felt the necessity of including in this compressed travelogue, the incomprehensibility of the Annunciation. I do not see this as a negative comment about the Catholic Church, or about any of its beliefs. What befits the character of the protagonist is rather his youthful hurry to see as much as possible in the manner of many a tourist; framed between the repetition of "From there," the incomprehensibility supports my view that Thomas' eye—the physical one as well as the one of his mind—was concentrating on the humanistic rather than the sacred beauties which Italy had to offer. Added emphasis is provided by the final sentence of the subsequent paragraph, which describes Thomas back again in Salamanca, where he graduated as a licenciate in law.

At this point Thomas meets a lady who falls in love with him, but since "he was more devoted to his books than to anything else, he did not respond at all to the lady's fancy" (p. 128). The relationship to Don Quixote is evident, but it would be overly hasty to see the two situations as duplications. We know that Alonso Quijano felt a desire for Aldonza Lorenzo and that he did not have the nerve to test his manhood by approaching her. We do not have any evidence to support a similar sexual fear on Thomas Rodaja's part. Their kinship lies in their love of books but it is of importance to note that Don Quixote's illness is ascribed to reading too many of them, whereas Thomas' illness is the result of a "love potion" devised by the lady and described by Cervantes as poison, "as if there were herbs, charms or words in the world powerful enough to force free will."

The major portion of the novel which now follows Thomas' recovery (after six months) from the immediate effects of the potion deals with his life as a madman who believes himself to be made not of flesh but entirely of glass. It is for this reason that he is now called El Licenciado Vidriera or Graduate Glass. This central and longest part of the tale is in reality a series of witty and biting comments on nearly every level of society. I am in total agreement with Casalduero's analysis that this constitutes a series of aphorisms and that, in fact, it is another version of the Dance of Death (*Sentido de las Novelas*, p. 140). In addition to constituting a series of sarcastic criticisms of current society, the "Dance of Death" performed by the citizenry as they eagerly await the licenciate's latest acerbic remark is at the same time a portrait of the types of individuals who make up that society: in short, despite the lack of originality in most of the witticisms themselves, Cervantes presents us with a nearly complete catalogue of the components of the society of the common man, including not only occupations (tailors, poets, gamblers, notaries, actors, etc.) but as well the varieties of people (those who dye their hair, those who are jealous, those who gossip, etc.).

Behind the mask of apparent insanity, then, lies a perceptive mind ready to make judgments about the variety of possibilities which this life holds. When he is finally "cured," he maintains that his name is now Licentiate Rueda (no longer Littlewheel, but Wheel). Having first seen a good deal of this life, then learned a great deal more through his studies, the protagonist may thereupon observe the almost infinite range of possibilities open to man as he walks through the streets and applies his knowledge to the various facets of human behavior. Once that analysis has reached its limits, he is "cured" and seeks a way to deal with his existence. Perhaps it would be more accurate to say that during his "glass period" he was probing the realities of this life rather than seeking eternal truths, and so what passed before him was a Dance of Life. This would explain the ending of this tale, at which point "he thought he would avail himself of the strength of his arm, since he could get no advantage from that of his mind." It is at this time that he heads for Flanders to rejoin the captain and where, as cited above, "he added eternal fame by deeds of arms to that which he had begun to acquire by his learning" (p. 146).

We should not lose sight of the basic aspect of individuation which the present chapter attempts to illustrate: the choice of the kind of life and the choice of name both are the result of the individual's own decision. This is not to say that every protagonist in the multifarious works of Cervantes feels a need to change his name as he evolves into a state of self-assertion (although there are many who do). What is of importance is to note that even as the various people in Cervantes' literary world seek self-knowledge and an acceptable (to themselves, at least) *raison d'être*, the results may vary, ought, in fact, to vary if we are dealing with individuals, but the processes are comparable and at bottom depend on the individual's choice to be himself. Accordingly, Cervantes describes Thomas' initial reaction to his glass state in a manner consistent with the desire to be individuated: ". . . for really and truly he was not like other men . . ." (p. 128).

It would require an inordinate amount of space to follow this process in every one of Cervantes' works. (The fact that many of the characters not remarked upon thus far will appear as examples of other aspects of the individuation process will also serve to show that the principle is not limited to my selected examples.) Before proceeding to other matters, however, a few more instances from the *Exemplary Novels* will serve to illustrate the variegated fashions in which Cervantes allows his characters to seek their niche amid the richness of his world.

Following an experience with a woman whose machinations had given him an illness which in turn enabled him to observe a "dance of life" pass before his eyes, Thomas Rueda chose the soldier's life in Flanders, presumably having accepted the commission as ensign originally offered him by the captain. Exactly the reverse situation describes the opening paragraphs of *The Deceitful Marriage*: Ensign Campuzano, recently returned from Flanders, emerges from a hospital and comes upon his friend, Licentiate Peralta, and explains that he has been undergoing treatment for syphilis.[35] As I shall detail in Chapter 2, the use of colors by Cervantes should clarify the fact that Campuzano's complexion is described as yellow; moreover, that the woman in question had asked a captain "to take some letters to Flanders for her for another captain who she said was her cousin, although he knew he was only her lover" (p. 183), will also be clarified in Chapter 2. In the same vein there is comprehension and not confusion when it turns out that the woman Campuzano had married does not really own the house in which their first nights of lovemaking took place, for it really belongs to another lady who "came into the room then, dressed in green satin lustre with lots of gold lace edging, a cape of the same material and the same trimmings, a hat with green white and red feathers and a rich gold band, and with a fine veil covering her face" (p. 186). Finally, we should not be amazed to learn that at the Ensign's wedding, his bride brought along as a witness "a youth she said was her cousin" who turns out to be the one to carry her off after Campuzano learns of the deception and who "had been her steady lover for a long time" (p. 190).[36]

But the use of erotic green and the device of the "cousin" are not employed here as they are in *Don Quixote* other than to arouse our awareness of eroticism and duplicity in both works. Like Graduate Glass and unlike Don Quixote, young Campuzano is not seeking eternal truths. We do not know enough about Graduate Glass' relationships with women (other than that he preferred his books to one of them), but we do know that Campuzano not only married but had sufficient intercourse to contract syphilis and thus he is not to be compared with Don Quixote on these matters. Yet he is also opposed to Graduate Glass who was a success as an ensign in Flanders, whereas Campuzano's experience in similar circumstances are passed over in a few words with no indication of having gained fame. In fact, it is the very opposition of his syphilitic state to the deeds that were expected of him which serves as his introduction: Licenciate Peralta, "crossing himself as if he were seeing a ghost, said when he got up to him, 'What is this, Ensign Campuzano? Are you really in this part of the world? Upon my word I thought you were trailing a pike in Flanders, not dragging your sword along here. What is the meaning of this awful colour and this weakness of yours?' " (p. 181).

When we add to this Cervantes' opening sentence, which describes the Ensign "using his sword as a staff, and with legs so weak and his face so yellow that you could see quite clearly that . . . he must have sweated out in three weeks all the fluid he had probably got in an hour," the eroticism that follows begins to take on a relationship consistent with this introductory page. Readers of my Chapter 2 will have no difficulty equating the image of the pointed military weapon known as a pike, with a phallic symbol of masculine sexual prowess which Cervantes contrasts with "dragging your sword." No explanation of the drainage of his fluid is required, particularly when added to the weakness of his legs and the color of his skin.

In contrast to Don Quixote's inability to perform sexually, Ensign Campuzano has left his place on the battlefield for the pleasures of the bedroom and his punishment is his limp sword (phallus) which he drags along with him. Amezúa sees in this description what he calls a great comicity. At first blush I would tend to disagree, but given Amezúa's own definition, I find myself in agreement: "Because if the comical is aesthetically naught but antithesis, opposition and contrast— strong and swift—between two contrary values, ideas or situations, what greater comicity can be found than that of the sound, brave, virile, euphoric figure representative of the military, proudly displaying the plumes and bright colors of his outfit, in contrast with that poor Ensign Campuzano as Cervantes depicts him, 'weak legged, yellow faced, stumbling and staggering,' while his sword, symbol and instrument of his office, serves him only as a cane?"[37]

Casalduero, on the other hand, sees tragedy and relates the invalid soldier-author (since it is Campuzano who is presented as author of *The Dogs' Colloquy*) to Cervantes' biography: "Cervantes offers us all the tragedy that progresses from man to author. If at the beginning we have before our eyes an invalid ('a soldier who, because of using his sword as a cane and because of the weakness of his legs and yellowness of his face'), who can barely support himself, we later find the self-confident author who says the last word, precisely in order to go for a walk."[38]

As my note elaborates, I can only accept the very last point of the passage quoted, and I shall return to that shortly. First I wish to inject my own reading into a controversy whose bibliography is longer than the tale we are discussing, namely the connection between *The Deceitful Marriage* and the novel it introduces, *The Dogs' Colloquy*. I shall not stray into the debate which deals with the structure and unity of the two stories other than to relate this question to my study of the individual. In this context, I must side with those who see the connection as inviolable and most certainly, intentional. Whether it is one novel in two parts, or whether the first serves merely as a prologue to the second (and hence the only) novel of the two is not relevant to my analysis. That the significance of *The Deceitful Marriage* depends upon *The Dogs' Colloquy*, however, is central to my views and there are two reasons for my conclusion.

It is not my purpose to seek sources for Cervantes' works. Even Cervantes, however, through the medium of his character Peralta, refers to Aesop when Campuzano explains that his story deals with two dogs who had the ability to speak. So it is that I, too, cannot help remarking that inasmuch as it is generally accepted that Cervantes was familiar with Apuleius' *The Golden Ass*, we should not overlook the fact that Lucius' transformation into an ass was the result of his lascivious relationship with Fotis. As is typical of his style, Cervantes is less concerned with attempts to mimic his sources than to adapt them to suit his purposes. There was no need, then, blindly to follow Apuleius or anyone else, and convert one of his human characters into an animal. Rather, he allowed his human personage to suffer a human punishment, namely syphilis, followed by an excruciating treatment with the resultant debilitation and emasculation. Campuzano elected to be a soldier; he preferred sex. As his animal instincts got the better of him, so he lost his manly prowess, followed by a forced passive participation in the conversation of animals. *The Dogs' Colloquy*, then, follows naturally upon the brief misadventure of a scoundrel who gave up his patriotic mission for the sake of animal gratification.

Campuzano's punishment, accordingly, is not only a confinement for his exhausting treatment during which time he must listen to a conversation between two dogs; he can only listen to them without participating (although interestingly the proof he offers of the veracity of his tale is that he was "wide awake and with all my five senses" and that he both heard and saw all this [p. 192]). The gist of the tale told by the dog Berganza to his companion Scipio is a satirical series of adventures he had had in a number of different societal settings. Once again, the situation depicted by Cervantes leaves room for suspecting that, like Graduate Glass during *his* illness and like Don Quixote in the Cave of Montesinos, Campuzano may either have dreamed it all or have been temporarily insane.

The significance once more is the same: the nature of the individual. At one point in the *Colloquy*, the dog Berganza relates the possibility that an old witch named Camacha could convert men into animals and vice-versa. The answer given by the dog Scipio provides, in my opinion, the key to this tale of the parade of society or Dance of Death: "I tell you then that the true meaning is just a game of ninepins [bowling], in which those who are standing are quickly knocked down and those who fall down get up again, and this by the hand of him who is able to perform it" (p. 239).

Were it not for the final clause, one could dismiss this sentence as an analogue to the wheel of fortune. The final words, however, whether we wish to interpret them as a reference to God or to the ability of men to take an active part in the game, balance the earlier reference to the vicissitudes of life. In short, we are presented with a description of life as a combination of chance and skill. Some of us are knocked down and some of us are able to raise ourselves. This is the lesson of *The Dogs' Colloquy* which the knocked-down Campuzano must hear through his window in the hospital, and it is significant that Cervantes has chosen for this purpose the Hospital of the Resurrection.

The foregoing clarifies my basic reason for seeing the necessary connection between the two tales in the context of the individual's self-knowledge and subsequent quest for his place as an individual member of society. It is in this context that my second reason agrees with part of the above-quoted passage from Casalduero. Although the conversation of the dogs was apparently not invented by Campuzano but rather used as a source for his jottings which eventually became the manuscript entitled *The Dogs' Colloquy*, the fact remains that he may now call himself an author. In fact, just as the Cave of Montesinos revelation is allowed to be doubted, so here Cervantes permits a similar conclusion to be left hanging. The Licentiate having read the *Colloquy*, his critique is as follows: "Although this colloquy may be a fake and may never have happened, it seems so well put together that you may continue with the second, Ensign."

"Since you think that," answered the Ensign, "I shall pluck up courage and prepare to write it, without disputing any more with you about whether the dogs did speak or not."

To this the Licentiate replied, "Ensign, don't let's return to this argument. I appreciate the art of the colloquy and the invention you've shown, and that's enough" (p. 252).

In other words, just as in the Montesinos adventure, the veracity of the events is not the salient point; what matters—in addition to the art—is the concept and the intent of the adventure. Having found his niche as a writer of talent, Campuzano no longer is described as hobbling but, as Casalduero pointed out, the story ends with Campuzano on his way for a walk with his friend.

VI THE PROCESSES

As I have noted a number of times, I have generally avoided the word "individualism." As I have also reiterated, not only the word but the concept was a phenomenon associated socially and politically with the late eighteenth century, and artistically with the nineteenth century, particularly in the cultural movement known as Romanticism. The writings on individualism are so voluminous that any attempt on my part to summarize or synthesize would not only be a herculean task but would convert this book into something it was never intended to be. Nonetheless, a few words about it are in order, so that we may be clear about our subject.

Even in the mid-nineteenth century, de Tocqueville had to explain that "'Individualism' is a word recently coined to express a new idea."[39] De Tocqueville, of course, was describing a social phenomenon, a society beyond the ken of Don Quixote or Cervantes. Yet, some of his observations bear upon the chapters that follow. Writing in a socio-political vein, de Tocqueville speaks of what he calls democracy as something which not only makes "men forget their ancestors, but also clouds their view of their descendants and isolates them from their contemporaries. Each man is forever thrown back on himself alone, and there is danger that he may be shut up in the solitude of his own heart."[40]

Not unlike de Tocqueville's views are those expressed by Ortega y Gasset half a century later: "The individual invariably adapts his reactions to a communal repertory which he has received by transmission from a venerated past. The medieval man, when he has to decide upon a course of action, puts himself into relation with what his 'fathers' did."[41] Ortega goes on to make the following important distinction as he describes the evolution of this process:

> So long as the empire of tradition lasts, each unit of mankind remains embedded in the close corporation of communal existence. He does nothing on his own account, apart from the social group. He is not the protagonist of his own acts. . . . Hence, in traditionalist centuries figures of outstanding personal physiognomy are not, as a rule, to be found. . . . The only important differences are those of position, rank, employment or class.
> However, within this communal mind, whose texture is that of tradition, . . . a small central nucleus begins, after a time, to form: this is the sentiment of individuality. . . . It used to be asserted that human beings are originally aware of themselves as individuals, and that the next step is to seek out other human beings with the object of associating with them. The truth is just the opposite. The subjective personality begins by feeling himself to be an element of a group, and it is only later that he proceeds to separate from it and achieve little by little the consciousness of his singularity (pp. 107-108).

Finally, Ortega speaks of the individual's production of "some new thought which is to be valued on the grounds, only, of its own independent content. Such a thought, not proceeding out of immemorial communistic life, not to be referred to 'our fathers,' an ideation lacking lineage, genealogy and the prestige of hereditary emblems, *is obliged to derive its parentage from its own works,* to sustain itself by its own convincing efficacy . . ." (pp. 108-109; italics mine).

This is the process of individuation which I propose to examine in the chapters that follow. The *cada uno es hijo de sus obras* theme which I outlined at the beginning and which Ortega has placed in a nonliterary context in the passage quoted above, is the underlying motif. Its very definition, however, suggests a variety of ways in which to become an individual. That process of sustaining one's existence, without any necessary recourse to the political connotations of the word "individualism," is the need of humanity to find a niche in one's lifetime which carries meaning for the individual. (Such an interpretation does not preclude, of course, that the meaning finds its ultimate realization in death or in the hereafter.) That process is the subject of this book.

Before moving on to the manifestations of that process, it is worth observing that the *cada uno es hijo de sus obras* theme is so pervasive that in addition to its appearance in philosophical and sociological contexts, it is found as well in an artistic—specifically, literary—context. Although this may seem to be a tautology given the author's concerns as author, we find here a typically Cervantine twist, as books are treated as though they were people. With respect to *Don Quixote,* this is generally viewed as the protagonist's confusion of life and literature, as well as the multilevel effect given by Cervantes to his work by having the characters discuss literature as though they, the invented characters, were as real as—if not more real than—the author, a technique which in turn makes us ponder our own place in this schematization. On matters of this sort, I refer the reader to the excellent study by Mia Gerhardt.[42] The perspective from which I see this commingling of people and books is one which Cervantes allows not Don Quixote but the latter's niece to originate, for it is she who first suggests that it would have been better had she notified the curate and barber sooner, so that they could have burned the books as if they were heretics.

"That is what I say, too," said the curate. "I swear that tomorrow shall not pass without a public *auto de fe* for them to be condemned to the flames . . ." (I, 5). This suggestion by Don Quixote's own niece, accordingly, sets up not only the burning of the books but implants the suggestion that books may be indistinguishable from people. As Wardropper has observed: "Whenever the *cura* refers to the *grande escrutinio* he does so in terms of burning heretics."[43] Not surprisingly, the inquisition commences with the prototype of such literature, the *Amadís de Gaula*.[44] The curate avers that "this book was the first one of chivalry printed in Spain, and all the rest have their beginnings and origin in this one; and so, it seems to me that, in view of its role as dogmatic founder of such an evil sect, we should without any excuse whatsoever condemn it to the fire."

"No, sir," said the barber, "for I have also heard that it is the best of all the books of this genre that have been composed; and so, in view of its being unique in its art, it ought to be pardoned."

"That's true," said the curate, "and for that reason we shall allow it to live for the time being" (I, 6).

It is interesting to note that despite the evident function of the scrutiny of the library as a parody of the inquisition with an aim toward ridding the world of the "false" books of chivalry, the founder of this literary "sect" is initially condemned because he is the originator. For this reason alone—the label given by the curate to the first book of chivalry is *dogmatizador*—the curate deems it proper and "without any excuse whatsoever," to condemn *Amadís de Gaula* to the flames. Yet, after the brief evaluation by the barber, the curate does not merely modify his views, but proclaims in parallel terms that it is for the very reason that the book is "unique in its art," that it ought to be spared. What exculpates the *Amadís*, which had initially been unpardonably condemned for being first, is the qualification that it is the best. In addition to the evident irony in having those who supposedly seek to condemn books of chivalry agree to preserve the genre's prototype because it is judged to be good, we should note a distinction which is more readily attributed to Cervantes himself than to his parodic characters. To be the first and to be the best are so radically different that it may literally be a matter of life and death.

The relevance to the matters I am discussing becomes clear when the next volume in Don Quixote's library is subjected to scrutiny: the *Sergas de Esplandián* or *Exploits of Esplandián*, described by the barber as the "legitimate son of Amadís de Gaula." The curate's response is unhesitating: "The merits of the father are not going to be of avail to the son."[45] The child (*Esplandián*) is not being condemned because it is not the father (*Amadís*), but because it is judged as having

29

nothing *other* to say for itself than that it is the child. *Amadís*, as we have seen, is spared because of its being judged best, *after* having been condemned as being first. Accordingly, the *hijo de sus obras* theme reflects a manner of judging not only social status, moral worth and esteem of people; it reveals to us as well the perspective from which Cervantes probes the value of creatures and creations generally.

Chapter 2

Sexual Sublimation: Don Quixote's Human Need for Manhood

I WHAT'S IN A NAME?

An assumption upon which I shall insist throughout is that although Cervantes or his printer may indeed have made an occasional mistake or failure to revise, the vast majority of "errors" or "lapses of memory" in Cervantes' works are intentional and not in need of "correction" by lesser imaginations. Rosenblat makes an important contribution in this respect, following the lead of Américo Castro.[1] Castro's insistence on ridiculing those who see lapses and carelessness on Cervantes' part has, as its particular focus, the many names for Don Quixote at the beginning of the novel. Castro uses the example to emphasize his view of the work as one of *becoming*, of the process of being and existing, a view he makes known elsewhere. I believe Castro's thesis to be coherent and relevant to Cervantes' portrayal of existence. My own point is simply an additional one, and my particular application to the names of the protagonist will be taken one step further shortly, and yet another step at a later stage of my study. My general response to the feigned inability to know the name is that of stressing as well (not instead) the process of literary creation, whereby the potentialities and their implications are thrown our way, forcing us to focus first on what the *author's* insight was, and then on what the significance of his ultimate choice is. The background of the suggesting and discarding of names, so long as "we do not depart one iota from the truth" (I, 1), is

31

indeed a combination of the Aristotelian poetical-versus-historical truth precept; a parody of the extensive and precise lineage of the heroes of the novels of chivalry; as well as the analysis of Castro and the rich interpretation of Avalle-Arce, who sees here a sort of reproduction of the baptismal sacrament, even a kind of auto-baptism. Unfortunately, he purposely dismisses ("dejando de lado") the potential names which are presented at the very beginning of the novel.[2] More akin to my own view is that of Rosenblat (p. 171), who points out that the knight's name was neither common nor capricious, but the expression or symbol of his true being. What that expression or symbol may be will be the concern of several sections of this book. What is to the point at this juncture is to stress that the *function* of these and other metamorphoses (not "lapses") is to alert the reader to the creative process of the author of a work of art, thereby allowing us to share in the evolution of the artist's intention.

In any great work of literature, the discovery of metaphorical connotations of whatever sort should come as no surprise. In fact, the writer is one of the few artists whose very craft may be shown to (and therefore, shared by) the observer, in this case, the reader. The composer of music may devise variations on a theme but the sculptor must be satisfied with the product, as must the painter. The process of the plastic arts can only be hinted at by creating yet another work with a different result. But it is another and a different work. The writer, on the other hand, like the musician, may show us the very process of his creativity and allow us to take part in the imaginative workings of his genius.

It is in the very first chapter of Part I that Cervantes displays this process. The examples are many, but for the matter at hand, the best is Cervantes' feigned struggle with his hero's name: Quijada, Quesada, Quejana (to which must be added Quijana in I, 5 and Quijano in the final chapter of Part II). It would not be to the point at this juncture to debate these versions and their meanings. What *is* relevant to my topic is that by allowing us to see the possible variations, Cervantes is begging the reader to see the multiple interpretations, so that by the time the hero chooses his own new version for his knightly exploits, we can share in the creative process. As Comneno has aptly pointed out, we must accept the names not in a literal but in a metaphorical sense.[3]

As I indicated earlier, Cervantes' feigned equivocation in his treatment of the name is a good example of the folly of ascribing so many of his apparent errors and inconsistencies to his alleged carelessness. That he was careless on occasion and that his printer made errors are matters that need not be disputed; but to dismiss as mistakes the very essence of a writer's skill, i.e., his use of words, is to overlook the process of the literary mind. It should be noted in this regard that in I, 1, Cervantes first settles on Quejana as the correct version according to the most likely conjectures ("por conjeturas verosímiles se deja entender que se llamaba Quejana"); shortly thereafter he maintains that the "real name must undoubtedly have been Quijada" and in I, 5, he believes Quijana to be the real name ("que así se debía de llamar"); yet most critics who have cared to refer to the protagonist in his "normal" state tend to heed Don Quixote's own assertion at the end of the book that his name is really Quijano.[4]

With respect to the place, Rosenblat (pp. 70-71, especially 71 n.) provides a concise summary of the scholarship concerning the vagueness of its name in the famous opening line of the novel. In addition to other interpretations (some of which are analogous to my earlier suggestions concerning the name of the hero), what stands out is that in contrast to a relatively typical custom of beginning tales by being *unable* to recall the place, Cervantes plays on this commonplace by claiming to be *unwilling* to recall it. This in turn has initiated a number of interpretations as summarized by Rosenblat, whose own addition is to suggest an act of will, filled with mystery. This may be going a bit far: an act of will it must be, but is not the intention clear, particularly as we see a parallel process for determining the name, i.e., a message to the reader to seek the author's creative meanings? A similar analysis could be made of the opening words of Part II: "Cid Hamete Benengeli relates. . . ." Since we have been repeatedly told not to trust Moors while being assured that this is a true history, is not Cervantes telling us once again and right at the outset to look for the true history which is there but which requires interpretation because of his (apparently hidden) art? A resistance to Cervantes' repeated invitation to us to seek his intentions would lead us into the sterile trap summarized by Perry: "The cardinal sin of positivistic criticism was to forget that art is a function of intention, that if Romanesque sculpture or Indian icons are 'unrealistic,' this shows not ignorance or inability but simply a desire to do something else."[5]

The importance of his ability to bestow names in accordance with his own intentions is reinforced by Don Quixote in II, 67, as he attempts to try out the pastoral life, "taking for myself the name of 'the shepherd Quixotiz,' while you will be 'the shepherd Pancino.'" A few moments later he adds that Sansón Carrasco may call himself Sansonino or Carrascón, the barber Nicholas can be Niculoso and the curate Curiambro. "As for the shepherdesses whose lovers we shall be, we can pick their names as we would pears. . . ." Sancho's response that he could rename his wife Teresona instead of Teresa is not merely an echo nor a mockery of Don Quixote's latest attempt to live literature. Sancho long ago learned the potency of bestowing names, for his "enchantment" of the peasant lass was accomplished in one bold stroke: he simply dubbed her Dulcinea! It should also be recalled that it was Sancho who invented Don Quixote's first alias, the Knight of the Mournful Countenance (I, 19), a chapter which follows a significant exchange on the subject. In I, 18, Sancho had refused to accept the blanket-tossing episode as the work of ghosts or people under enchantment, for as he insists, "it is my opinion that those who had such sport with me were not phantoms or human beings under a spell as your Grace says, but flesh-and-blood men like us. *They all had names*, for I heard them calling one another by them as they were tossing me" (italics mine). The theme of names is picked up only moments later by Don Quixote as he refers to Amadís' alias of the "Knight of the Flaming Sword." More importantly, this same chapter goes on to relate the adventure of the two droves of sheep which Don Quixote converts to soldiers by implicitly accepting Sancho's criterion for the "flesh-and-blood men like us": they shall all have names. Don Quixote proceeds to identify the sheep-turned-soldiers, sprinkling his commentary with a series of names, nicknames, and names of places of origin. It is a mutually profitable experience: Don Quixote has learned quite rapidly that in order to convince a Sancho of the reality of people, he must give them names. Sancho, whose "common sense" reaction to the alleged phantoms had originated the process which he now observes as Don Quixote converts animals to men, shows his understanding of its function in the following chapter as he bestows the nickname upon his master. In the second part he will raise the level to that of quixotic irony when he converts the peasant lass into Dulcinea.

II DON QUIXOTE'S SEXUAL TIMIDITY

With this understanding of Cervantes' fondness for playing on and with names, we can better appreciate the name Quixote itself, bearing in mind Comneno's warning that the name must be accepted in a metaphorical sense. The word *quijote* means that piece of armor which covers the thigh. It is hardly necessary to turn to psychologists, symbolists, or etymologists in order to associate the thigh with that portion of the anatomy surrounding the genital area and traditionally used in literature as a euphemism for the sexual center of the human body.[6] In short, Don Quixote's very name suggests sexuality and the fact that the author allows the recently-turned knight to so name himself would support the notion that our hero is trying to cover and protect his sexuality. This is not to say that he is attempting to deny his masculinity, but that his manliness will assert itself on the battlefield of knighthood rather than in that other possible assertion of manhood, namely sexual intercourse.

Levin (*Quixotic Principle*, p. 54) reminds us that "Smollett not only translated the authentic *Don Quixote* into English but also modeled his own *Sir Launcelot Greaves* upon it, even to the point of the heroic agnomen—inasmuch as a greave, like a *quijote*, happens to be a piece of leg armor." That this leg armor protected Don Quixote from nudity on at least one occasion (thus reinforcing his purpose of covering) is shown in the unhappy ending to the adventure of the galley slaves: "They then stripped Don Quixote of the doublet which he wore over his armor, and would have taken his hose as well, if his greaves had not prevented them from doing so, and made off with Sancho's greatcoat, leaving him [Sancho] naked" (I, 22). Rocinante was protected in a similar manner, for Sancho had been ordered that unless they were indoors, Rocinante "was under no circumstances to be stripped. This was in accordance with an old and established custom which knights-errant faithfully observed: the bridle and saddlebow might be removed, but beware of touching the saddle itself!" (II, 12).

We know very little of the protagonist's first fifty years. We do know that as he approached his late forties, he turned to reading novels of chivalry, novels of manly exploits. Why? None other than Unamuno explains it: "Idleness, and an unfortunate love affair . . . led him into reading books of knight-errantry. . . ."[7] More significant is Unamuno's lecture to Don Quixote after several pages of extolling Dulcinea as the incarnation of Glory:

> And now, my Don Quixote, take me somewhere where we can be alone together, for I want to have a heart-to-heart talk and speak to you as many men do not dare to speak even to themselves. Was it really your love of glory that led you to invest Aldonza Lorenzo, of whom for a while you were enamored, with the image of Dulcinea, or was it your unhappy love for the

comely young peasant girl, that love *which she never never knew of nor paid any heed to*, which turned into love of immortality? [italics by Unamuno]
. . . .

And that repressed love, that love whose current was turned aside, found in you neither the dash nor the boldness to urge it along to its natural culmination. That poor love perhaps shaped your soul and came to be the well spring of your heroic madness (pp. 80-81).

Don Quixote's response could well have been that which he gave to the ecclesiastic (II, 32): "I am enamored, for the very good reason that knights-errant must be. I am not, however, one of those vicious lovers, but rather, chaste and platonic."[8] As Unamuno had suggested, the notion of timidity is Olivera's explanation for Alonso Quijano's failure to achieve love and consequently to seek refuge in the depths of his own being.[9] Michael Predmore has discussed Madariaga's agreement with this line of reasoning, namely that a timid soul, silently in love with a peasant girl of a neighboring town, was unable to assert himself and instead sought refuge in books.[10] This timidity in matters of love is, I believe, indeed why Alonso Quijano turns to literature where he may experience vicariously whatever his library has to offer. Seen in this light, a scrutiny of Don Quixote's library, carried out with greater insight and understanding of the owner than that of the barber and the curate, might prove fruitful. I would not, therefore, agree with Unamuno's decision to pass over I, 6 because "it is a matter of books and not of life" (p. 52). On the contrary, the rest of Don Quixote's life finds its source in that world of books. What is more, he turns specifically to books of many exploits and then attempts to live them, i.e., to assert his manhood.

But he is not so insane as to think it all done so easily. He may indeed have come to believe that he can carry out knightly and heroic feats, but his timidity as a lover remains with him always. This explains why he sends Sancho and not himself whenever the opportunity to confront Dulcinea presents itself. It similarly explains why, despite his expressed intentions, he did not interfere in the Leandra episode (a flesh-and-blood woman) but had no reluctance to rush to the defense of the Virgin Mary shortly thereafter (an image). The parallel in this regard is made more evident by the goatherd's listing of the many men who had fallen in love with Leandra and had taken up a pastoral life because of her having scorned them, "and their madness is carried to such a point that there are some even who complain of her scorn *who had never had a word with her*" (I, 51, italics mine).

One need only think of Don Quixote's reactions to situations which he believes require sexual response to understand that his attitude toward sex is one of evasion. The examples are many, but let the well-known one of Maritornes stand out as the epitome of his desire to flee from sex. His rationalization for this behavior is well known: chastity corresponded to the knightly conduct he had read about. So he knew all along that, in addition to his responsibility to right wrongs, give aid to damsels in distress, together with other heroic exploits, a traditional part of being a knight-errant (in literature) included avoiding unchaste encounters. By preserving himself for his lady, who had been raised to ideal and hence unattainable status, Don Quixote at once set out to test his manhood on the battlefield and avoid his manhood in the bed. (We should also recall that among the poems he reputedly composed during his isolation in the Sierra Morena, one of the few to be preserved [I, 26] includes a reference to himself as "the most loyal lover / who from his lady himself he hides.") An indication of how ideal and, therefore, to what extreme of inaccessibility Don Quixote has depicted Dulcinea is provided by a comparison with other ladies and with other novels of chivalry. In the latter, the knights rendered homage to all lovely ladies, although naturally each reserved his preference for his own chosen lady. Don Quixote, in contrast, repeatedly and right on through his ultimate (physical) defeat, insists that Dulcinea is peerless. (Interestingly, he uses the romances of chivalry as he sees fit and does not always blindly obey their model.) Although Cervantes refers to the beauty of so many of the female characters in his novel, Don Quixote will not admit that any woman can compare with Dulcinea. The purpose, in my opinion, is to insist upon her uniqueness, so that he may rationalize his making no approaches to other lovely ladies (he is reserving himself for the most beautiful of all), while being able to avoid Dulcinea whose very uniqueness makes her unattainable even for him.

Cervantes gives us more than enough preparation for such an understanding of his protagonist. Although like most prefaces and introductions, the prologues to *Don Quixote* were written after the book was completed, their intended purpose was of course to precede the reading of the book.[11] In the final paragraph of the prologue to Part I, Cervantes explicitly introduces Don Quixote de la Mancha as "the most chaste lover and the most valiant knight that had been seen in those parts for many a year." It is easy to dismiss this as parody. which indeed it is; but, as with most of Cervantes' writings, further reading

37

reveals so much more, and often the "more" is the obvious and simple. Our hero, who, we are to learn shortly, is nearly fifty and has loved only from afar, is presented as heroic *and* chaste. Alonso Quijano has found in his readings the answer to his masculine frustrations: he can undertake manly endeavors by attacking whatever his evident imaginative powers will allow him to view as a challenge, and he will not—with significant exceptions—turn his back on such opportunities to exhibit his prowess; by the same token, his interpretation of the novels of chivalry has provided the solution to his timidity with regard to women. It is for this same reason, I suspect, that after his defeat toward the end of Part II, he briefly wants to turn to an imitation of the pastoral life, an existence for those lamenting unrequited (hence unrequired) love. The experiment with the pastoral as an escape from sexual reality is another consequence of his years of reading.

"The point of departure for Goethe's Faust, as for Don Quixote, is a book-lined study; but the two explorers, each of them measuring *das Wort* against *die Tat*, accumulated theory against the practice of life, take opposite courses."[12] I must agree, but the parallels are closer than Levin suggests. There is a prior reason for the book-lined study in each case, and what Barzun has written about the one applies to the other:

> Unlike most heroes, Faust has in fact two lives, and by their juxtaposition he learns what is missing from each. In the first, before the play, too much conventional occupation and withdrawal into bookish lore have withered his heart. He feels cut off from both the grand and the dark forces of Nature and holds life worthless. In the second, appetite and a desperate courage bring him closer to the heart of Nature and carry him through the heights and depths of feeling, but he forgets until too late that he is not alone in the universe. If he were a youth on his first pilgrimage . . . he could find excuses for his behavior. . . . But his being a man with an intellectual and moral past doubles his guilt, and he suffers a new form of anguish far worse than doubt and emptiness of soul, for it involves more than himself. His powerlessness is now no longer a defect but a punishment.[13]

Now, as Unamuno might have said, now we know. Timid Alonso Quijano, converted into Don Quixote, is indeed the Knight of the Lions (Cervantes' valiant knight who knows no fear of physical phenomena) *and* the Knight of the Mournful Countenance (Cervantes' chaste knight who has known no women). Let me attempt to clarify my views by applying my analysis to some well-known adventures. The episode at the estate of the Duke and Duchess can serve as a starting point.

In an insightful observation, Margaret Church comments that "Don Quixote's fantasy of knight-errantry far surpasses the Duke's extravaganza; one [the Duke's] is done for idle amusement, the other [Don Quixote's] for lofty purpose. Cervantes creates the Duke and Duchess, as he has created other figures, as foils for Don Quixote. Is the man who mistakes inns for castles more foolish than the idle exploiter of a madman? The hunt of the innocent boar is in a sense symbolic of the hunt the Duke and the Duchess are conducting for their amusement at the expense of Don Quixote. Sancho's fears, if not Don Quixote's, surely stem partly from his awareness of being the object of the ducal hunt."[14] The word "hunt" is here used, of course, in the larger sense of quest, the ducal pair's search for a meaningful existence (which they perceive only in terms of entertainment and amusement), for which they have temporarily ensnared Don Quixote and Sancho.

The spectacle put on by the Duke and Duchess is, of course, pure sham and the reader must avoid the trap of becoming part of the audience and forgetting that it is presented for an audience. As Green points out, "we are thus completely within the realm of entertainment, of play-acting for amusement, not edification. . . ."[15] On the other hand, some details chosen by Cervantes should not be lost upon us, such as the fact that Dulcinea's role is portrayed by a male youth: is Cervantes suggesting that the Duke and Duchess have correctly read at least one aspect of their guest's personality?

As readers of the novel know, the upshot of all this is that Dulcinea's disenchantment will now depend upon 3300 lashes administered to Sancho. The irony lies in the fact that Sancho himself must apply the punishment. I agree with Margaret Church when she calls this poetic justice, since it was Sancho who "enchanted" Dulcinea and it is he who must now "disenchant" her. "Cervantes," writes Professor Church, "shows us in this episode that each man must come to his own defense as well as recognize who his real enemies are." Generally speaking, this is so, although I am not convinced that this is what Cervantes shows us in this chapter. Even less am I persuaded that "valor without the ability to apply that valor with insight is as useless as insight coupled with cowardice, [is what] Cervantes seems to be saying" (Church, p. 121).

In the first place, there is, in my opinion, a subtle irony far more significant to the total novel and more readily apparent when the protagonist's character throughout the novel is used as the means to view specific episodes. I suggested before that the ducal pair's intent, when they selected a male to play the role of Dulcinea, may be Cervantes' way of letting us know that the Duke and Duchess saw through Don Quixote's sexual difficulties. We shall never know whether Cervantes wanted us to make such an observation about the insight of the Duke and Duchess; the fact that Cervantes is the author of it all, however, strongly suggests that the choice was not a mere crudity, but a deliberate reinforcement of a theme elaborated upon earlier.

There is more, however. The fact that the original Aldonza Lorenzo (whom Don Quixote had converted into the ideal Dulcinea del Toboso), is subsequently reconverted, so to speak, by Sancho to a peasant lass, and now presented as an *apparent* peasant lass portrayed by a male, is a stroke of genius on the part of Cervantes. Rather than remain on the obvious level of Don Quixote's valor having been rendered useless, the ultimate parody of Dulcinea's enchantment is now tied to her newly enchanted version upon which rests Sancho's irrational ideal: the governorship of the island.

III   THE QUEST FOR DON QUIXOTE'S ROLE

Don Quixote, the post-Montesinos Don Quixote,[16] already knows that Dulcinea is unattainable. The cave episode revealed this to him, although he is still groping to find the proper niche in the drama of life. As Casalduero puts it, Don Quixote is the spectator of his own destiny (with regard to Dulcinea) and her disenchantment depends not on him, but on Sancho.[17] I would take the argument one step further: Don Quixote recognizes the unattainable nature of the ideal contained in the concept of Dulcinea; Sancho still sees a connection between the peasant lass and *his* ideal, the island. Don Quixote is becoming more fully aware of reality and thus he fails to disenchant because he recognizes it as outside his own destiny, as he had earlier with the braying towns and the enchanted boat. He is not Amadís:

> . . . every failure to cope with a life situation must be laid, in the end, to a restriction of consciousness. . . . The whole sense of the ubiquitous myth of the hero's passage is that it shall serve as a general pattern for men and women, wherever they may stand along the scale. . . . The individual has only to discover his own position with reference to this general human formula, and let it then assist him past his restricting walls. Who and where are his ogres? Those are the reflections of the unsolved enigmas of his own humanity. What are his ideals? Those are the symptoms of his grasp of life.[18]

Don Quixote has seen Dulcinea in all her guises. Through his experience in the Cave of Montesinos, as well as his experiences in his earlier life and the transformations of her identity first by Sancho and now by the Duke and Duchess, Don Quixote is reaching self-knowledge, which in turn will lead him to his individuality:

> Woman, in the picture language of mythology, represents the totality of what can be known. The hero is the one who comes to know. As he progresses in the slow initiation which is life, the form of the goddess undergoes for him a series of transfigurations: she can never be greater than himself, though she can always promise more than he is capable of comprehending. She lures, she guides, she bids him burst his fetters. And if he can match her import, the two, the knower and the known, will be released from every limitation. Woman is the guide to the sublime acme of sensuous adventure. By deficient eyes she is reduced to inferior states; by the evil eye of ignorance she is spellbound to banality and ugliness. But she is redeemed by the eyes of understanding. The hero who can take her as she is, without undue commotion but with the kindness and assurance she requires, is potentially the king, the incarnate god, of her created world.[19]

It is with this in mind that we must view the defeat of our hero by the Knight of the White Moon, as Don Quixote, basing himself on the premise that "it is not right that my weakness should serve to defraud the truth," maintains that "Dulcinea del Toboso is the most beautiful woman in the world" (II, 64). Don Quixote has recognized the make-believe world of the Duke and Duchess—which is why "adventures" such as that of the Distressed Duenna are "resolved" by what in effect are nonadventures, in this case the "ride" on the wooden horse, Clavileño. A mere sitting, while Sancho's imagination is allowed to roam, puts an end to the presumably difficult undertaking. That Don Quixote has, intuitively if not consciously, seen the futility of disenchanting the Duenna and her entourage by merely sitting still on the wooden horse is symbolized by his willingness to remain blindfolded. Unlike his scrutiny of the Cave of Montesinos, he does not need to see *a ojos vistas*, whereas Sancho finds it necessary to peek. Therein, I believe, lies the significance of Don Quijote's whisper in Sancho's ear: "Sancho, . . . if you want us to believe what you saw in Heaven, then you must believe me when I tell you what I saw in the Cave of Montesinos. I need say no more" (II, 41).[20]

Don Quixote can insist, despite physical defeat, that Dulcinea is as beautiful as ever. As I have indicated, the unattainability of the woman he created in his dreams at the outset is and has been clear to him for some time. That woman has been converted into Sancho's ideal, an ideal on a different plane and with a different set of reference points. (It is for this reason, as well as that of a friend's attempt to revive the

41

faith of a dying man, that Sancho, in II, 74, begs his master not to die: "Who knows but behind some bush we may come upon the lady Dulcinea, as disenchanted as you could wish.") The Dulcinea of Don Quixote has been revealed to him as an ordinary woman, and his faith ultimately will be aimed at higher and more transcendental realities.

"The first problem of the returning hero is to accept as real, after an experience of the soul-satisfying vision of fulfillment, the passing joys and sorrows, banalities and noisy obscenities of life."[21] From the braying of people to the surroundings of the nobility, such has been Don Quixote's experience of the world during his gradual understanding of the nature of his own self. "Why re-enter such a world? Why attempt to make plausible, or even interesting, to men and women consumed with passion, the experience of transcendental bliss? As dreams that were momentous by night may seem simply silly in the light of day, so the poet and the prophet can discover themselves playing the idiot before a jury of sober eyes" (*ibid.*).

It is for such reasons that I cannot accept Don Quixote's insanity. Nor can I accept him as a saint. I would stress instead his *humanity*, ranging from all the errors and misconceptions which limit human understanding, to the God-given attributes which allow those with sufficient wit and motivation to come to know better (albeit not totally) the world in which humans live and how that world relates to any more lasting truths that may be discoverable. Yet, as Campbell says in the quotation above, such people "can discover themselves playing the idiot before a jury of sober eyes."

I mentioned earlier the gradual and evolutionary aspect of the protagonist in this vein as opposed to the supposition that only in one of the last chapters (perhaps after his expression "I can do no more," in II, 29; perhaps after his defeat by the Knight of the White Moon in II, 64; perhaps in the final chapter at the moment of his death in II, 74) does a reversal occur. This is the error not only of some critics but of personages in the novel itself: "The characters who witness the death of Alonso Quijano are not so aware as Cide Hamete is of this continuity and what it implies, for they now refer to him as Alonso Quijano the Good while the Arabian historian continues to designate him by his more familiar title. . . . Without doubt, the literary, philosophical, humane, and even Christian preoccupations of the infidel historian have led him to conclude that Don Quixote has achieved what his soul most desired."[22]

IV THE NAME AND THE ROLE

Let us focus for a moment on this new name, for although I agree that there has been a continuity throughout, I am not willing to dismiss this final self-baptism so hurriedly. In fact, I think it of supreme importance that we fix attention on this last significant act of the protagonist.

I have already remarked on the feigned inability of the author to know his hero's name at the beginning of the novel. To this must be added the following observations: Whether or not we accept the various explanations concerning the earliest hesitations about the name, there is only one character in the novel who unhesitatingly calls the protagonist by a name he has come to know him by during the hero's first fifty years of life. The character himself is of little importance and therefore the naming of the protagonist ought to reflect a fixed form. I am referring to the neighboring farmer in I, 5, who finds our hero after his ill treatment at the hands of the merchants. This farmer, who "knew him very well," calls him Señor Quijana, to which Cervantes adds that "such must have been Don Quixote's real name when he was in his right senses and before he had given up the life of a quiet country gentleman to become a knight-errant." A few moments later, the farmer repeats that the protagonist is "a respectable gentleman by the name of Señor Quijana." (It is at this point that Don Quixote utters his famous reply that he knows who he is and who he may be.)[23]

It would seem reasonable to suppose that his neighbor ought to know the correct name. Nonetheless, not only is Quijana not one of the several versions suggested in the opening chapter; it is, more significantly, not the one mentioned by the protagonist himself at his death. As we have seen, at this point he calls himself Alonso Quijano the Good.

There are at least two levels on which I see this change. First, all of the names suggested in the early chapters end in -a (Quijada, Quesada, Quejana, Quijana), a suffix which in the Spanish language is generally—though not invariably—associated with the feminine gender. In this connection, the contrast is heightened in the final chapter during the reading of the will. Having revealed that his name is Alonso Quijano, he then dictates to the notary that he is bequeathing his estate to his niece, Antonia Quijana. He repeats that her name is Antonia Quijana in the subsequent paragraph. It is, of course, true, as many editors point out, that it was not unusual for female members of a family to bear a feminine form of the family name, particularly if the name lent itself readily to such conversion. The fact, however, that this was not necessarily done, added to the previous feminine versions of the name for the hero, cause the contrast to stand out when one reads, for the first time in 126 chapters, that the protagonist's name ends in the masculine -o, namely Quijano. (Cervantes' awareness of the significance of such linguistic playfulness on the sexuality of names is revealed on a farcical level in *El retablo de las maravillas*, in which he presents Juana Castrada [Jane Castrate], wife of Juan Castrado who, in turn, is the son of Juana Macha [Jane Male].) Bearing in mind my previous analysis of the name Quixote or Quijote as an asexual self-baptism, there is good reason to be consistent and consider this final masculine version as evidence of an ability and a confidence to call himself at last a man.

I obviously do not agree with Sieber that the "final acceptance of himself as Alonso Quijano 'el Bueno' is an admission that his will cannot change or protract the time of death."[24] More to the point is Levin's observation ("The Example of Cervantes," pp. 84-85): "From first to last the narration is colored by his [Don Quixote's] own self-consciousness." We should also not lose sight of Don Quixote's own views on the significance of the naming process: After having dubbed his lady Dulcinea, he believes it to be "out of the ordinary and *significant*, like the others he had chosen *for himself* and his things." In this way Cervantes ends the opening chapter. I follow Groult (*op. cit.*, p. 173) in emphasizing the italicized words, for they reveal how important these names, including his own, are to Don Quixote.

That this device is yet one more of Cervantes' many literary recourses is dealt with at length on another aspect of the novel in the previously cited article by Carroll Johnson. In that case, the discussion centers around Cervantes' (apparent) equivocation with respect to the gender of the animals ridden by the three peasant lasses, one of whom is "enchanted" by Sancho to represent Dulcinea. This same device, begun in I, 1 with respect to the gender of the protagonist's names, used later for the animals in II, 10, and now employed by the hero himself as he affirms his name to be masculine, has been at work between the first and last chapters of *Don Quixote*. Between these points, the protagonist has endowed himself with a name whose lexical meaning I have already commented upon, and whose final vowel is an asexual one. Furthermore, we should recall a salient point in I, 1, about which little comment has been made. I am referring to Don Quixote's criteria for the naming of Rocinante: "The kind of name he wanted was one that would at once indicate what the nag had been before it came to belong to a knight-errant and what its present status was." If we apply this standard (which took him "all of four days") to his own name of Don Quixote (which "required another week"), it becomes still easier to understand why the name Quixote would similarly indicate what he had been before (asexual) and what his present status was (mimesis of famous knights, such as Lanzarote), the combination being a parallel to the paradoxical meaning of Rocinante (a former nag and now the foremost nag, yet still a nag). In the same way, the protagonist was a former asexual gentleman and now a gentleman of heroic aspirations, yet still asexual. It is not until the final moments of his life, that his manhood can be asserted without specific reference to sexual exploits.

To take this analysis one step further, I would submit that not only has the hero come to accept himself as a man in his own eyes; he has as well felt confident enough to add the sobriquet, "the Good." His self-awareness is confirmed in his last words to his niece: "My mind now is clear, unencumbered by those misty shadows of ignorance," and clarified by Ramirez' observations that this "is to compare and almost equate insanity with the darkness of ignorance."[25]

How does Don Quixote achieve this awareness of the nature of things and, concurrently, his self-knowledge? As I have indicated, I cannot ascribe such learning to one magical moment. What is apparent even to the cursory reader is that the protagonist's "true history" begins at a point in his life when there is no history at all: he has spent close to five decades and his own biographer is not certain of his name (for the obvious reason that he has not earned a name) and the narrator does not wish to recall the name of the town. This combination, while frequently commented upon, rarely is accepted at face value. It is well known that several scholars have attempted to locate the place, thereby ignoring the fact that Cervantes specifically expresses his *wish* not to recall the town's name. Clearly, there is a purpose, as I have already indicated, and that is to begin the tale by stressing the nonentity who is to be the "hero" and the intentionally anonymous place which his lack of exploits have not "put on the map."

The protagonist's many hours of reading of the exploits of others have made him aware of his own nothingness. He is simply "un hidalgo," *a* member of a social class, whose dietary habits are briefly

45

described, but whose name is unclear. In short, he is not an individual. His readings, which include pastoral as well as chivalric novels, make him aware that his manhood is in doubt. What better way to begin than by seeking the ideal time in an ideal paradisiacal setting, the very subjects of his first discourse to the goatherds?

V THE "LOCUS AMOENUS"

In a study which barely touches upon Cervantes' masterpiece, Patrick Cullen mentions "the great reservoir of Renaissance commonplaces, the *Quijote*, where commonplaces are set up and reduced to rubble, though sometimes sympathetically."[26] One commonplace, not only of the Renaissance but of European literature in general, is the *locus amoenus*, described in detail by Curtius in "The Pleasance," a section of his chapter, "The Ideal Landscape,"[27] and subsequently summarized by Evett, who writes that "the *locus amoenus* is comprised of three essential elements: trees, grass, and water. It is a landscape of the mind, an aid to conceptualization, imitated from books, not life, and if it is based on a real place, that place assumes an extraordinary dimension. . . . [The theme] comes to have certain traditional expressive capabilities as well, to connote any or all of the categories of refection, numinous creativity or generation, and eroticism. And it becomes morally ambiguous."[28]

Evett goes on to observe that this "combination of grass, shade, and water is, quite simply, gratifying to the senses; it constitutes a powerful, universally recognizable emblem of rest, relaxation, retirement" (p. 506). . . . The *locus* is distinctly conceived as a refuge from the processes of time and mortality (indeed, in its generative aspects, as an antidote to them). . . . Hence the *topos* encourages nostalgic melancholy, especially when reinforced by its traditional associations with the myth of the golden age" (p. 507). As Heninger so concisely defines it, the "milieu is Arcadia in terms of space, or the Golden Age in terms of time."[29] Levin also speaks of the Golden Age as a concept which "takes us back to genesis, the beginning of all things in whatever version. . . . Similarly, on a spatial plane, the backward glance at Eden has its classical counterpart in Arcadia and its exotic counterparts elsewhere. . . ."[30] Moreover, "its actual function is to project an attitude" (p. xvii).

In the discourse to the goatherds, Don Quixote speaks of all these matters. But there is more here, I believe, than a nostalgic yearning for Eden. What Don Quixote presents is, of course, an undisguised panegyric of the *locus amoenus*, but we should not lose sight of which elements he stresses. He speaks of "clear-running fountains and rivers in magnificent abundance [which] offered [a man] palatable and transparent water for his thirst; while in the clefts of the rocks and the hollows of the trees the wise and busy honey-makers set up their republic. . . . The vigorous cork trees of their own free will and grace . . . shed their broad, light bark with which men began to cover their dwellings . . . against the inclemency of the heavens" (I, 11). Moreover, his first reason for calling it a "golden" age, he explains, is that "those who lived in that time did not know the meaning of the words 'thine' and 'mine.'"

"Then, it was," continues Don Quixote, "that lovely and unspoiled young shepherdesses . . . went roaming from valley to valley and hillock to hillock with no more garments than were needed to cover decently that which modesty requires and always has required should remain covered." Subsequently, he returns to the matter of young girls: "Maidens in all their modesty, as I have said, went where they would and unattended; whereas in this hateful age of ours none is safe. . . ." His own profession, he concludes, was instituted for the safety of these maidens.

The relationship in Don Quixote's mind seems clear. Just as he felt the need to create an unattainable woman (Dulcinea), so he must seek the inaccessible time and place (*locus amoenus*) where there is no necessity to prove his manhood in the two most conventional ways: the battlefield (in the Golden Age "all then was peace") or the sexual arena (in the Golden Age maidens did not have to be pursued). It is no coincidence, then, that this discourse is followed by a modern-day counterpart of such pursuit (the episode of Marcela). Don Quixote tries to find Marcela but he cannot. What he does find is his first encounter with the reality of a physical *locus amoenus*: "Don Quixote and his squire entered the same wood into which they had seen the shepherdess Marcela disappear, and . . . having journeyed in the forest for more than two hours, looking for her everywhere without being able to discover her, they finally came to a meadow covered with fresh young grass, alongside the cool and placid waters of a mountain stream which irresistibly invited them to pause there during the noontide heat. . . ."

Not only has Don Quixote failed to encounter the beautiful Marcela, but he has landed in a *locus amoenus* which Cervantes immediately inverts morally. What occurs in this Arcadian setting is Rocinante's abortive attempt to "have a little sport with the ladies," the ladies being some female ponies. It is, of course, correct, as Casalduero observes (*Sentido y forma del Quijote*, pp. 89-91), to view this misadventure as a burlesque deformation of the pastoral as well as a parody of chivalric love (the extra pun being lost in translation, since *amor caballeresco* reflects the etymology of *caballero*, which originally meant "horseman"). In the context of the present study, however, we need not reject Casalduero's interpretation; it merely becomes necessary to relate the burlesque to what preceded it in the novel, namely, Don Quixote's eloquent description of a *locus amoenus* with its chaste vision of love, followed by his entrance into a real place of pleasance, in turn succeeded by the base moral inversion to animal desire for the satisfaction of sexual drive, which the female ponies wanted no part of.

Casalduero's reference to this adventure as a preparation for the parody of chivalric love in the adventure at the inn (Maritornes) is also correct. Once again, however, I prefer to tie this scene to Don Quixote's *first* inn. Having just begun his quest for virtue, his first encounter is with two prostitutes. He had, of course, been looking for either "some castle or shepherd's hut," a paradox rich with meaning.[31] The castle, it goes without saying, is symbolic of his knightly ambitions. To restate this in the context of the present chapter, the castle represents confirmation of his need to be manly. The shepherd's hut, on the other hand, represents his search for a *locus amoenus*. In this respect, there is added significance in Cervantes' description of either the castle or the hut as a place where he might "attend to his pressing needs." Of course, Don Quixote finds neither the castle nor the Arcadian hut but a common inn.

The inn which he finds in I, 2 must therefore be compared with the inn that he encounters in I, 17. These two places—the first being the residence of two prostitutes, and the second being the domicile of Maritornes, the lascivious lass who, though on her way to keep a date with the muleteer, walks into the bed of Don Quixote—are Don Quixote's experience with lust even as he seeks to defend virtue. The two places of iniquity balance the episodes described above, namely, Don Quixote's description of another kind of place (*locus amoenus*) and his subsequent entering such a place of pleasance only to witness animal lust. It should not be overlooked that Don Quixote's eloquent description of the *locus amoenus* is unintelligible to his listeners, for theirs is not an Arcadian setting but a real goatherds' dwelling, precisely what Don Quixote had sought, but not in its literal sense. So it is early in his adventures, although we may not be certain how well he absorbs the lesson, that Don Quixote finds his ideals—virtue, chastity, the *locus amoenus*—inverted.

VI   THE CAVE OF MONTESINOS

Let me now turn to an adventure about which many scholars have written and to which I shall return in a subsequent chapter. I refer to the Cave of Montesinos episode and the events which lead up to it. As we shall see, this adventure may readily be related to the introductory elements I have just commented upon, ranging from Don Quixote's sexual needs (and inabilities) to the *locus amoenus* and the ideals he seeks.

Everything that prepares the reader for the Cave episode is calculated to arouse his awareness of the sexual implications of the adventure, along with warnings not to accept the text literally. The first reference to the Cave takes place at the home of the green-cloaked Don Diego de Miranda. It would take an inordinate amount of space to cite all those who have interpreted this gentleman as either the "perfect knight," or the sane antithesis to Don Quixote, or the degenerate modern knight who substitutes the hunt for knightly adventures. What is to the point of my argument is that Don Quixote expresses his desire to explore the Cave after having spent time with someone whom Cervantes took pains to represent as a lascivious individual.[32]

In addition to what may well have been Cervantes' personal intention concerning the real-life Diego de Miranda, the prolonged stay at the home of a man repeatedly referred to as the green one (or the man in green and other variations stressing the color) must have had a profound effect on Don Quixote. Chamberlin has pointed out the erotic symbolism of the color green and that it was readily recognized as such in Cervantes' time.[33] Given, then, the contrast established by Cervantes between a modern *caballero* whose exploits revolve around his sexual prowess while presenting to the world a picture of respectability (Don Diego), and an out-of-date knight-errant whose attempt to prove his valor in a desperate effort to display manliness while sublimating his sexual impotence (Don Quixote), it becomes easy

49

to interpret the subsequent adventure, that of the lions, with more than the accustomed sense of irony.

The various interpretations of this adventure are beyond the scope of the present study.[34] Suffice it to say that they embrace the extremes which range from Don Quixote's supreme moment of courage (how could he have known that the lions would be too decrepit to be dangerous?) to his supreme moment of folly (only a madman would insist on challenging lions who are securely caged and a threat to no one). In between lies the enticing theory that for some time Don Quixote has "recovered" from his knightly insanity and is here pursuing a death wish. The death wish factor is not irrelevant to my own view but, for the moment, I should like to keep the adventure of the lions within the sequence of themes described in this section of my analysis.

Whether or not Don Quixote—who is introduced to us in I, 1, as *amigo de la caza* ("fond of hunting")—was able to recognize the infirmity of the lions, we shall never know. What we do know is that even in the case of animals (and in a metaphorical sense animals generically represent the nonintellectual, i.e., instinctual, desires of humans), Don Quixote calls forth the male lion, completely disregarding the female of the species. It is of some significance, therefore, that after the lion yawns and proves to be uninterested in combat, "he turned his back and presented his hind parts to Don Quixote" (II, 17). I leave to others any homosexual interpretations to be made of this; I would find them irrelevant to my own thesis, which does suggest to me that Cervantes is presenting to his protagonist a reminder of sexually associated parts, but in a gesture which is symbolic of sexual failure. This may astonish those who see in this adventure an example of Don Quixote's heroism. However, given my previous statements in this chapter, together with the cited comments concerning Don Quixote's timidity with respect to women and sexuality, is not the avoidance of the lioness (a metaphorical turning of Don Quixote's back) followed by the presentation of the lion's rear to Don Quixote, an antecedent by Cervantes of Unamuno's comments on the same weakness of the protagonist (despite Unamuno's subsequent interpretation of the lion adventure as a "marvelous feat")? It is, incidentally, in the very paragraph just cited that Unamuno suggests, "Might it not have been that while Don Quixote demonstrated his courage in this form, within him Alonso the Good, overwhelmed by the disillusion suffered at the meeting with the longed-for Aldonza, sought death at the claws and jaws of the lion, a death not nearly so agonizing as the slow death he suffered from his unfortunate love?" Otis Green is also somewhat ambivalent as he first dismisses this episode as "an adventure purposely sought in all foolhardiness with no other end in view than the conquest of renown," and then on the same page refers to "the shameful exposure, by the challenged lion, of his buttocks to our hero (who had hoped to meet claw and fang)," but draws no conclusion other than to include this among a series of disasters to which Don Quixote is subjected by Cervantes.[35]

Whether it be windmills or lions, whether Don Quixote recognizes them for what they are (lions) or transvaluates them (giants), he is not afraid to demonstrate his virility under battlefield conditions. Virility with respect to women, on the other hand, is something he avoids. So the lion adventure is indeed, as Unamuno suggests, a marvelous feat, for who would care to challenge even a weary lion? But a closer look confirms Unamuno's earlier suspicion: our hero avoids the female, the male recognizes that lack of Don Quixote's desires, and shows him his rump in a symbolic gesture of contempt. Though it was Don Quixote who had called them *leoncitos* ("little lions" or "cubs"), it is the lion who has the last (symbolic) word by suggesting that it is Don Quixote who is not, in animal terms, a man.

That the temporal sexualities and the eternal verities have been converging and have already caused a change in Don Quixote is delicately demonstrated by Cervantes in the reversal of the order in which the hero commends himself to his lady and to his God. In I, 13, Don Quixote had explained that a knight first commends himself to his lady, then to God also. Here, in the adventure of the lions, Cervantes specifically states that Don Quixote drew his sword and faced the cart which bore the lions, "meanwhile commending himself to God with all his heart and then to his lady Dulcinea" (II, 17). This inversion of the order not only parallels Don Quixote's gradual realization and self-knowledge concerning his inner response to the concepts represented by Dulcinea (whom, he now knows, he will not find and cannot have), and God (who, he slowly becomes aware, is his true destiny and destination), but foreshadows the order in which he will commend himself first to God and then to Dulcinea prior to undertaking the adventure of the Cave of Montesinos.[36]

It is shortly following the adventure of the lions that Don Quixote expresses his desire to explore the Cave of Montesinos (II, 18), and it is in II, 22 that Don Quixote repeats his request for a "guide who would conduct him to the Cave of Montesinos, as he had a great desire to enter it and see with his own eyes (*a ojos vistas*) if the marvelous tales they told of it throughout that region were true or not." The guide given to him is a first cousin of the swordsman-licentiate they had met earlier, whom Osuna calls "the so-called cousin."[37]

Osuna does not clarify why he qualifies the cousin in this manner, but he may have picked up one of the many clues to the Cave adventure which I believe Cervantes has left for us. It was a commonplace in the literature of the time that the way in which to entertain a lover without giving rise to local gossip was to let it be known that one's "guest" was a cousin. In short, the word "cousin" suggests two things: generally, a duplicity, and specifically, a sexual encounter. We shall never know whether Cervantes intended us to think in this way, but why was it necessary for him to invent the cousin in the first place? Could not the licentiate have served the purpose as well? Both the change of character and the new personage's identity as a cousin cause us to focus on the process of substitution and camouflage.

Let us take a closer look at this cousin, whose first appearance is alongside "an ass in foal, with a packsaddle covered with a multi-coloured rug or sack-cloth."[38] The presentation of this addition to the plot cries out for metaphorical interpretation. The animal's pregnant state is the first element mentioned by Cervantes in describing the newcomer, clearly an image of sexuality, combining animal passion, sexual potency and its consequences in pregnancy. This is to be the guide of our timid, impotent and self-described platonic lover! Any doubts about Cervantes' meaning are dispelled by the packsaddle, not merely because of its relationship to the rider's (and the animal's) backside but because it was part of the erotic color code of the times for horses to wear colors in a symbolic way. Moreover, "in the latter part of the sixteenth or in the early part of the seventeenth century this symbolism came into such common use that the kaleidoscopic costume of the amorous young men became rather a laughing-stock and offered a fit subject for the attacks of the satirist."[39] The use of an ass rather than a horse only serves to make Cervantes' intended parody that much more apparent.

It is not so, of course, to Sancho, who has—perhaps unwittingly—picked up the sexual signals and proceeds "to stuff his saddlebags to keep company with those the newcomer had brought with him."[40] Sancho, then, who is married and the father of two children (and who symbolically rides a male ass), does not await anyone's order or suggestion to prepare to travel. Rather, Cervantes leaves no break between the introduction of the cousin as arriving on a female ass covered with erotically meaningful colors and Sancho's immediate saddling of Rocinante and his own ass and filling his saddlebags. The imagery of filled saddlebags as connoting potent genitals does not require elaboration.

Nonetheless, Cervantes wants to make certain that we have not missed the point. As they set out for the Cave, the cousin explains that he composed books, one of which is entitled *The Book of Liveries*, "in which were depicted seven hundred and three different liveries with their colors, mottoes, and ciphers, from which the gentlemen of the court might pick and choose the ones that suited them best for their feasts and revels. . . ." If we have been oblivious of color symbolism— particularly as it pertains to erotic interpretations—the cousin's first book requires us to bear it in mind now.

It was in the green-clad gentleman's company that Don Quixote first expressed his desire to explore the Cave of Montesinos, and it was at that time that he indirectly alluded to Ovid. The connection is now made, for the cousin plans to call his next book *Metamorphoses, or the Spanish Ovid*. The contents of this book can easily be interpreted as an entire series of erotic symbols (statues of women which function as weather vanes, stone figures of bulls, sewer conduits, mountains and fountains), and I strongly suspect that this is exactly what Cervantes expected us to see. Accepting them as such, then, without elaboration, we must ask the question, why the title of the book? Since Ovid is as famous for his *Art of Love* as for his *Metamorphoses*, one answer surely is that this is another clue to be on the lookout for erotic meanings. The examples from the contents serve to reinforce this interpretation.

Yet, there is more. The very meaning of the word "metamorphoses" is an unadorned signal to be on guard for changes, substitutions, transformations, inversions and reversals. As if he feared this warning might be lost, Cervantes has the cousin's second reference to this book entitle it *Transformations* (*Transformaciones*). We are being warned not only to read between the lines and be wary of literal meanings; we are being prepared for changes. Added to my previous interpretation of why Cervantes introduced a cousin in the first place, this latest detail confirms the notion of substitution and conversion as a leading motif of this adventure.

The cousin's next book is called *Supplement to Virgilius Polydorus*.[41]

This new volume is supposed to set forth "certain things of great moment that Polydorus neglected to mention. He forgot to tell us who was the first man in the world to have a cold in the head, or the first to take unctions for the French disease. . . ." Again, a bawdy interpretation could be made of "head," and the relationship of syphilis to sexual matters is clear. That this is not pushing my interpretation too far is manifested once again by Sancho's quick leap into this exchange, for he immediately asks whether the cousin knows "who was the first man that ever scratched his head? For my part, I believe it must have been Father Adam." To this the cousin replies affirmatively "seeing there is no doubt that Adam had a head with hair on it, and being the first man, he would have scratched it some time or other."

In addition to some of the bawdy interpretations that one might wish to make of the preceding, a relevant interpolation at this point could well be the words of Falstaff (1 *Henry V*, III, 3): "Dost thou hear, Hal? Thou knowest in the state of innocency Adam fell, and what should poor Jack Falstaff do in the days of villainy?" Both Falstaff and Sancho remind us of the golden age *topos*, but whereas Falstaff goes no farther than to present the contrast between the age of innocence and the current one of corruption as an excuse for hedonism, Sancho's reference to "Father Adam" not only relates the biblical to the erotic (because of the possible bawdy connotation suggested above as well as because Adam's fatherhood takes us beyond the Fall) but goes on to refer to another fall as he immediately asks the cousin who the first tumbler in the world was. The cousin is at a loss for an answer, but Sancho has no trouble in pursuing the connection: the first tumbler was Lucifer "when they cast him out of Heaven and he came tumbling down into Hell."

Although most commentators remark that the word "tumbler" specifically refers to "acrobat," I doubt that the semantic distinction detracts from the significance connoted by the image of a fall from Heaven to Hell, particularly since it is another moral fall from grace. It is interesting to note that both Putnam and Starkie use the word "Hell" (for the obvious reason that this is where Lucifer is believed to have landed), whereas only Cohen exactly translates the original *abismos* as "abyss." I find it of interest because as the translations appear to reveal—when viewed simultaneously rather than as the individual efforts they obviously are—there is a ping-pong effect between "Hell" and "abyss," an effect which Cervantes created by referring to "abyss" in the example just cited, followed a few moments later by Don

Quixote's insistence that he intended to see the end of the cave, even if he went as far as the abyss (which this time only Starkie renders as "abyss," but Putnam and Cohen preferring "Hell"), which in turn is followed by Don Quixote's commending himself to God and Dulcinea as he prepared to descend to the abyss (all three translators agree) and concluded by Cervantes' reference (via indirect discourse) to the Hell (again all three translators agree) which Don Quixote had visited, a name that Don Quixote immediately rejects. Is it simply an abyss or is it Hell? In other words, is it the exploration of a cave of the known world or is it the symbolic descent into Hades which presents such an inviting and almost ready-made interpretation?

I stated above that I find of interest the interplay of the words "Hell" and "abyss" on the part of the author as well as of modern translators. In addition to viewing this typical stylistic device of Cervantes as playing with the reader's perception of reality,[42] I find inescapable the clue laid down for us by the author in selecting a personage who, besides his place in people's minds as one of the many guises of the Devil—in a confusion resulting from a misinterpretation of Isaiah 14:12, in which the reference is to the King of Babylon— carries a name which means "bearer of light." Although this may require some etymological knowledge on the part of some readers, no special insight is required of the Spanish-speaking reader, in whose language the word for "light" is *luz*. (One might add that the Isaiah verse reads, "O Lucifer, son of the morning!" which accounts for the other confusion of Lucifer and Venus as both symbolic of the morning star.) That Sancho's question and answer are indeed open to subtle interpretation is suggested by Don Quixote himself, who recognizes that the meaning lies beyond the intelligence of his illiterate squire: "'Sancho,' said Don Quixote, 'that question and answer are not your own; you've heard them somewhere.'"

Previously, we were prepared for a *locus amoenus* and we found its antithesis. Concurrently, we have seen a development of sexual themes ranging from Don Quixote's inability to cope with a sexual relationship to the series of bawdy and erotic references which have been gathering momentum. Now we have been alerted to two famous cases of falls from grace, thus joining the biblical with the human (i.e., the divinely perfect with human flaws), together with the allusion to light. Finally, amid all these motifs, a recurrent series of warnings by Cervantes has made us aware that we are not to take things literally, not only because one of his well-known overall themes is the question of reality and how it relates to appearance but because of the more immediate insistence that we seek the significance of the work, particularly through an understanding of the motivating forces which propel the characters.

The cousin, whom I have associated with substitution and eroticism, is to guide our hero's way, "delighted to conduct him to the mouth of the said cave and show him the Lakes of Ruidera. . . ." To see the metaphor of the "guide" who will conduct him to the "mouth" of the "cave" in erotic terms does not require much imagination. With regard to the lakes, Don Quixote had, in his first request to see the Cave of Montesinos, included a desire "to look into the true source and headwaters of the seven lakes that are commonly known as the Lakes of Ruidera" (II, 18). To be consistent in the metaphor, then, it seems appropriate to explain this desire as voyeurism, particularly since we shall shortly be told that these lakes are women. To want to see the source of their waters, then, can readily be interpreted as a desire to see the female genital area. That it reflects the general desire (since he speaks of them as a group) of a man uninitiated in sexual matters to see naked femininity rather than the specific desire to have an affair with a particular woman, is consistent with the timidity mentioned earlier. It is important in this regard to recall Don Quixote's insistence on seeing the cave with his own eyes. Furthermore, as I indicated above in the discussion of the word "abyss," Don Quixote expressed his intention of seeing where the Cave ended. (If the sexual analysis I have expounded is valid, Don Quixote's need to see where the cave ended confirms his inexperience.)

This motif is picked up by the guide—Cervantes specifically calls him "guide" here, not "cousin," the two words being interchanged at the author's will, a device I have noted earlier as typical and which serves to underscore the literal and metaphorical levels that the reader is continually being asked to perceive. To repeat, the visual motif is picked up by the guide as he begs Don Quixote "to view thoroughly and inspect with a hundred eyes what you find down there; who knows, maybe it will be something that I can put in my book on *Transformations*." (I have already commented on the translation of the Greek title to the vernacular; that it appears in the same passage in which the cousin is called the guide, reinforces both my earlier suggestion and my observation in this paragraph.)

The cave's mouth is described as "broad and spacious, but clogged with boxthorn, wild fig trees, shrubs, and brambles, so dense and tangled an undergrowth as wholly to cover over and conceal the entrance." If Cervantes has succeeded in making us aware of the erotic symbolism thus far, it is a simple matter to see in this description the image of the female genital area concealed by pubic hair. The image is supported by the choice of species which cover the opening, fig leaves being the traditional covering of the genitals ever since Adam and Eve ate the apple (Genesis 3:7) and the bramble a symbol of virginal purity.[43] Such symbols, of course, serve only to add to, rather than create, the erotic symbolism of the cave opening.

Cervantes then describes how Don Quixote used his sword to cut away all this undergrowth, causing a large number of crows and jackdaws to fly out. What symbolic meaning we may wish to attach to the sword is limitless. Even a cursory glance at sources which deal with such matters reveals the astounding range of meanings that the sword has held for various peoples. I think it safe to say, however, that for a knight eager to prove his manliness, the sword is an obvious reference to his masculinity, whether it be of a warrior nature or of a sexual one. Of the many other things which the image of the sword may connote, the only one that also applies is, I believe, that of the cross. This dual applicability to a Christian knight does not detract from my interpretation of the book; rather, it strengthens it. For the moment, however, the function of the sword to cut away the undergrowth in order to reveal the opening makes the sexual imagery predominate. It will not be long, however, before events cause the cross imagery to assume primary significance.

A similar dual symbolism exists with regard to black birds which emerge as they are disturbed by Don Quixote's sword. Leaving aside the obvious interpretation, namely that they foretell bad luck—because Cervantes himself warns us away, as he explains that had Don Quixote "been as much of a believer in augury as he was a good Catholic Christian, he would have taken this as an ill omen and would have declined to bury himself in such a place as that"—I should like to concentrate on their color.

Cirlot (p. 55) quotes Jung to the effect that "the profoundest meaning of black is occultation and germination in darkness." He also cites Jung as pointing to "the relevance of the 'dark night' of St. John of the Cross and the 'germination in darkness' of the alchemists' *nigredo*."[44] Moreover, according to Ania Teillard, "the dark earth-mother—the Diana of Ephesus—was depicted with black hands and face, recalling the black openings of caves and grottos."[45] Although color symbolism can be debated endlessly and the symbolic meanings of most colors are not universally agreed upon, certain general statements may be made: "Black, in fairly generalized terms, seems to represent the initial, germinal stage of all processes, as it does in alchemy. In this connection, Blavatsky points out that Noah released a black crow from the ark before he sent out the white dove. Black crows, black doves and black flames figure in a great many legends. They are all symbols closely related to primal (black, occult or unconscious) wisdom which stems from the Hidden Source."[46]

All of the above fits well into the sexual motif which I have been tracing. Having uncovered the female opening, Don Quixote is confronted with the primal color, leading him to the next potential stage, entry and germination. As he tells us upon his return, he was greeted by Montesinos himself, "clad in a hooded cloak of mulberry-colored stuff that swept the ground. Around his head and bosom was a collegiate green satin sash, and on his head a black Milanese bonnet."[47]

Kenyon (p. 328) indicates that mulberry (*morado*) "is par excellence the color of love." We have already seen that green symbolizes eroticism. As Kenyon points out, "because of the close connection of the two colors, green and violet are often combined" (p. 330). When we add the black of the bonnet in light of its generative connotation, it would appear that all the signs point to a successful and erotic act of love, even to the possibility of childbirth. It is tempting to suggest that the arrival of the guide on a pregnant animal, which in turn was preceded by the adventure of Camacho's wedding, all served to prefigure a sexual union in the Cave. Yet, we need to take a closer look at color symbolism.

In the first place, the green sash which goes around Montesinos' bosom is also described as encircling his head, thereby causing it to come in direct contact with the black bonnet. Kenyon (p. 330) observes that "dark green, being a mixture of black and green, denotes the loss of hope, or that one's hopes are greatly diminished." Furthermore, as Cirlot points out, "when two colours are contrasted in a given symbolic field, the inferior colour is feminine in character and the superior is masculine. By 'inferior' we mean that which is lower within the alchemic order or series. . . . Any symbolic composition that, spatially, does not conform with this order presents us with a clear-cut example of Symbolic Inversion. . . . For example, in the normal symbolic pattern, white will be placed above black . . . and so on" (p. 57). If we reread the description of Montesinos, we note that the color white is significant: his beard is snow-white and falls *below* his waist, whereas on his head, well *above* the white beard, we find the black bonnet. The Cave episode presents us, then, with what Curtius (pp. 94-98) calls "The World Upsidedown," and the various colors, which, when examined in their total array, represent one of this *topos'* characteristics: the "stringing together impossibilities." On the other hand, those who stayed behind and did not share Don Quixote's experience in the Cave, have generative interpretations (Sancho, in II, 22: "Welcome, master, we are glad to see you again. We thought you had stayed down there to found a family") or erotic ones (the cousin, in II, 24: "I . . . look upon this journey . . . as having been exceedingly worth while. . . . I have learned what lies hidden in this Cave of Montesinos and have heard of the mutations [into women] . . . of the Lakes of Ruidera, all of which will stand me in good stead in connection with my *Spanish Ovid* . . . [and] I have established for a certainty what the source of the Guadiana River is").

Don Quixote's own experience has been quite the contrary. The color symbolism which first greets him is an indication of inversion. No wonder, then, that Don Quixote's immediate reaction is to ask Montesinos "if the story was true that was told in the world above, to the effect that with a small dagger he had cut out the heart of his great friend Durandarte and had borne it to the lady Belerma as his friend at the point of death had requested him to do." Don Quixote—who had maintained a steadfast faith in the tales of chivalry—recognizes the ambience of inversion and thus it is of significance that his very first words question the veracity of one of these tales.

The love between Belerma and Durandarte can be traced back through several variants which apparently have their origin in the Carolingian ballads, a subject outside the concerns of the present study. Let us, however, not forget that they do represent one of those many faithful pairs of lovers of tradition and poetry. One of the best known of such couples is the legend of Pyramus and Thisbe. It is undoubtedly part of Cervantes' careful elaboration that two paragraphs prior to Don Quixote's first mention of his desire to see the Cave of Montesinos, a sonnet based on the Pyramus and Thisbe story is recited. Somewhat later, in the adventure immediately preceding the Montesinos episode, another reference is made to "revive for the world the forgotten romance of Pyramus and Thisbe" (II, 19). One might be tempted to dismiss both references as mere reflections of Cervantes' reading of Ovid, were it not for the specific details contained in the sonnet, of which I shall cite only a few:

The beauteous maiden now bursts through the wall, she who in Pyramus's gallant breast hath left a gaping wound. . . .

. . . .

Desire grows, rashly the amorous maid, seeking her pleasure, hastens to her death. Ah, what a tale is here for hearts that strive! Two lovers dying by a single blade to find a common grave, and yet the breath of memory doth keep them still alive. (II, 18)

The parallel is clear; the comparison truly odious. What in the poem is metaphor becomes in the Cave grotesque literal enactment. The hero literally has his heart cut out, yet is still alive, while the heroine wanders about carrying the "mummified heart, all dried and withered" and undoubtedly still with the salt put upon it by Montesinos "so that it would not have an unpleasant odor."

Belerma's appearance follows the pattern I have been describing. She is clad in black with a large white turban on her head, a suggestion that the superior-inferior order is rightside up. But she also wears "a flowing white veil so long that it touched the ground." The fact that the white extends from head to toe may not be sufficient to suggest inversion but it assuredly blurs the white-above-black order. Furthermore, the veil is itself symbolic of concealment, a motif which has been with us at least since the arrival of the cousin, in a more subtle way all along, and in a dramatic way in the Cave. Moreover, her complexion is that of sallowness (*amarillez*) or greenish yellow.

There is an illness called "chlorosis," which the *Random House Dictionary of the English Language* (1967) defines as follows: "Also called *greensickness* . . . a benign type of iron-deficiency anemia in adolescent girls, marked by a pale yellow-green complexion." The inversion of values in the Cave scene is emphasized by the fact that this condition is normally found in adolescent girls, whereas Montesinos makes a point of explaining that Don Quixote must not think "that her sallowness and those circles are due to an affliction that is common to women at a certain period of the month, for it has been many months and even years since she has had that experience. It is, rather, the grief that she feels in her heart for that other heart she holds in her hands."[48]

Aside from being a parody on the imagery of love poetry,[49] what the Cave episode portrays to Don Quixote is yet another transvaluation. If he had hoped to have an amorous experience, a traditional personage of love has been presented to him in a state of putrefaction: Belerma, with her sallowness and her "few and uneven" teeth, carrying the desiccated heart of the heroic Durandarte who lies heartless with a cavity in his chest—all this depicts the literal representation of the figurative sonnet which described the lovers in a common grave, still alive and slowly decaying. Don Quixote's question, while revealing his doubt about the Durandarte ballad, reveals as well that the sonnet in II, 18 prefigured correctly that the memory of the lovers is what gives them continued life. This is that "second life of fame and honor" of which Jorge Manrique speaks; it does indeed survive the "first" life and last longer, but as Manrique himself made clear, it is not eternal either. Moreover, yet another *topos* is stood on its head in this scene. Manrique, like many others of the later Middle Ages and thereafter, raised the famous *ubi sunt* motif. Unlike most works, *Don Quixote* answers the question: "*there* they are," the episode seems to be saying, in a state of decay, still alive but on their way to yet another death. (The anachronism observed by many critics as the result of the confusion of characters from different eras spanning hundreds of years is obviously not an "error" by Cervantes; rather, this device allows us to see the various stages of decay.) As one critic has observed of Dante's *Purgatory*, "It is true, what Dante asserts in the letter to Can Grande, that 'the subject, then, of the whole work, taken according to the letter above, is simply a consideration of the state of souls after death.' It is equally true that the subject is the state of souls in their mundane condition, and vested in particular forms."[50]

With this preparation, the reader may readily expect the climax of this adventure: Dulcinea is also in the Cave—where else would she be, if the adventure includes among its variegated aspects the perhaps hidden hope on the part of our timid hero that here he may at last experience a sexual union? It is only to be expected, then, that Dulcinea, too, appears in an "enchanted" form. Moreover, it follows naturally that Dulcinea is first spotted in the Cave with her two girl-friends "gamboling and disporting themselves like goats." The ending could not be more fitting; it recalls his last view of "Dulcinea" as she rode off on her ass "sitting there astride it like a man" (II, 10), as well as his adventure with the lion. Dulcinea in the Cave turns her back on him and flees. That she finally sends one of her friends back to him to borrow six *reales* only to have Don Quixote realize that he has no more than four, invites an interpretation that I am not the first to make, but which clearly fits into the pattern of my arguments thus far. Don Quixote is unable to achieve a union with Dulcinea because he is unable, that is, impotent, and cannot provide her with what she asks for. Moreover, it is the final confirmation of his views on sexual matters: they are beyond his reach. (As this book was being readied for the press, I was privileged to hear a paper delivered by E. C. Riley at the 1977 congress of the International Association of Hispanists in which he made a convincing case to indicate the symbolism of femininity contained in the image of the hare. In the penultimate chapter of Part II, Don Quixote comments, "A hare flees, the hounds pursue it, Dulcinea appears not." Sancho, in his reply, similarly understands the relationship between the hare and Dulcinea. That this incident can be related to the matters discussed in the present chapter is, it seems to me, patent.)

Within the context of the foregoing, we can better understand the many comments about the negative consequences of passion which are sprinkled throughout the novel. This is by no means a new topic but its relevance to an understanding of the protagonist's character and behavior is, I believe, made clear by the preceding pages here. As Predmore (*The World of Don Quixote*, p. 90) has observed:

> The passion of love is another great upsetter of rational conduct. How many characters refer to its power and its effects! Vivaldo, for example, speaks of the "end to which come all those who plunge down the path that unbridled love sets forth before their eyes" (I, 13). Leonela speaks of the "snare of love" (I, 34); Lothario, of "so powerful an enemy as love" (I, 34); Altisidora, of "the powerful force of love" (II, 44). Referring to the love affair of Lothario and Camila, the narrator affirms: "the passion of love is overcome only by flight; let no one test his mettle with so powerful an enemy, because divine strength is needed to conquer its human strength" (I, 34). Don Quixote, who began to speak of the "amorous pestilence" in his discourse on the Golden Age, treats of it again and again: "love and liking blind the eyes of understanding" (II, 19); "the power of love is wont to unhinge the soul" (II, 46).

Somewhat later, Predmore says of the Cave episode: "All of this goes very well with knight-errantry, but not everything witnessed there does. Out of keeping with the romances of chivalry is the capering of Dulcinea and her damsels, and especially the request of one of these to borrow a few coins for Dulcinea, using her skirt as security" (p. 111). I cannot but agree that Dulcinea's capering is not in keeping with chivalric literature. On the other hand, my arguments here have, it seems to me, shown the connection between her behavior, the inversion of values, and Don Quixote's sexual timidity. Moreover, the literal association of money, that is, *gold*, with the quest for a "golden" age, not only reveals the inversion of even this metaphorical epithet to the *topos*, but is one more example of Cervantes' skill in adapting a source to suit his own style, for the play on the word "gold" in the sense of noble values as well as that of purchasing power is already present in Ovid's *Art of Love*.[51] Levin (*Golden Age*, p. 143) makes the interesting point that Cervantes, following the Spanish prose version of Ovid's *Metamorphoses* by Jorge de Bustamente, "marks the culmination of a voluble concern for the golden age which, in Spain, was coextensive with the extraction of gold from the New World."

As we return to "the world above"—to use Don Quixote's own words—and recall that the hero's first words were that he had been taken away from "the most delightful existence mortal ever knew and the pleasantest sight human eyes ever rested upon," the question that must be raised is not whether it was all a dream, or a true happening or an invention on the hero's part. I agree with Sieber's quotation and commentary from Riley: "'It is useless to ask if what Quixote related was a dream, a wilful fabrication, or anything else. Cervantes never intended us to know.' And I would add that knowing the truth or falsehood is not necessary for an understanding of this adventure. What is important is merely its existence in the novel where it is presented as a *unique* product of Don Quijote's consciousness."[52] The question to be considered, then, is that whatever its definition, Don Quixote reports it as such a delightful and pleasant experience and, as Riquer points out, the most curious aspect is the attitude of Don Quixote, who goes on explaining what Riquer calls his "vision" without fully realizing the grotesque elements in it (*Aproximación al Quijote*, p. 145). Why?

The answer lies in the beginning of the novel. Realizing that his nearly five decades on this earth have produced a nonentity and therefore having at first falsely concluded that the purpose of a man is to demonstrate his manhood, the protagonist has finally apprehended at least some of the eternal truths. These have been revealed to him directly and indirectly, but the ultimate purpose lies in his differentiation of the temporal (which includes the sexual) from the eternal (which places the individual in a context of God's truths). The adventure of the Cave of Montesinos is nothing more (dream or no dream) than a dramatization of this undeniable truth.

Chapter 3

The Eye of the Beholder

I INVERSION

The various inversions of the *locus amoenus* motif find their significance in the reversal of the protagonist and, although the change is neither sudden—Cervantes has prepared us for a long time—nor total—the final chapter will produce that—the climactic moment is, in my estimation, Don Quixote's experience in the Cave of Montesinos.

"Reversal" in literature brings to mind the words of Aristotle, who defines it as "a change of the situation into the opposite . . . this change being . . . like the man in the *Oedipus* who came to cheer Oedipus and rid him of his anxiety about his mother by revealing his parentage and changed the whole situation. . . . A 'discovery,' as the term implies, is a change from ignorance to knowledge. . . . A discovery is *most effective when it coincides with reversals.* . . ."[1] The italics here are mine, for Cervantes has added another dimension: not only does Don Quixote undergo a reversal in the Cave and reach a fundamental discovery, but the very fabric of the novel has presented an inversion—reversal, if you will—of the world above *and* the world below. The discovery is that *neither* is what was sought or expected. Thus plot, style and character are interwoven with *topoi*, symbolism and change.

Francis Fergusson refers to the "imagery of light and darkness [which] runs through the [*Oedipus*] play. . . . It is based on the *analogy* between the eye of the body and the eye of the mind—sight: blindness :: insight: ignorance."[2] To analyze the light-darkness imagery would be to step outside the scope of my study, and to a large extent, Casalduero has

64

already done much of this throughout his work. It is to the point, however, to recall the emphasis on *seeing* in the Cave as described earlier. To this must be contrasted the fact that Don Quixote returns from the Cave *with his eyes closed* and that his first words refer to the *sight* he has witnessed. To explain it away as a dream or a vision hardly deals with the issue—particularly in a work of literature—and still leaves us with Riquer's question about Don Quixote's failure to see the grotesque. If we do not answer this question, it is we who have lost sight of the significance of the adventure created by Cervantes.[3]

An analogue may be found in Erasmus. As one observer recently put it, "to live one's life by [the illusion of man's happiness] is to live a life of unavoidable insecurity. A single flash of insight can blindingly illuminate Plato's cave. Micylluses may dream, but their passivity exposes them to rude awakenings. Man's uncontrollable impulses will push him face to face with truth and will force him to open his eyes."[4] Rebhorn goes on to say that the Christian fool's metamorphosis is not to be "identified with that of those worldly fools who think themselves content in the bondage of Plato's cave, committed totally to the values of this world and consequently its inevitable victims. Through faith and God's grace, the Christian fool is able to rise above the limits of earthly life and achieve a foretaste of the true, unending bliss that God prepared for him and that, once experienced, completely transforms his life" (p. 471). Rebhorn continues:

> The sun shining outside Plato's cave is the Light which illuminates the universe, and heaven holds the promise of endless youth and eternal spring. For the Christian fool, life will still be a shadow play, the world still dominated by opinion, but now experience has a sure, transcendent meaning. For him it does not matter whether life is comic or tragic, because he does not live life for its own sake, but as a prefiguration of and preparation for the eternal life which he has just barely tasted in his mystical transformation. . . . The work embodies a strategy of conversion. It brings man to a full perception of the ambivalent, inadequate, futile character of life on this earth, and then it leads him beyond that comi-tragic vision to a fuller, more all-encompassing one. (p. 472).

Another commentator on Erasmus and the literature of the "fool" has observed that "Don Quixote would take us back into Plato's (or Montesinos') cave, to gaze on shadows as though they were realities and to be happy."[5] To some extent, particularly with respect to happiness, this is accurate, for we have heard Don Quixote's description of how pleasant and delightful was the sight he had witnessed. On the other hand, the "shadows" which he saw and which to us seem so grotesque, demand enlightenment. It is Don Quixote himself who, in response to one of the several occasions on which Sancho casts doubt about the veracity of the adventure in the Cave, answers that time will tell, "for time, the discoverer of all things, never fails to bring them to the light of the sun even though they be hidden in the bosom of the earth" (II, 25).

Otis Green, after summarizing St. Augustine's views on the sinner who loses all hope, observes that "the sinner who turns his back on despair and heeds God's voice may be regenerated and returned to God's friendship: 'When once that voice is heard and believed,' wrote St. Augustine, 'those who were submerged in that profound abyss emerge therefrom.'"[6]

The foregoing comments lead us to the answer to what Don Quixote saw, and why, despite the grotesque aspects, he was able to see it as a pleasant sight. Let us retrace some of our steps and take a second look at the process which led Don Quixote to the Cave of Montesinos.

In view of my previous hypotheses with respect to the author's (or, if you will, the biographer's) inability to know with certainty the name of his leading character (although the writer is, ironically, intimately familiar with the details of the protagonist's dietary habits), the resultant anonymity of the hero is rather consistent with Cervantes' characterization. Aside from his eating and reading habits, we know next to nothing about Alonso's pre-quixotic life, which is in consonance with his not having made a man of himself in any way in which that term is commonly understood in society. His sexuality is in doubt and his only masculine attempt in any other direction has been confined to the hunt, a substitute for warfare. In short, his life has been a total sublimation, an awareness of which began to dawn upon him in middle age, whereupon he first sought refuge in the literature of chivalry through which he could vicariously experience heroic and manly undertakings. His mistake, as nearly everyone knows, lies in the confusion of this vicarious experience with a belief that he is now one of these heroes, perhaps even the greatest one of all. For this reason, he is interpreted alternately as a fool, a madman or, in spiritual terms, a hero. That he himself entertains doubts is demonstrated repeatedly, beginning with his refusal to test his helmet a second time, and his choice of name which, as I have indicated earlier, may indeed be patterned after Lanzarote (Launcelot) but nonetheless remains a word whose simple meaning is that piece of armor which covers the thigh. In summary, he begins his adventures without a name, without a known deed, without any sexual experience, and the author of his history must recount for us the hero's own invention of the name to be used henceforth.

II EXISTENCE

"Alonso Quijano's attempt to transform himself entirely into his self-invented character, Don Quijote, is as unsuccessful as Ginés de Pasamonte's attempt to unite his active self with his own analytical self-portrayal. The scene of Don Quijote's penance in the mountains (I, 25) is enough to show that Alonso Quijano is not entirely absorbed into his character Don Quijote."[7] I have made several references to the highly important triad as best described by Jorge Manrique.[8] The so-called "first life" is that which the protagonist of *Don Quixote* has nearly finished. Recognizing this piece of common knowledge, namely that our physical life on earth is temporary, he now realizes that his failure to have achieved fame has not prepared him to have a "second life," a life of fame which is more enduring than the physical life, since, metaphorically speaking, man lives on in the form of the memory he leaves behind him. Having read of the heroic exploits of chivalry which help to create such fame and extend one's existence, the protagonist attempts to live out his physical life by performing the requisite feats to leave such a memory behind him. The parody represented by such well-known episodes as those of the windmills, the armies of sheep, etc., is not merely a parody of the books of chivalry. Cervantes is also parodying the attempts of his contemporaries to gain fame for the sake of the "second life," and what he is doing by means of these adventures is to point out the real folly of believing the display of masculinity to be as important as (if not more than) the purpose of moral behavior. This is the meaning behind Don Quixote's words "that one man is worth no more than another unless he does more" (I, 18).

Consequently, underneath all the literary devices, there exists the simple story of an individual who has sufficient self-awareness to recognize the emptiness of his life and who desperately seeks meaning in his attempts to imitate the knights-errant of old. Even here, as noted previously, despite many protestations to the contrary, he never quite believes it all and therefore retains that bit of self-knowledge which will enable him to see the light. (At a different level, Cervantes makes a similar comment on people's doubts about beliefs in his short play, the *entremés* entitled *El retablo de las maravillas*, in which legitimacy and pure Christian blood are the attributes that enable people to "see" the "marvels" which the traveling charlatan presents. That they pretend to see the "marvels" and obviously do not, reveals their doubt: a doubt not only about their own particular claims to legitimacy and pure blood but—and herein lies the ultimate irony—doubt about the validity of the underlying assumptions.) It is noteworthy to recall, therefore, that even Cervantes waits until the adventure in the ducal palace, long after Don Quixote has begun to see his way to a purposeful existence, before venturing to say that "it may be said that this was the first time that he really and wholly believed himself to be a true knight-errant and not a fanciful one" (II, 31).

Underlying nearly all of both parts of *Don Quixote*, whether upright or upside down, has been the theme of the *locus amoenus* and the Golden Age, that is, a *state* (more than a place or time) of grace, inasmuch as an obvious reference point for both myths is the Eden of Genesis. A scrutiny of *Don Quixote* reveals not two or three but dozens of references to pleasances and utopian settings. There can be only one state to which man can aspire and this is the *third* life to which Manrique alludes, the only one which is eternal, namely the heavenly one.

I suggested earlier that the *ubi sunt* theme—which, if it is answered at all, is usually answered indirectly by referring to the fact that all humans, from the lowliest to the most powerful, disappear (die)—is answered by Cervantes in the Cave of Montesinos (also indirectly) by saying, "*There* they are." The Cave thus reveals the truth about the second life by confirming its existence (people are still in various stages of a "second life" because of the memories they have left behind, a motif begun by Don Quixote's opening question as he greets Montesinos). The grotesque aspects confirm something else: as Manrique had pointed out, this "second life," while better and longer, is not eternal either. Don Quixote's *discovery*, then, is that the attempt to gain a worldly glory also results in ultimate corruption and a second death. He need not display his manliness (literally or figuratively) after all! The eternal life lies elsewhere, with God; the false life of literary heroes is a life enchanted by Merlin, son of the Devil.

On comparing some aspects of Lope de Vega's *comedias* with Cervantes' novels, Rivers observes that "Lope's theater is highly lyrical, appealing to the dreams, illusions and wishful thinking of his audience, which easily 'identifies' with his romantic characters, who make love in high flown language and who defend with passion their sexual honor, that is, their social reputation for male aggressiveness and feminine chastity."[9] Rivers goes on to remind us that both Lope and Cervantes wrote a pastoral novel, "which may be taken to represent their common point of departure. But for Lope we may say that the pastoral myth of rustic innocence and harmony is eventually identified, as in *Fuenteovejuna*, with the Spanish social myth of the 'blood purity' and innate superiority of the 'old Christian' peasant. For Cervantes, the pastoral myth, like the chivalric myth, is eventually relegated to the realm of literary dreams, which lead in extreme cases to mad quixotic fanaticism" (p. 117). Finally, Rivers points to Cervantes' genius in synthesizing contraries: "Cervantes himself is clearly unable to accept in a final way either of the extreme positions in the incipient debate between ageless classicism and historical relativism. His great novel is based precisely upon the hilarious interplay between heroic archetypes of literary myth, on the one hand, and the pathetic boredom of life in the villages, inns, courts and highways of contemporary Spain, on the other. The anti-historical worlds of knights errant and of lovelorn shepherds were of course, in a sense, unreal to him, as were the dashing young gallants and madly jealous husbands of cape and sword in Lope's comedies" (p. 118).

At first blush it would seem that I have relegated Cervantes' masterpiece to a novelistic treatment within a long tradition, namely the stories or confessions of those who had led a life of sin, only to "see" the true glory of God, repent, and find the everlasting life amid the heavenly host. The first part of such a pattern clearly does not apply, for if nothing else, the protagonist's life prior to the opening of the novel could not have been more chaste; in fact it bordered on the ascetic. Nevertheless, much can be said about his quest for the eternal values, which he eventually "saw" toward the end of his life. Such is the thesis of Otis Green: "The clearest example of *desengaño*—of becoming undeceived and coming to oneself that can be found in all of Spanish literature is the gradual return of Don Quijote from the world of phantoms, born in the minds of the authors of the romances of chivalry that he read with such absorbing avidity, to the changeless eternal world of God's truth that from the beginning was destined (by the artistic will of Cervantes) to be the Knight's ultimate center of repose."[10]

My conclusion does not depart from Green's above, but my interpretation of how and why the protagnoist reaches that ultimate truth differs completely. Green's reasoning is consistent with his earlier essay, a thought-provoking analysis (which I had the privilege of hearing prior to its publication when the author visited the University of Colorado in the summer of 1957), based on Huarte de San Juan's theory of the four humors and their corresponding effects upon an individual's psychological behavior.[11] Moreover, Green's view of the Cave of Montesinos episode is simply that of serving to reinforce Don Quixote's own continuing doubts as he asks, at various intervals, for confirmation of the truth of what he saw.

My own view, as the present study shows, agrees that Don Quixote's progress is gradual, as Green affirms, that he ultimately reaches "the changeless eternal world of God's truth," and that this will be his "center of repose." But the path I have observed is not the then accepted psychological theory of the four humors. The protagonist simply becomes aware of the emptiness and futility of his life, a life of failure in any arena, but particularly in those connected with virility (sexual and warrior prowess), and, fearing it is too late to attempt any real sexual conquest, he invents an ideal lover who, as his thorough reading of the novels of chivalry has informed him need not be physically attainable. What is more, having declared such an ideal courtly love for Dulcinea, he is now free to avoid any other real love entanglements with the convenient pretext that any amorous desires he may feel must be limited to Dulcinea. So it is that he risks being the object of ridicule by declaring himself a knight-errant, attacking windmills as he converts them into giants in an attempt to be recognized as a man. No matter how foolish his behavior may appear, the one accusation he thereby avoids is that of insufficient valor and virility. What he sees in the Cave of Montesinos confirms what he has already been on his way to suspecting: the manly name and the resulting fame of these heroes is disintegrating.

There lies Durandarte, "flower and mirror of the brave and enamored knights of his age." The connection is readily apparent: Durandarte was in his day what Don Quixote proclaims himself to be in his. Durandarte's memory has kept him in a "second life" which is steadily, though less swiftly than the "first life," corroding. Manly feats are not sufficient. "Patience, and shuffle," moans Durandarte, an expression which commentators either ignore or dismiss as a common expression of gamblers. The cousin believes the comment to be of historical value for his book, since it helps to fix the date at which playing cards were invented. I believe there is much more significance.

III   RECOGNITION

Earlier I made reference to one of the most important statements in the novel, namely Don Quixote's insistence in I, 5 that he knows who he is: "I know who I am and who I may be, if I choose." Casalduero puts this affirmation in contrast with Hamlet's doubt and cites the well known lines, "O, that this too too solid flesh would melt, / Thaw, and resolve itself into a dew!" (*Sentido y forma del Quijote*, p. 25). This, it seems to me, is too traditional and too hurried a look at Hamlet's character as seen from his first monologue. As Watson points out "Hamlet becomes more courageous as the play draws to a close. The man who leaps into the grave with the cry, 'This is I, / Hamlet the Dane,' is an altogether different figure from the youth accusing himself of inaction and cowardice earlier in the play."[12] What Hamlet and Don Quixote have in common is not merely a few similar lines asserting their identity but, more importantly, a nearly desperate attempt to find and maintain such an identity. Their manner and circumstance vary completely; their human need to proclaim and believe in their individuality is far more similar than most observers care to recognize.

Returning again to Watson's excellent study, we note that patience "upholds Antonio [in *The Merchant of Venice*], Brutus, and Coriolanus in their hours of trial. But it does not prevent the heroes of the great tragedies from being torn asunder. Their response to their particular predicament is heroic and they show superhuman endurance in bearing misfortune. But the burden becomes too great. They are torn by a sense of inner disintegration which finally makes it impossible for them to maintain self-composure" (p. 315). Watson then quotes lines 47-64 of Act IV, Scene 2 of *Othello*, followed by the observation that "*King Lear* presents an inner, spiritual conflict in which the hero is fighting primarily the possibility of his own disintegration. . . . The mainspring of Lear's disintegration is precisely the same as Othello's or Hamlet's— these heroes are torn apart by the realization of evil in those whom they had loved so intensely, so wholeheartedly, with such a great degree of emotional identification, that the awareness of evil in the person loved destroys their own mental stability. Patience and fortitude can not prevent this disintegration" (p. 316).

Finally, Watson quotes the Renaissance moralist William Cornwallis

71

to the effect that patience "keepeth the reputation unspotted; though outward forces be destroyed, this makes the mind invincible." Watson points out that "unless we keep in mind this typically humanist counsel for adversity, we lose sight of much of Lear's tragedy. . . . Weak and infirm he is, but, for the Renaissance moralists, magnanimity did not depend upon bodily strength, but on greatness of soul, of mind, heart and will, which Lear manifests in abundance" (p. 318).[13]

This distinction serves to illustrate as well the differing attitudes between the heroes of the *Comedia*, for whom patience was equivalent to a failure to exact immediate vengeance, which could mean loss of honor and inaccessibility to the "second life," on the one hand, and, on the other, the humanistic tradition in which Cervantes' writings generally have their roots. We should also recall that the guide for the Montesinos adventure introduces himself as a humanist.

With the foregoing in mind, let us return once again to the Cave, this time to the finale of the adventure, when Don Quixote finds himself unable to pay the required sum of money which would enable him to "disenchant" (i.e., attain) Dulcinea. He immediately promises "not to eat bread off a cloth, along with other trifling stipulations which he added, until vengeance had been had." This apparently ludicrous promise is easily placed into context when we recall that it is a portion of a famous vow, having its origins in the *romances* or ballads of the Cid. Cervantes' contemporary, the Valencian dramatist Guillén de Castro (who, incidentally, was among the first to put excerpts from Cervantes' works on the stage), used it in his *Las mocedades del Cid* (*The Youthful Deeds of the Cid*), Part one, Act III, lines 1993-96: "*Rey que no haze justicia / no devría de reynar, / ni pasęar en cavallo, / ni con la Reyna folgar*" ("A King who does not do justice should not reign, nor ride around on horseback, nor to go bed with the Queen").[14] The source can be found in the *romance* which reads, "*Rey que non face justicia / non debía de reinar, / ni comer pan a manteles, / ni con la reina folgar.*"[15] The difference lies in the penultimate line, which, unlike the Castro reference to horseback riding, includes the vow made in the Cave by Don Quixote not to eat bread off a tablecloth. What is of significance for the present study is not only that readers of Cervantes' time and tradition were familiar with the complete *romance*, but that any reader of Cervantes' book should recall that Don Quixote himself had employed the original version when, having noted the irreparable damage done to his helmet by the Biscayan, he swore "not to eat bread at table, nor lie with his wife" until he had taken vengeance (I, 10).[16]

The apparently nonsensical vow not to eat bread off a tablecloth until vengeance has been had, which Don Quixote makes in the Cave of Montesinos, can now be placed in context. The indirect reference is an example of Cervantes' greater skill in subtle artistry in 1615 than the more direct statement of 1605. The words in the Cave are sufficient to connect Don Quixote's vow to the traditional source which is a vow of sexual abstinence. That this is consistent with his character is, I trust, obvious by now. Moreover, it comes immediately after his display of impotence (the failure to provide the money) and the obvious loss of any possibility for union with Dulcinea, who has just turned her back on him. More than that, his vow, which in reality is a vow *not* to exact vengeance since there is no one to avenge himself upon, is linked to the mutterings of his hero, Durandarte, "Patience, and shuffle." The lesson of Durandarte is another one of the realities which Don Quixote "sees" in the Cave of Montesinos. Not only is Durandarte's "second life" passing away, but his final words of advice are not a call to action; rather, they are a plea for the virtue of patience.[17]

To summarize: Don Quixote, in the Cave of Montesinos, sees with the eye of the mind. It is irrelevant, therefore, whether it is a physical experience, a vision or dream, or an invention. (Cervantes' allowing the adventure to be called apocryphal assumes added irony when it is recalled that Cervantes considered his own greatest talent to be that of invention.)[18] What does hold fundamental significance is that the experience is the climactic point in a gradual development of an anonymous person who, in a desperate striving for self-knowledge while never totally unaware of his limitations as a man, comes upon a setting which is an inverted picture of everything he had hoped to find. What he does find, through this inversion, in an adventure that one critic has described as a point at which "the entire structure teeters on the edge of sanity,"[19] is the discovery that sexual exploits are as grotesque as their realistic description (the salted heart); that reputation and the memory one leaves behind are eventually corroded by time; that a Christian virtue such as patience is of more importance than the worldly need to prove one's virility; in short, he has seen what he has long suspected and therefore the reversal of his personality from blind belief in the need to assert masculinity—in turn an earlier reversal from five decades of nothingness after his discovery of the literature of chivalry—into an individual whose eyes have been opened to a higher goal, if he will but follow through, despite the obstacles of mortal tribulations which are still to befall him during the time left to him.

The inexorable passage of time was one of the concerns of the age. It also provides one additional explanation of the protagonist's original intent to revive times past, particularly an ideal Golden Age. Approaching old age, both author and protagonist become increasingly aware that one's earlier ages, whether simply the youth's disregard for time (an underlying motivation of the Don Juan complex), or true exploits, such as Cervantes' heroism at Lepanto, do not hold back the clock or the calendar. As Heninger observes: "The Renaissance . . . most frequently expressed the enigma of perfection's finitude in terms of mutability: time brings inevitable change, but this change is itself part of the pattern, indeed is essential to realizing the pattern. This cognizance of finitude haunted the poet, and frightened him into explaining it. . . ."[20] This need to explain the feared passing of time is one of the motifs of the Cave adventure.

In addition, then, to Cervantes' use of the word "apocryphal"—with which he frames this adventure—we should recall that the other occasion on which the author had surrounded an episode with this word was II, 5, in which the stated reason was the difficulty of believing that Sancho was capable of speaking so wisely. In other words, Sancho's intelligent *language* caused the so-called *translator* to judge the episode to be apocryphal. The word "apocryphal" is not native to Spanish any more than it is to English. It is of Greek origin and refers to a hidden or secret language, and part of its etymology is derived from the word meaning "crypt." Don Quixote's experience in the crypt has enabled him to discover, to understand, to see.[21]

It is interesting, by way of concluding this chapter, to recall Unamuno's words about the veracity of the adventure. How ironic that in his attempt to belittle Cervantes for not believing Don Quixote, Unamuno is himself the victim of Cervantes' art, for despite Unamuno's knowledge of Greek, any purposeful intent behind Cervantes' use of "apocryphal" evidently escaped him and he ends up by defending what he thinks he is attacking. In the face of Cervantes' consistent hints about metamorphoses, hidden meanings, symbolism and ultimate belief in his own creation, particularly his inventiveness, Unamuno asserts that with respect to the Cave adventure, Cervantes "feels himself obliged to doubt its authenticity, in which attitude he demonstrates his little faith; and he even goes so far as to claim that at the hour of his death Don Quixote retracts his story. . . .[22] Oh timid and mean narrator, how little you understand the matter of visions" (p. 194). Unamuno gives his own interesting twist to the *ubi sunt* theme by suggesting that if we believe in the visions described in the Bible and in the lives of saints, how can we doubt a knight?

> I invite the reader [writes Unamuno] to reread . . . the narrative of the astonishing visions of Don Quixote . . . and let him tell me later if these experiences are not more believable than others no less astonishing which God is said to have granted to certain of his servants, dreamers in the profound enchanted cave of ecstasy (p. 193).
>
> . . . .
>
> How, in all truth, can we deny that Don Quixote saw what he saw in the cave of Montesinos, since he was a Knight incapable of lying? . . . If life is a dream, why should we obstinately deny that dreams are life? And whatever is life is truth. Is what we call reality anything more than an illusion which leads us to act and which produces deeds? The practical effect is the only worthwhile criterion of the truth of any vision, of whatever kind" (pp. 195-96).

IV   INTERLUDE: THE PURPOSE OF RECOGNITION

In this and in the two preceding chapters, I have tried, from several perspectives, to relate the process of individuation to the need for recognition and awareness of oneself as a human being. That such a need to see oneself as a "somebody" in a society which was emerging from medieval, hierarchical, fixed structures and beliefs to a questioning of these concepts—political, geographic, cosmological and even religious—does not need documentation here. A cursory glance at the new shape of the world, at that world's position in the solar system, at the apparent reality of utopian myths in a "new" world; at names such as Columbus, Luther, Copernicus, Erasmus, Cortés, Pizarro and Gutenberg; even such a partial list gives an inkling of what must have been going through the minds of the common people in the age of Cervantes. I hasten to reiterate my earlier caveat: socio-political revolutionary thoughts would not emerge with any potency until nearly two centuries later. Revolutionary thoughts about one's existence as an individual within the structure of the prevailing society, however, were indeed making themselves felt.

In Spain, for example, as Américo Castro, among others, has shown, the common people of peasant stock could find pride and self-esteem in the belief that they were of pure Christian blood (the *cristiano viejo* or "old Christian" concept). In addition to the many ramifications of this concept (which appears throughout Castro's works) as one more reason for commoners to see themselves as belonging to an "in" group, the phenomenon has its other side. It is not an individualistic concept for the very reason that it once more depends upon a defined group. Its importance to my study is simply that it did contribute to the several bases for challenging the supremacy of the titled classes and thus it gave added impetus to any individualistic thinking with which it may have coexisted.

As for the concept itself, the previously cited *entremés* by Cervantes, *El retablo de las maravillas*, is a well known example of how it could be ridiculed. Less often commented upon, however, is a line which follows a famous one in *Don Quixote*. Sancho, basing his remark on the concept just mentioned, tells his master that he is an old Christian and in order to become a count, that is enough for him (I, 21). This sentence appears frequently in analyses of the novel. Don Quixote's response is less often remarked upon: "Enough and more than enough for you." In works like the *entremés* mentioned above and in lines like Don Quixote's rejoinder, there is more than a mockery of the pure blood concept. Cervantes is once more showing that such people are basing their existence on being *hijos de algo*, that they are as deserving of being ridiculed for their lack of accomplishments and dependence upon ancestry as those whose titles reflect similar nothingness on their parts. (A favorite theme which appears throughout Cervantes' works is that of the idle rich—witness the Duke and Duchess; as well as the nobleman who cannot point to any deeds: witness the knight of the Green-Colored Greatcoat—as objects of ridicule.)

The individual, therefore, could be anybody, provided that he himself made of his own being a somebody. The new breed of hero, consequently, could emerge from nowhere (La Mancha, not known as the birthplace of heroes in general; and, as Cervantes pointedly tells us in his famous opening line, in just *some place* of La Mancha) if his deeds accorded to him the necessary steps on the way to individuation. One always speaks of irony when dealing with Cervantes; the deeper irony of having his "hero" be a nobody without a past lies not so much in the parody of the various lineages, be they nobles or *cristianos viejos*, but in the freedom which the lack of a past gave to such characters.

The picaresque novel had forged a beginning half a century earlier when the anonymous *Lazarillo de Tormes* was published in 1554. We do get to know the protagonist's family name, but it is as meaningless as Smith: Gonzales Pérez. As the many manuals of literature point out, we can explain away the autobiographical format of the picaresque novel with the simple observation that who else would write the biography of a nobody but the nobody himself. As Gilman has observed, Lazarillo's parents are "genealogical nobodies."[23] Cervantes' added touch is that Don Quixote's life as we come to know it does not begin until nearly fifty years after his birth. In addition to an absence of ancestors, whose only trace is the rusty armor left in the house, Cervantes' protagonist has no past of his own after five decades of existence. As Silverman has put it, the absence of "the specifics of a genealogy" has *freed* Don Quixote from having a past.[24]

Freed from having a past! Therein lies the opportunity for individuation. Chapter 1 of my study has attempted to discuss the process, its relationship to one's works and the urge to become an individual. In Chapter 2 I have concentrated on Don Quixote's dependence on stereotyped ways of achieving status (heroic deeds or sexual success) and his discovery that such achievements are not within his grasp. The present chapter has concentrated on a literary *topos* and shown its inversion as a means to recognition. The following chapter will attempt to deal with the individual on the final path to individuation as he confronts the challenge of being alone.

Chapter 4

Isolation and Desolation

I   BROAD AND ALIEN IS THE· WORLD
    —*Ciro Alegría*

Isolation and desolation are different conditions: the former is a physical state and does not, *ipso facto*, carry either a pejorative or an ameliorative connotation; the latter is, in contrast, an emotional state and is generally considered to be undesirable. The concept of isolation, however, is not necessarily limited to the physical absence of other people: one may feel isolated in a crowded room, in which case the isolation assumes a metaphysical significance, although it need not reach the extreme of desolation. The individual in such a situation may feel left out of things or feel discomfort as a result of sensing a strange or incomprehensible milieu, in which case modern analysts would probably speak of alienation. It may also occur, however, that such an individual is unaware of any sensation of strangeness, in which case one may still describe him as isolated, but without any attendant reason to suggest alienation.

Two other words demand brief discussion: solitude, which is again the physical state of being alone and hence similar to isolation, although it is the more frequently used term when being alone is viewed optimistically; and loneliness, which approaches desolation in its emotional aspect of sensing the undesirable aspects of *feeling* alone, despite the company of others. Loneliness is less pessimistic (and often of shorter duration) than desolation, and either of these may be related to alienation, or a sense of not belonging. Weiss has remarked upon the failure to relate and differentiate such conditions: "Sociologists have given a great deal of attention to 'alienation,' by which most mean something like the social or psychological estrangement of an individual from an activity or social norm with which he is nevertheless at least nominally associated. There seems to be very little overlap between the phenomena considered in discussions of alienation and the experience of loneliness."[1] The feeling of being alone—regardless of actual physical isolation—which may occur when "life is no fun anymore" adds an impressionistic aspect which encourages the individual to withdraw simply because *he* believes himself to be depressed and this syndrome adds to the difficulty of differentiating among the various kinds of isolationist responses: "Unfortunately there is a confusion of terminology since one can 'have' a depression without 'being' depressed. In other words, there are often 'substitute' or 'equivalent' symptoms for the depressive ones. The most prominent of these is anhedonia—the absence of pleasure."[2]

In a writer whose works deal with as vast a panorama as does Cervantes, it is to be expected that we should come upon characters who display all of these conditions, sometimes more than one to a character. Although Weiss, as he clarifies almost immediately, is really speaking of the emotional and desired kind of solitude (as opposed to what I have defined as loneliness, desolation and alienation), his rarer clinical cases coincide with the process I am describing:

> Sometimes the term *loneliness* has been used to describe a not at all disagreeable condition in which a sense of one's separateness from others offers "a way back to oneself." This sort of loneliness refers to a time in which one is not only alone but also able to use one's aloneness to recognize with awesome clarity both one's ineradicable separateness from all else and one's fundamental connectedness. It is a time of almost excruciating awareness in which one sees clearly the fundamental facts of one's small but unique place in the ultimate scheme, after which one can recognize one's true self and begin to be that true self.[3]

Finally, Weiss makes the interesting observation that "very unusual individuals may be able to function in response to the concerns of imagined or anticipated communities,"[4] referring us to Erikson's description of "George Bernard Shaw's sustaining himself in his early life through imagined membership in the company of great writers."[5] Clearly Shaw would qualify as a "very unusual individual" in any age and, if we were to grant his existence, so would Don Quixote. In the present chapter my task is to investigate the individual's search for himself in a period when even such accepted and formerly understood concepts as "world," "universe," "race," and "religion" were open to new and startling interpretations. This is why

> the first great novel of world literature stands at the beginning of the time when the Christian God began to forsake the world; when man became lonely and could find meaning and substance only in his own soul, whose home was nowhere; when the world, released from its paradoxical anchorage in a beyond that is truly present, was abandoned to its immanent meaninglessness; when the power of what is—reinforced by the utopian links, now degraded to mere existence—had grown to incredible magnitude and was waging a furious, apparently aimless struggle against the new forces. . . . Cervantes lives in the period of the last, great and desperate mysticism, the period of a fanatical attempt to renew the dying religion from within; . . . the period of truly lived but already disoriented, tentative, sophisticated, occult aspirations.[6]

The enormity of the changes in fundamental beliefs which affected the people of Cervantes' time simply cannot be overlooked or overstated. Within the span of one century, the beliefs of a millennium were reshuffled and attempts were made to make sense of, while maintaining faith in, a universe whose very definition was being rewritten. Small wonder that Cervantes, Calderón, Quevedo, Lope de Vega and others (not to mention Shakespeare and his fellow Elizabethans) found the theme of appearance and reality so welcome to their pens: on both sides of the Atlantic reality was being crushed or censored while it simultaneously revealed ever more convincingly— and thereby creating further doubt—how false so many of the alleged realities were when divested of their trappings. The phrase "paradoxical anchorage in a beyond that is truly present" in the quotation above could not be more fitting.

A people who had struggled for nearly eight centuries to regain their national territory succeeded in 1492 in recovering and uniting their country. In return, it seemed only natural that God would reward them by giving them a "New World" with the clear mandate to convert the heathen population there to God's true religion. At the same time it was necessary to readjust one's concept of the planet as a sphere and concurrently to wonder whether the newly discovered half of it did not really bring to fruition the age-old dream of the Golden Age in all its ramifications: El Dorado, Amazons, untold wealth and nothing to do but pluck it. (For a people used to thinking in terms of a four-year World War I, a four-year involvement in World War II, a three-year

Korean War and a decade of direct involvement in Vietnam, the concept of putting an end to an eight-century struggle against infidels cannot help but give us some idea of the magnitude of the significance of the final Battle of Granada.) Yet, just around the corner lay the Reformation and when the century reached its end, inflation and the fiasco of the Armada had taken their toll. Added to this was the slow re-evaluation of the order of the universe as a result of the declarations of Copernicus and subsequently of Galileo, and so we find men either desperately clinging to long-held beliefs or just as desperately attempting to adapt to the new ones.

Certainly this explains the fallacy of supposing the "Cervantes smiled Spain's chivalry away." No, Cervantes was not laughing. He began his masterpiece by writing about an alienated man. Despite humanity's consistency in the ability to create revolutions—usually inspired by liberal causes—man is basically a conservative creature. He may speak eloquently against tyranny and other evils of this world, particularly if he sees a better world for himself as an outcome, but at bottom he is more comfortable with what is familiar to him. (This is why alienation is considered a problem to be dealt with by clinicians: the very meaning of the word suggests that to be or to feel oneself to be in an alien environment may be the cause of a mental dysfunction.) Alonso Quijano's "problem" was his feeling at home in the world in which he grew up and about which he had read so much and which was changing before his eyes. His "insanity" was his attempt to preserve that world and so he converted himself into part of the old hierarchy: a knight-errant. His attempt, I must repeat, was a desperate and ultra-conservative one: had he succeeded, he would have preserved or restored along with his grandfather's rusty old armor, the entire establishment which was already on its way to decay. It took his experience in the Cave of Montesinos to open his eyes to that. From then on he had to make his peace with the new order which no longer would call for knights-errant despite the popularity of the honor-conscious *caballero* in Lope's plays. But he helped to open the way for a new heroic ideal. To be or not to be was *not* the question: the new challenge was whether to be or to become.

II   THE "LOCUS AMOENUS" ONCE MORE

What am I to say, then, of Cervantes' final work, the lengthy *Persiles*, finished shortly before his death in 1616 and published posthumously

81

in 1617? I raise the question somewhat rhetorically, for what strikes the eye is that in the very first paragraph the hero, with a rope around him, is being raised from the depths of a cavernous dungeon! The *Persiles* is not well known outside the world of Cervantes specialists and remains obscured by its more famous relative, *Don Quixote*. I suspect that even among people who recall that Cervantes wrote a collection of *Exemplary Novels* and some works for the stage, few are aware that he wrote another full-length novel—strictly speaking, it is a prose epic or romance—whose title means *The Travails of Persiles and Sigismunda*. And indeed, its plot not only begins in a cave but continues to recount a series of episodes in other caves.

Forcione concentrates his attention on three of these caves. These three instances are the dream of the hero in which the "demonic cave looks backward to the cave-dungeon of the opening scene and forward to its apocalyptic counterweight, the cave of Soldino. . . ."[7] To put the ambience of this episode in a context consistent with the present book, I quote further from Forcione:

> The description of the cave of Soldino as underground paradise is rich in literary overtones. . . . Cervantes uses Soldino's account of his life to celebrate the ethical values which had originated in the writings of classical antiquity and had been revived and Christianized by the humanists of the Renaissance. Here we observe the traditional themes of the sixteenth-century reworkings of the Horatian *Beatus ille*. . . . The streams and fruit-bearing trees of [Soldino's] *locus amoenus* are linked imaginatively back [to previous adventures]. . . . Thus it takes place in the series of triumphant visions, which begin with Periandro's gaze toward heaven as he is hoisted from the underground sepulcher. . . . The adventure of Soldino's cave is Cervantes' final monument to the synthesis of the classical and Christian traditions which Christian humanism had achieved. . . . In this world-weary soldier who has faithfully served Charles V for many years, we observe the harmonious coexistence of classical antiquity's ideal of moral perfection on earth and the Christian awareness that earthly existence is but a prelude to the life that is to follow.[8]

The episode of Soldino's cave has a function which in many respects is similar to that of Montesinos' cave. In fact, each appears at approximately the same point in their respective novels: the Montesinos adventure occurs at approximately three-quarters of the length of *Don Quixote* and the Soldino episode appears at about the two-thirds point. (That this emphasizes the importance of the two passages is reinforced by the baroque concept of pictorial representation, which views the center of importance as belonging not in the center of the work.) The similarity is increased as we read the description of Soldino: "a man, whose long white beard made one put him at over eighty years of age; he was dressed neither as a pilgrim nor as a *religioso*, although he seemed to be both; his head was bare, bald in the center with long and very white hair hanging down the sides. . . . In short, all of him represented a venerable old man, worthy of every respect. . . ." The proprietress of the inn where Soldino makes this appearance introduces him as "this mountain of snow and this statue of white marble . . . , the famous Soldino, whose fame is spread not only in France, but throughout the whole world."

Soldino asks her not to praise him, "for perhaps a good reputation (*la buena fama*) is born of an evil lie; not the entry but the departure makes men fortunate; virtue which has vice as its end is not virtue but vice" (III, 18). The three parts of the sentence which I have here translated must be viewed as interconnected. It would be simple to extract the middle portion and infer from it alone that it is a Christian *topos* of the times, so often associated (in literature) with the works of Calderón, namely that life is not so important as death. Simple, but also simplistic. The words do not contrast life on earth with the life everlasting; they oppose birth and death, that is to say, the manner in which one enters this life and the manner in which one leaves it. The significance becomes clearer as we look at the parts of the sentence which frame this middle portion. Soldino is suspicious of that most esteemed attribute of the times, *la buena fama*, because it may be *born* of a lie. The reference, in my view, is to the subject of my first chapter, namely that to be the child of ancestors who have earned fame is not so important as to earn fame by oneself. To seek fame because that is the way in which to be admired is hypocritical, which is the meaning of the third part of Soldino's sentence. Taken all together, then, Soldino is saying that what one does during one's life is more important than being born with a silver spoon in one's mouth, so to speak, and if fame is earned for the sincere reason that it is merited, it is well earned; otherwise it is vice in disguise.

A reading of this brief episode makes its relevance readily apparent. I have remarked that Soldino and his abode bear a certain resemblance to Montesinos and his cave. I have also ventured that the two episodes perform analogous functions in the two novels. Yet, while similarities and parallels clearly exist, the Soldino's cave adventure is, to an important degree, the converse of the Montesinos adventure. It will be recalled that the description of what Don Quixote first beheld had all the characteristics of a *locus amoenus* and that subsequent events and depictions served to disillusion the protagonist with respect to his earthly and eternal values.

In the *Persiles*, Cervantes once again cautions us not to take literally everything we are about to read. (He does not use the word "apocryphal" here and I agree with most commentators that the warning refers to Cervantes' understanding of poetic truth as opposed to historical truth, i.e., the Aristotelian precept.)[9] This time it is not one individual who descends into a cave to find a bearded old man and knights and ladies; in the Soldino adventure, "he who wrote this history says that Soldino, with that whole group of ladies and gentlemen (*damas y caballeros*), descended the steps of the dark cave. . . ." We are then told that Soldino himself had dug the cave and we are given a description of the *locus amoenus* to which the cave is an entrance, as well as of Soldino's life style, which approximates that of the legendary Golden Age:

> I made that valley mine, its waters and fruits giving me bounteous sustenance. Here, fleeing war, I found peace; the hunger which in that world above . . . I felt, found here its satiety; here, instead of the princes and monarchs who rule the world, whom I served, I have found these silent trees which, although tall and stately, are humble; here the disdain of emperors and the annoyance of their ministers don't resound in my ears; here I don't see any lady who scorns me, nor any servant who serves me badly; *here I am lord of myself*, here I have my soul in my hands, and here, straight and true, I direct my thoughts and my desires to Heaven. . . . (Italics mine.)

Soldino goes on to predict good things for the travelers, based not on any books but "only on the experience that I have acquired with the time of my solitude."

I have used the word "converse" to describe this brief episode in comparison to the Montesinos adventure. In addition to what I have already said, here we have no grotesque distortion of the *locus amoenus*: Soldino has found peace here and it really is pleasant. Moreover, there is a fundamental difference which explains Cervantes' attitude toward isolation. Montesinos, Durandarte, Belerma and the rest were simply waiting to be disenchanted, their thoughts exclusively on their worldly fame. (The little byplay in which "Dulcinea" asks for the most mundane of all things—money—takes on added weight in this larger context.) The error of these views was graphically epitomized in the antipoetic image of Durandarte's heartlessness, the never-healing wound (another inversion of a *topos*), and the grotesque depiction of Belerma wandering for centuries holding Durandarte's heart in her hands. Don Quixote was able to see through the grotesqueness and his isolation in the cave enabled him to see the truth with his mind's eye and find it beautiful. The characters in the *Persiles*, in contrast, actually behold a beautiful scene and a comforted soul. (Soldino's affirmation that here he has his soul in his hands, while its meaning clearly is that he is his own master with respect to his behavior, must be metaphorically contrasted to Belerma and the heart she holds in her hands.)

Soldino is not thinking exclusively of worldly fame, as he made clear in the above-quoted passage on the nature of fame. Moreover, he has used his solitude to perceive truths, ranging from his assertion that here he is lord of himself—one cannot mistake the echo of Don Quixote's "I know who I am"—to his firm belief that this is the life "from which I intend to go forth to the everlasting one." The key to all of this lies, I believe, in the final sentence of the chapter: immediately following the words just quoted, Soldino ends the adventure by saying, "And for now no more, rather let's go back up; we shall give sustenance to our bodies, just as down here we have given it to our souls."

In the first place, these words seem to contradict the earlier *locus amoenus* description of the waters and fruits which provide bounteous sustenance. Clearly, then, we are meant to interpret the *locus amoenus* figuratively (or spiritually), not literally, as Cervantes had already warned us.[10] But the suggestion to go back up, particularly when introduced by the stipulation that "for now no more" of such introspection, lies at the heart of the matters discussed in the present chapter.

As I indicated at the outset of this chapter, there are various ways of being alone. Soldino's experience which is repeated in different portions of the *Persiles*, is obviously a healthy variety of isolation. Although, as I shall show further on, Cervantes also describes experiences of desolation, the "key" to which I have been referring relates to his views on isolation as a beneficial occurrence. In this respect, Cervantes tends to view solitude as a psychological restorative and while he does not preach this kind of isolation as an end in itself, he does believe that it is one of the several major steps in helping to recognize their individual selves. In so doing, the individual attains that all-important prerequisite for individuation, self-knowledge. It is essential, however, not to lose sight of the fact that isolation is only one step, and this explains Soldino's assertion that he is now at peace and lord of himself, followed shortly thereafter by his insistence on going back up.

We must ask, where did Cervantes receive the idea that self-knowledge—the importance of which goes back at least as far as Socrates—may be achieved by being alone with oneself (or, more accurately perhaps, alone with one's self)? That he was an observer of human nature hardly answers the specific question. Let us take a less narrow look at some examples of isolation in his works and see whether at a greater distance we may uncover some pattern to provide a clue, and let us begin with the instance just discussed: Soldino's cave.

Between the point at which Soldino relates the nature of his cave, his *locus amoenus*, and his having found peace and become master of himself, and the point at which he changes the subject to concentrate on present and future realities, he mentions the fact that he had served the "never sufficiently praised" Emperor Charles V, adding that he would have gone on serving him had the Emperor not wished to exchange mortal for divine militancy. (The reference is, of course, to the decision of Charles V in 1556—Cervantes was nine years old—to retire to the monastery of Yuste.)[11]

One of the several other caves in the *Persiles* is that of Antonio. Once again, a *locus amoenus* describes the surroundings: "it was made and fashioned from Nature, as if skill and art had put it together . . . all full of trees which offered up fruit . . . ; the grass grew high because the large amount of water that came forth from the rocks kept it in perpetual verdure" (I, 6). This cave also plays its restorative role, and it just so happens that its occupant had gone to war under the "Caesar Charles the Fifth" in Germany. What is more, Antonio asserts that although his good breeding comes from his mother's womb and therefore for this "I neither deserve to be praised nor blamed," the glory he earned in battle is something that "I carried off myself." This explains the apparently ambivalent statement that he is the "son of my works and of *hidalgo* parents" (I, 5), an illustration of another case of isolation, self-knowledge and the second connection with Charles V.

A passage in praise of solitude occurs in II, 20 of the *Persiles*. Renato had found solace by building a hermitage on an island and as he recounts his story, he gives thanks to "solitude, happy company of the sad." Another character of the novel joins him by adding, "Oh life of solitude! . . . Oh life of solitude," he said, "holy, free and safe, which Heaven instills in pleasing imaginations." But Mauricio, another personage in the novel, cautions him that although he is correct, the desire to seek isolation is praiseworthy only in those who have something to give up. To surrender because you are a failure, seek refuge and let others do your work is simply laziness, but if "I were to see a Hannibal shut up in a hermitage, as I saw a Charles the Fifth cloistered in a monastery, that would astound and amaze me." Mauricio goes on to say that a negative interpretation is not to be made of Renato's desire to live as a hermit, since he had to give up goods and took up this life from a position of strength. This portion of the *Persiles* ends with the arrival of Renato's brother who, among other things, gives news of the "glorious death of Charles V, king of Spain and Roman emperor, terror of the enemies of the Church and scourge of the followers of Mohammed" (II, 22). We thus have a third instance of isolation, self-knowledge and an allusion to Charles V.

It would be naive, and in fact impossible to substantiate, were I to attempt to build a case which would relate nearly every instance of ameliorative isolation to the self-imposed exile of the Emperor Charles V. What I am trying to suggest, however, is that these examples convey a pattern of thought in Cervantes' mind, a pattern whose model may well have been the seclusion of the Emperor (not to mention a similar penchant on the part of his son, Philip II), and whose traces appear from time to time as the writer creates an episode which deals with isolation. But I mention this primarily in an attempt to help explain Cervantes' evident and repeated concern for the isolation of his characters, not as a biographical digression to explain away artistic intent. (I might recall that in a chapter in which Don Quixote exalts eternal fame over human fame, a chapter which many believe to be a crucial one in his "return to sanity," namely II, 8, Cervantes includes an anecdote about Charles V which introduces the passages on fame, envy and the mortal sins.)

Whether or not, then, the examples of Charles V and Philip II were mere afterthoughts in Cervantes' mind, or whether they actually planted a seed for his observational powers to develop, is of course impossible to ascertain. What cannot be denied, however, is that Cervantes' literary production contains a plethora of situations in which some form of isolation plays a significant part. One of the observers to devote some attention to this phenomenon is Amezúa: "No one in our [Spanish] classical literary period has known or felt more deeply the value of silence, nor has found more delight in solitude; no one made more true Aristotle's aphorism, *Homo solitarius aut Deus, aut bestia*; . . . because Cervantes knew or guessed that silence and solitude are the climate which is propitious to great souls, where man finds himself, forms himself, prepares and invigorates himself for the highest endeavors."[12]

To restate a point made above: how the Emperor actually behaved in his retirement is irrelevant, particularly since it is unlikely that Cervantes had access to such facts. The image of the Emperor of the Holy Roman Empire relinquishing his crown and seeking the kind of solitude described here by Amezúa could not have been lost on Cervantes in any event. But, as I have also suggested, such an experience is only a step. Amezúa observes as well that "these states of quietism and passivity in Cervantes are fleeting and transitory, like peaceful oases in which to seek momentary restoration, in order to resume later the bitter struggle against an adverse reality. . . ." (p. 280).

III THE TREATMENT OF "TOPOI"

As one would expect of a pastoral novel, Cervantes' contribution to the genre, *La Galatea*, includes many a reference to the *locus amoenus* setting. The beginning describes "a delightful meadow, [the shepherd Elicio being] invited by its solitude and by the murmur of a delightful stream which ran through the field," as well as a specific assertion that "for sad, imaginative hearts nothing is more pleasant than solitude, the awakener of sad or happy memories." Avalle-Arce appropriately points out that this hymn to solitude is a commonplace in pastoral literature. He then refers to the passage from the *Persiles* quoted previously ("Oh life of solitude . . ."), and makes especial note of Cervantes' deeper penetration of the *topos* when he calls solitude holy.

Avalle-Arce interprets this as a "Christianization" of the Horatian *Beatus ille*, a conclusion not unlike that of Forcione, quoted earlier, concerning Soldino's cave.[13] There is some ambiguity in words like "Christianization." That we have here the application of a *topos* of antiquity to a Christian milieu is patent. However, Cervantes belongs to a more universal tradition in his treatment of conventional themes with respect to the human condition. I think that it is precisely because his attempts bore fruits which have achieved nearly universal recognition that we must look at these results in an all-embracing manner rather than that of a single religion. (I am not implying here that we should remove Cervantes from his milieu: it is indisputable that his writings are in keeping with the Catholic Spain of his time, despite—or even because of—some Erasmian influence which major scholars have perceived.) But whether or not Cervantes intended to "Christianize" commonplaces is to my way of thinking a narrow piece of a larger artistic product: not only his masterpiece but most of his literary works reveal a consistent talent for taking *topoi* of pagan times, *topoi* primarily concerned with human attempts to live with the confusing and sometimes indecipherable realities which confront man, and subsequently manipulating those *topoi* so that they enable his characters—and ultimately his readers—to lift their eyes to eternal truths. Such truths need not be Christian alone; they may encompass as well the wisdom of the Old Testament (not merely as prefiguring the New but as part of the greater, universal truths) and they may include—as Américo Castro has shown—Moslem wisdom, and of course continue to include the classics as well.

The purpose of the foregoing is not merely to repeat what we have already observed in earlier chapters, nor to take issue with respected scholars. Rather, it is within the context just outlined that I see Cervantes' use of isolation. To call solitude "holy," as a character in the *Persiles* does, is scarcely an artistic way of converting a pagan *topos* into a Christian truth. Moreover, Christianity has no monopoly on the beneficiality of solitude. (To trace this theme would be to go far afield. Let the example of Genesis 32:24-30 serve as one of the earliest as well as the best, for after "Jacob was left alone," he was permitted to see "God face to face.") What needs to be asked is why the topic of isolation is so frequently found in Cervantes' writings. It will then be seen that while in works of his earlier period (such as *La Galatea*, 1585) he appears to have a more conventional approach than in his last work (*Persiles*, 1616), the variations are not attributable to his maturation alone; one must take into account the obvious: the requirements of the genre. Despite Cervantes' great talent—perhaps even his greatest talent—of taking not only *topoi* but genres such as the one-act play (*entremés*), the novel of chivalry, the quest romance and the Boccaccio tale, and creating from them modern literary forms with entirely new possibilities, it must also be recognized that he could not ignore many necessary ingredients of what his predecessors had developed. In short, the praise of solitude in *La Galatea* conforms with the pastoral desire for escape, whereas in the *Persiles* the author adheres more closely to the quest for Truth.

The foregoing deals primarily with form and I am principally concerned with content and intent. I have already proposed that

89

Cervantes perceived the restorative function of isolation as one of several steps which lead to the self-knowledge that precedes individuation. In this light, then, we should re-examine the praise of solitude quoted earlier from *La Galatea*. This quotation, which Avalle-Arce described correctly as a pastoral commonplace, also contains the germ of an idea which I have been stressing from a number of perspectives. I am referring to potentialities available to people as they seek to know, and subsequently become, themselves. The quotation is more than the commonplace tribute to solitude found in pastoral laments, for it makes a point of affirming that solitude may awaken sad *or* happy memories. In this earlier work of Cervantes, then, we already find his perception of the possibilities inherent not only in the literary *topos*, but in the phenomenon of isolation: it may produce psychological good health by calling forth pleasant thoughts which enable the individual to be alone with himself, or it may be an occasion for unhappy memories, the negative side of the isolation coin. What is essential to bear in mind is that both possibilities exist, which is to say that Cervantes recognized the extremes of the spectrum outlined at the beginning of this chapter.

Just as it would be restrictive to interpret the praise of solitude in *La Galatea* exclusively as an adherence to pastoral tradition (although no one can dispute that pastoral literature is the immediate formal source), so it would be myopic to dismiss Don Quixote's imitation of storybook knights during his self-imposed isolation in the Sierra Morena as mere parody of chivalric literary convention (which is also clearly the formal source). I therefore find accuracy but limited vision in Riquer's analysis of the Sierra Morena episode as "a constant *topos* of the novel of chivalry." On the other hand, I must question his continuation that in such novels "it was frequent that the knight, in despair (*desesperado*) because of amorous disdain or for whatever other reason, would retire to the solitude of the woods" (*Aproximación al Quijote*, p. 118). Riquer is correct if we focus exclusively on the action. The emotional needs of an Amadís and an Alonso Quijano, however, remain in opposition.

IV SOLITUDE AND OPTIMISM

The view of solitude in Cervantes' works does not present a truly pessimistic ambience (which is not to say that there is no sadness); and as Casalduero has suggested, such an interpretation of hopelessness is anachronistic and would be more appropriate to the nineteenth century: "The figure surrounded by solitude. Once more we can observe the difference between the Baroque and the 19th century. The past century, from Romanticism to Impressionism, turns to solitude in desperation. . . . Such an amount of desolation is unknown in the Baroque period. With the 'penance' of Don Quixote we have one of the manners in which that age felt solitude. . . . His solitude is a plenitude, a spiritual concentration. Man feels himself more than ever tied to his eternity. What distinguishes one age from the other is that in the Baroque this solitude is aflame with hope" (*Sentido y forma del Quijote*, pp. 123-24).

It is hope, optimism and a desire for something which, in Don Quixote's eyes at least, will provide the solution to that nothingness of his past life, that Don Quixote seeks in his isolation. It will require, as I have shown with respect to the Cave of Montesinos, yet another kind of isolation before he can see the permanent truths. For the moment, at a point nearly parallel in the structure— the Sierra Morena adventure begins in I, 25, and the Montesinos episode is related in II, 23-24—Don Quixote's desire is still, to a large extent, worldly. He is still attempting to find his place in the annals of mortal fame. The structure is provided by the formalistic antecedents, hence the reference to a painter's achieving fame by imitating the great painters who preceded him; thus the knight-errant (and the author, whether in seriousness or in parody) will imitate the famous knights of the past. The substance, however, is the protagonist's hunger for fame and this is repeatedly and unequivocally insisted upon.

Don Quixote is quite explicit when he reveals to Sancho that "it is not so much the desire to find a madman that leads me to traverse these regions as it is the hope of accomplishing here an exploit that will win for me perpetual renown and fame throughout the whole of the known world. . . ." Sancho is to return quickly from his errand to Dulcinea, for "my labors will soon be at an end and my fame will begin to spread." Sancho still does not see the point of it all and asks Don Quixote what he "proposes to do in this lonely spot." The knight replies by giving a summary of some of the absurdities performed by knights of the books he had read. The description, as well as a number of discourses in flowery language that follow it, are clearly a parody of the novels of chivalry. But one must not read too hurriedly. Some of the most important lines in the entire novel are interspersed among what appears to be ridicule and parody.

Don Quixote plainly states that he means to imitate the famous knights "by playing the part of a desperate and raving madman." If Sancho returns with a negative response from Dulcinea, "I shall go truly mad and, being mad, suffer no more." We are given clear notice, then, that Don Quixote is going to play a role and that he is aware of the distinction between insanity and a façade.[14] Margaret Church (*op. cit.*, p. 33) makes some interesting comparisons between this multilevel madness and that in *King Lear*. She concludes: "I think Cervantes is saying here that play-acting in life for the sake of play-acting does not work, is not authentic." I am not in agreement if for no other reason than that there is no outcome to substantiate any criticism on Cervantes' part (other than the parody of the novels of chivalry). But there is more.

This same episode contains Don Quixote's famous explanation of his perception of the barber's basin as Mambrino's helmet: "this that appears to you as a barber's basin is for me Mambrino's helmet, and something else again to another person." I need not elaborate on the importance of this philosophical observation; hardly a scholar exists or has existed who has not in some manner made reference to this perspectivistic declaration. Yet, there are aspects which relate to my overall topic that warrant attention in the context of my observations. First, the statement is not merely an abstract philosophical thesis concerning the relativity of truth and perception. It is also a very explicit down-to-earth description of how the object was first encountered: because it was raining the barber had put his shaving basin on his head and it was this glittering object that Don Quixote espied from a distance as it was being used as a hat by the very barber who denied that it was anything but a basin. Consequently, on an even simpler level than that of philosophy, the object in question was adapted to a secondary use, and Don Quixote's statement here extends the possibilities. In other words, the view expressed about the multiplicity of potentialities for an inanimate object complements the thesis I have been expounding with respect to individuals.

Secondly, this important declaration appears in the same chapter with another oft-quoted affirmation by Don Quixote, after he has revealed that Dulcinea is Aldonza Lorenzo: "I am content to imagine that what I say is so and that she is neither more or less than I picture her and would have her be, in comeliness and in high estate." That this statement about his ideal must be linked to his similar statement about a symbol of his calling seems clear. What matters is not how a thing or a person was created until it, or he or she, is exposed to the potentialities which life affords. The two declarations are as individualistic in their implications as any of the more direct statements I have been quoting. Therefore, the playacting to which Church referred must be seen in this more optimistic context: to play a role is to attempt to live. My next chapter will give an indication of how this may be done; the present chapter emphasizes the precondition of testing out one's potentialities by being alone. This is the essence of the Sierra Morena adventure, as Casalduero has observed: "Don Quixote wants to be with himself, in the solitude of his silence" (*Sentido y forma del Quijote*, p. 120).

Thirdly, we must take a good look at the location—dare I say *locus*?—chosen by Don Quixote for his three days (the same length of time he would later insist he spent in the Cave of Montesinos) with himself. The spot selected is at "the foot of a tall mountain, which, *standing alone* amid a number of surrounding peaks, had almost the appearance of a rock that had been carved out of them. Alongside it flowed a gentle brook, while all about was a meadow so green and luxuriant that it was a *delight* for the eyes to behold. There were many forest trees and a number of plants and flowers to add to the quiet charm of the scene" (italics mine). Evidently, another *locus amoenus*. The combination of a really delightful setting, the desire of a man to be alone with himself, that same man's articulation of the potentialities inherent in the things and people of this world—all these within a context of Cervantes' approach to them severally, individually and in juxtaposition—cause us to see the acting of a role in a more positive, though admittedly tentative, light.

A fourth point to be made is one which Church not only observed but about which she has written a cogent and concise analysis, namely the fact that Don Quixote decides to adopt a less ludicrous type of penance: "His conscious reasoning is irrational, and more and more often he is trying to find means and reasons to shy away from direct confrontation of his fantasy. It exists more easily if it is not continually tested. More and more often, too, we are reminded that Don Quixote's interpretation of his role is changing. The pathos of his character grows as he slowly learns that the most that ever will be said of him is that he 'attempted' great things, that his intentions were good ones. And the pathos deepens because even his intentions are questioned by most men he meets" (p. 35).

93

With this extremely important background in mind, then, let us now look closely at Don Quixote's desired isolation, bearing in mind as well that—at least within the period of his life related by the novel—of all Don Quixote's periods of total physical isolation, the Sierra Morena episode is the only one in which he is not asleep. (I leave aside the question of whether or not the Montesinos adventure was a dream, having discussed this elsewhere.) As Van Doren observed, Don Quixote was a natural actor and quick to take his cues. On one level, then, he has found a setting for acting out what his reading of earlier "scripts" has informed him is required of his role; hence his bald statement that he is only "playing the part of a desperate and raving madman." At the same time, this gives the author a chance to ridicule such scenes in the books of chivalry.

On a different and more pathetic level, the attempt to send Sancho off as a witness to his having performed some of the requisites of knighthood constitutes, as I have suggested, a resort to achieving some sort of fame, an intention explicitly stated by Don Quixote himself, as we have seen. The pathos is heightened by Church's comment about his "trying to find means and reasons to shy away from direct confrontation of his fantasy," an observation I have made in earlier portions of this study and which Unamuno probably was the first to identify. Thus the desire to be somebody (i.e., to achieve fame) is pathetically linked to his avoiding Dulcinea here—as he also does later in El Toboso—by having Sancho deliver a letter instead. All the while he is revealing the true nature of things as he talks to Sancho about the perspectives that may be applied to a knight's helmet and to a knight's lady.

Reality and the truth—how desperately he wants to apply these concepts to himself Who is he? The helmet is a basin, Dulcinea is Aldonza, and he—he must be alone with himself, for he cannot avoid the confrontation with himself. Here, in the seclusion of the spot in the Sierra Morena, he will have his first moment of introspection since he set out as a knight. Here, then, and not later in Part II, is where the protagonist's attempt to remove his own mask and see his real self actually begins. (Of course, it *is* only the beginning, as we have seen.)

He starts by symbolically removing the helmet, leaving it in Sancho's care, "for I do not need it at present. Indeed, it is my intention to lay aside all this armor and remain naked as I was born." Next he allows Sancho to ride off with Rocinante, thus separating himself from his animal and social ties (once Sancho has seen enough to report that his master was indeed going through with his penance). Yet, when Sancho has departed and Don Quixote is left in absolute isolation, the knight halts his actions and begins a debate with himself over the question of whether to imitate Orlando (physical acts of a raving madman, such as tearing up trees and muddying the waters of springs) or Amadís (who went into seclusion in the company of a hermit). Don Quixote's solution is to imitate Amadís to the best of his ability, for "why should I go to the trouble of stripping myself stark naked? Why should I injure these trees which have done me no harm or disturb the clear water of these brooks which provide me with a drink when I desire it?" (I, 26).

The analysis which Church makes of this scene is to concentrate on the nature of madness and to compare Don Quixote's levels of madness with the three madmen in *King Lear* (Lear, Edgar, and the Fool). To pursue this aspect of Don Quixote's character would divert me from the present topic, but the comparison to Lear should not be totally dismissed. I raised this point earlier and it should be repeated here: Lear's stripping himself in order to seek his reality unadorned is the aspect which applies here to Don Quixote, who has divested himself of his horse (unbridled passion), his companion (society), his helmet (his profession) and most of his clothes (as with Lear, the discovery of his "unaccommodated" self).

Again, the interpretation of this behavior is easily seen to be consistent with his recent actions. On the level of his persistent desire for fame, he is content to cease his inanities as soon as Sancho has departed to spread word of his "penance." Concurrently, his ability to stop and apply his intellect to his behavior need not be viewed only at the level of a hypocritical display for Sancho's benefit. Nor need we simply see it as further proof that he is not so mad as he would have people believe. What is of utmost importance for the reader is the rare opportunity to observe Don Quixote when he has no audience, when he is in isolation.

In his isolation he fashions a rosary and prays, as well as composing some verses in praise of Dulcinea. This last-mentioned behavior must be considered as destined for an audience, for although Cervantes tells us that only some of them were found later to be legible, we must see these attempts at poetry in the light of having others read the results. It may also be viewed as evidence that the ideal of a Dulcinea to love is still with him.

Of greater interest are his rosary and his "round million of Hail Marys," which must be contrasted to the grotesque rosary worn by

Montesinos in the Cave adventure. In the Sierra Morena, everything is presented within a normal background, thus causing Don Quixote's initial antics to appear that much more irrational and absurd, and in this manner providing the significance of his more rational behavior in his subsequent solitude following Sancho's departure. As we have seen, the background of the revelation of Dulcinea's identity and the discussion of Mambrino's helmet each served to reinforce the theme of the multiplicity of potentialities inherent in what we call "reality." Alone with himself, Don Quixote still harbors a hope of attaining Dulcinea, but his prior attention to prayer suggests that in his isolation, even this early in his quest, his real search is for the greater truths of which God is the ultimate source.

The Montesinos adventure presents an inverted world to underscore the false realities of the limited truths of the storybook knights. Thus, just as Riquer can describe Don Quixote's isolation in the Sierra Morena as a "parenthesis of sanity" (*Aproximación al Quijote*, p. 120), I can refer to it as one of the earliest moments of self-awareness, a moment in which his parody of the knights of chivalric literature reflects his private doubts that such behavior will attain the goal he is seeking. He may still call that goal Dulcinea—although his sending a go-between is even here indicative of his perhaps subconscious distinction between her as a woman and as an ideal—but it is the rosary and prayers which first bring forth responses from him, and, to repeat, the fact that Cervantes chose this period of isolation for this to occur reinforces the importance of being alone as one moves along the road to maximal self-awareness.

I have already commented on the grotesque nature of the several aspects of the Montesinos adventure. The grotesque description of Montesinos' rosary as "a string on which the beads were larger than fair-sized walnuts, every tenth one being as big as an ordinary ostrich egg," is but one early revelation of the topsy-turvy nature of the world as reflected in the Cave. I should emphasize that inasmuch as I believe the inversion of some commonly held opinions as depicted in the Cave (all centering around the legendary knights and revealed through anti-poetic representations to contrast them with greater truths, an observation which applies as well to the avaricious Dulcinea of the Cave) to reveal the workings of Don Quixote's inner eye, so does the outrageous rosary suggest that God's world will not be found among Montesinos and his companions. That it is not found there explains, as I have already suggested, why Don Quixote describes it without reference to its grotesque distortions: his mind's eye has been focused on the eternal truths he has been seeking all along.

I referred earlier to Don Quixote's revelation of Dulcinea as Aldonza and the explanation of Mambrino's helmet as two facets of not only the relativity of truth theme, but of the concept of the multiplicity of potentialities inherent in what we tend to describe as reality. These two explanations constituted the first lectures to Sancho on the subject—although his experiences and several occasional remarks by Don Quixote had helped to prepare the way—and there is no hint in Part I that Sancho comprehended this in the Sierra Morena adventure, other than to laugh at the realization that the fair lady Dulcinea was really the hoarse and coarse Aldonza. However, that the lesson was not entirely lost upon him—despite the more frequently commented upon doubts he entertains about the veracity of the Montesinos adventure—is revealed by his response to his master's insistence that he spent three days and three nights in the Cave whereas Sancho has timed it as "a little more than an hour." Sancho concludes: My master . . . must be speaking the truth; for since all the things that happened to him came about through magic, who knows? what seemed to us an hour may have been three days and nights for him."

On the other hand, it is only a few moments later, when Don Quixote relates his having seen Dulcinea in the Cave and describes her as the one Sancho himself had earlier "enchanted," that Sancho forgets all about philosophical and psychological possibilities, focuses on the "reality" of the peasant girl and concludes, as he did upon leaving the Sierra Morena, that his master is truly mad. Although I can see varying degrees of validity in both sides of the age-old debate about Sancho—that on the one hand he is the earthy, sane and common sense antithesis to his master, or on the other, that he complements the quixotic personality and even becomes more quixotic than his master—I suggest an analysis which fits better within the framework of the present study. Is not Sancho as well an individual? More precisely, does he not, as does his master, start out as a type and subsequently carve out his own niche? That individual may or may not be as discernibly or dynamically different at the end of the work as is the protagonist, but I submit that he is indeed a more self-conscious individual than the *tabula rasa* (relatively speaking) of the Manchegan peasant encountered at the start. Let us, then, take some looks at isolation in the evolution of Sancho Panza.

97

V SANCHO'S ISLAND

I cannot stress too heavily the significance that must be attached to the description with which Cervantes initiates Sancho's governorship: the Duke and Duchess "sent Sancho . . . to the place that for him was to be his island" (II, 44).[15] Clearly what strikes us first is the expression "for him." We need not labor long to note the perspectivist (as well as the more remarked upon parodic) tone of these words. We are once again in a world where windmills are giants, sheep are armies, a barber's basin is a helmet and where, for Sancho, a place in the middle of Spain is to be his island. What matters for the focus of my study, of course, is not whether it *is* an island (I said I would not debate windmills), nor even the jocular tone of Cervantes. What matters is that *for Sancho* it is an island, and that this will constitute his experience of finding his niche, his place in the sun. It will be *for him* a portion of the process of his individuation.

As readers of the original Spanish are aware, references to Sancho's island are consistently made with the antiquated form *ínsula*, rather than the modern (even in Cervantes' time) form *isla*. Again, I would not dismiss the observation made by most commentators that this is in keeping with Cervantes' parodic use of archaic forms when dealing with matters of chivalry. However, the use of this particular word merits further attention. Cervantes himself draws our attention to it *as a concept* on at least three occasions. The first such reference occurs in the final chapter of Part I, as Don Quixote is returned home in his cage. Sancho's wife is anxious to know what material things her husband has brought back with him: a new cloak, shoes, things she can see. Sancho, for his part, has something better in mind: soon he will govern an island, an *ínsula*. His wife confesses that she doesn't understand about *ínsulas*. Aside from the many interpretations that have been and can be made of this conversation, we cannot escape Cervantes' finger pointing at the word and its connotations: what, after all, is an *ínsula*?

In II, 1, Sancho is once more confronted with the question. This time it is Don Quixote's niece who phrases the query even more crudely: "What are *ínsulas* anyway? Are they something to eat, glutton that you are?" The third of the many references which I wish to stress is contained in the sentence cited above: "the place that for him was to be his *ínsula*." We have then three instances in which the meaning of *ínsula* is dealt with: first, in contrast with tangible things which Sancho's wife had expected; second, in contrast with food, an association the niece has come to make with her uncle's companion; finally, Cervantes' own declaration that a certain place would serve as Sancho's *ínsula*. Why select these three, when the word *ínsula* appears throughout the book? Partly because of what I have already stated, namely, that it is on these occasions when the *concept* of an *ínsula* is discussed; but also because each of these same instances is related to a period of isolation for Don Quixote himself. I shall return to this shortly, but the connection must not be lost, for it helps us to see Sancho's island in its proper perspective. I am saying nothing new when I agree with all those who have seen the island as Sancho's counterpart of Don Quixote's Dulcinea. They are the unattainable ideals which correspond to the scope of the imaginations of the two men. The focus on *ínsula* is too insistent for us to dismiss as a mere archaism; the word *isla* would suffice to tell the same story. The remoteness, the exotic quality of an *ínsula* suggests Sancho's level of a *locus amoenus,* and because it is simpler to smile away, the concept of the island has been scoffed at by the reader all along. (This is confirmed by the amazement shown by readers who have never touched the second part, when mention is made of Sancho's governorship of his island.)

The parallel, then, lies not only in the ideals and dreams of the two wanderers; it lies as well in the inversion with which they are confronted.[16] This is why discussions of the word *ínsula* are tied to episodes of Don Quixote's insulation: in his home to which he is taken in a cage; in his home where he is kept from all references to chivalry; in the ducal palace where he is separated from his companion. And what Sancho finds, as did Don Quixote in the Cave of Montesinos, is the literal meaning of an island: isolation.

Isolation, when he is surrounded by his "subjects"? But we must remember our earlier excursion into the definitions of being alone. It is possible to be amid a multitude and still be emotionally or socially isolated. That is the insulation which is imposed on the gregarious Sancho Panza from the moment he begins his governorship. Sancho, it will be recalled, was proud of his "old Christian" blood, considering that sufficient to become a count. More than sufficient, Don Quixote had warned him, but Sancho failed to understand. Now, as governor, he is proud to reiterate that he cannot read or write, and asks that a newly made inscription be read to him. Upon being told that it is a notation of the day when the governorship of the island was assumed by Don Sancho Panza, he immediately becomes enraged:

99

Well, then, brother, I will let you know that there has never been any "Don" in my family. Plain Sancho Panza they call me, and Sancho was my father's name before me, and my grandfather's before him; they were all panzas, without any "Dons" or "Donas" tacked on. (II, 45)[17]

Whether he likes it or not, Sancho has also been "freed" from his past. In his case, he must learn to live without the security of pure blood. His isolation has begun and he is among a class to which he does not care to belong. His island is not the ideal he had believed it to be. His persistent yearning—to eat well—is the next privilege he is deprived of, as he attempts to dine at the head of the table, only to have the physician assigned to him declare everything unfit for Sancho's good: "Señor Governor, one may eat here only in accordance with the usage and custom in other islands where there are governors. . . . I am far more attentive to their health than I am to my own. . . . My chief duty is to . . . permit [the governor] to eat only what is good for him while depriving him of anything that may do harm or injury to his stomach" (II, 47).

It is not long after this that Sancho receives a letter from the Duke (which of course must be read to him), warning him that his very life is in danger, particularly at night: "Keep your eyes open, observe closely all who come up to speak to you, and eat nothing that is offered you." Sancho's two enduring pleasures—eating and sleeping—are now represented as potential sources of pain and even death. He is told explicitly that he is surrounded by enemies. Although he continues to show good judgment through his commonsense arbitration of disputes, he is gradually becoming aware of his isolation and that the governor is being governed by a set of principles which allegedly are there to protect him from himself.

VI   FREEDOM AND INDIVIDUATION

Earlier I referred to Don Quixote's insistence on freedom. Naturally enough, such expressions of the need for freedom are usually linked to Cervantes' own experiences of captivity. Aside from political freedom, however, the question of freedom has its ethical and intellectual aspects. Sancho Panza, the nonintellectual peasant who believed that the pure blood of his forebears was sufficient to earn him a title and whose symbolic ideal was possession of land, now finds himself caught unwittingly in the midst of a philosophical debate. Perhaps the clearest description of the humanist position is Pico della Mirandola's *Oration on the Dignity of Man* as summarized by Cassirer:

> The dignity of man cannot reside in his being, i.e., in the place allotted man once and for all in the cosmic order. The hierarchical system subdivides the world into different levels and places each being in one of these levels as its rightful place in the universe. But such a view does not grasp the meaning and the problem of human freedom. For this meaning lies in the *reversal* of the relationship we are accustomed to accepting between *being* and *acting*. The old Scholastic proposition *operari sequitur esse* is valid in the world of things. But it is the nature and the peculiarity of the human world that in it, the opposite is true. . . . The being of man follows from his doing; and this doing is not only limited to the energy of his will, but rather encompasses the whole of his creative powers. For all true creativity implies more than mere action upon the world. It presupposes that the actor distinguishes himself from that which is acted upon. . . . And this opposition is not a process that takes place once and that closes when certain results are achieved, but rather one which must be completed over and over again.[18]

Cassirer also cites Carolus Bovillus (Charles de Bouelles) from the latter's *De sapiente* (1509): "Being, as the most abstract element, is common to everything that exists; consciousness of self, as the most concrete and the most developed, is the property only of the highest creature, man. And between these two extreme poles stands nature as a preliminary level and as a potency of the mind. Nature embodies the various forms of *life*; but it only leads to the threshold of reason, of *reflexive knowledge*, knowledge of self" (p. 89). Finally, Cassirer explains the Renaissance concept of the microcosm: "If this idea requires that the Ego of man be understood by means of the world, it also requires, conversely, that genuine and true knowledge of the world must pass through the medium of self-knowledge" (p. 112).

The foregoing enables us to understand the theoretical basis upon which a writer like Cervantes could create his art. In an atmosphere of intellectual freedom, the species known as man could acquire self-knowledge and be the actor of his existence. Earlier I quoted Silverman's insightful observation that the absence of a specific genealogy freed Don Quixote from having a past. Silverman used these words in a different context but his perception is applicable to the concept developed in the present study. By not having a genealogy, Don Quixote is free to become the child of his own works if he will use that freedom to seek his role in life. This aspect is not Don Quixote's alone: we have already observed that Thomas in *The Glass Graduate* does not wish to reveal the name of his homeland or of his parents until he can bring honor to them both; we have seen that Ginés de Pasamonte's autobiography cannot be finished until his life is ended; and these are by no means singular cases.

The other extreme of this position is the ambience in which Sancho Panza finds himself. It is a posture assumed by those who wish to restrict the individual's freedom to act by protecting him from himself, a posture which would, centuries later, be described in political terms as in the concise statement by Proudhon: "To be GOVERNED is to be watched, inspected, spied upon, directed, law-driven, numbered, regulated, enrolled, indoctrinated, preached at, controlled, checked, estimated, valued, censured, commanded, by creatures who have neither the right nor the wisdom to do so."[19] This statement loses its anachronistic aspect if we do not carry it to its libertarian or anarchistic interpretation and instead consider it simply as an observation about a paternalistic form of constraining the behavior of the individual, which is to say that he loses his individuality. Although Proudhon capitalized the word "governed," his perspective is shared by Cervantes if we de-emphasize the political meaning and give it its broadest application of control over people's behavior, be it in a political or in a social circumstance.

Seen in this light, the irony of Sancho's governorship merits a new look. The entire adventure of Don Quixote and Sancho at the ducal estate is generally accepted as a contrived farce at the expense of the two wanderers, and the episode of the island becomes another play within a play. Sancho is often described as the deceiver deceived because the Duchess has him doubt his own mischievous "enchantment" of Dulcinea, which serves as a prelude to his gullible belief that he has at last been given his island and that he is its governor. But is he so credulous as to be taken in by it all?

The lengthy affair at the ducal estate, to which Cervantes devotes over one third of the chapters in Part II, has its beginnings in a mood of disillusionment. Don Quixote's inability to cope with the "enchanted bark" had ended with his famous confession: "God help us all, this world is nothing but schemes and plots, all working at cross-purposes. I can do no more" (II, 29), whereupon Cervantes leads us into the first of the more than two dozen chapters concerned with the ducal estate, a chapter which begins by describing Sancho's sense of disillusionment, that is, the beginnings of awareness, "for while he may have been a simpleton, he could not help perceiving that all or most of his master's actions were quite mad" (II, 30). As master and squire are about to meet the Duke and Duchess, then, Sancho Panza as well as Don Quixote is portrayed as disillusioned, as having experienced *desengaño*.[20]

The farce that is enacted at the ducal estate is, of course, that of allowing Don Quixote and Sancho to experience a realization of their ideals: recognition as a knight-errant in Don Quixote's case ("this was the first time that he really and wholly believed himself to be a true knight-errant and not a fanciful one" [II, 31]), and the attainment of an *ínsula* to govern for Sancho. (It is of some significance for an understanding of the characters of the Duke and Duchess to note how *their* values have been superimposed upon those of Don Quixote. Whereas they may understand the peasant's desire for land ownership, they do not comprehend that the corresponding ideal for Don Quixote is the intangible symbol of Dulcinea, an image which they cannot grasp and therefore prefer to present in the coarse "enchanted" guise.) That I should describe this adventure as an experience and a realization in the same sentence in which I label it a farce is neither inconsistent nor a relegation of the novel to the literature of buffoonery. As was my view in the Montesinos episode, the question of reality or dream becomes immaterial when one deals with the behavior of the person who believes that he experienced it; the charade at the ducal estate is no less an experience for Don Quixote and Sancho.

It is in this experience that we may see Sancho's growing awareness of realities which are of importance for his character and for his eventual self-awareness, no matter how limited. The *leitmotiv* which persistently underscores this process is contained in the personage of the Duke's majordomo. It is this man who impersonates the "Countess Trifaldi," supposedly one of a group of ladies forced to sprout heavy beards as the result of the magic arts of the enchanter Malambruno. Earlier I referred to the choice of a man to impersonate the "enchanted" Dulcinea in this same adventure. Now, as the plot is transposed downward, so to speak, to the role of Sancho, another man in the employ of the ducal pair is chosen to portray a distressed woman, whose disenchantment will depend primarily upon Sancho's steerage in the episode of the flying wooden horse Clavileño: "Indeed, without your [Sancho's] presence I do not think we shall be able to accomplish anything" (II, 40).[21] The connecting link between the two "enchanted women" is of course that it is Sancho who must disenchant each of them (in Dulcinea's case, the 3300 lashes he must administer to himself).

Sancho's growing awareness is reflected in the use of the eyes. Whereas Don Quixote had insisted on seeing the Cave of Montesinos with his own eyes and had been advised to scrutinize the Cave with a hundred eyes, he now insists on the blindfold: "Cover your eyes, Sancho." Shortly thereafter he asks La Trifaldi to "cover his eyes very carefully," followed by an angry exhortation to Sancho: "Cover your eyes, you spiritless animal, cover them I say." Sancho, in contrast, wants very much to see during the "flight" and suggests: "I've a mind, master, to take a peep and see where we are." Don Quixote gives him several examples to show why he should not uncover his eyes.

The motif of the eye is continued; Cervantes begs us to apprehend it: the Duke reads the inscription concerning the adventure "with half-closed eyes"; he assures Don Quixote that he is "the best knight ever seen in any age." Throughout this, Sancho is "gazing about in search of the Distressed One [La Trifaldi], for he wished to see what she looked like without her beard." Sancho confesses that while they were "flying through the region of fire, or *so my master told me*, I wanted to uncover my eyes a little. . . . I have a little bit of curiosity in my make-up and always want to know anything that is forbidden me; and so, very quietly and without anyone's seeing me, I lifted the handkerchief ever so little, close to my nose, and looked down at the earth" (italics mine). Following several other references to the sense of vision, Sancho sums it up: "I had a peep at [the earth] from one side and saw it all."

The connection which Don Quixote makes between the Clavileño and the Montesinos episodes is more than a parallel of imaginative adventures. Each is designed to portray the character in a state of curiosity, a desire to see. What is more, Cervantes presents each of the characters with a manner of seeing that befits his individual traits: Don Quixote with his eyes wide open, discovering eternal verities; Sancho Panza peeking at the world, discovering mundane realities.[22]

I have said that the *leitmotiv* is personified in the Duke's majordomo. Not only is he the link to Don Quixote's illusion and enlightenment because of the representation of an enchanted lady by a man as suggested earlier; the majordomo is a constant reminder of Sancho's curiosity and of his scrutiny of those realities within his grasp. The first inkling is contained in the cited quotation to the effect that Sancho wanted to see what La Trifaldi looked like without her beard. That is to say, he wanted to pierce the illusion and find the reality. What causes him trouble is that he has seen the reality (a bearded man) which was presented to him as an illusion (a bearded lady).

Cervantes hammers the *leitmotiv* home by insisting upon the connection as Sancho is led to his governorship:

> Now, it happened that the one who was in charge of Sancho and his train was a major-domo of the Duke's, a fellow with a keen sense of humor who was at the same time very discreet (for there can be no humor where there is no discretion). He it was who had played the part of the Countess Trifaldi so amusingly, as has been related, and so was well suited for his present role. . . .
>
> The moment Sancho laid eyes upon the major-domo, he had a vision of La Trifaldi. [There follows a brief discussion with Don Quixote, who admits the resemblance but ascribes it to the wiles of enchanters. Sancho then replies:] "a while ago I heard him speak, and it was like La Trifaldi's voice sounding in my ears. Very well, I'll keep silent; but from now on I intend to be on my guard to see if I can discover any other sign that will tell me whether I am right or wrong in what I suspect" (II, 44).

This explains what appears to be a *non sequitur* in the letter which Don Quixote writes to "Governor" Sancho Panza: in the middle of a paragraph of his letter, Don Quixote inserts a request that Sancho inform him "as to whether the majordomo who is with you had anything to do with the business of La Trifaldi as you suspected" (II, 51). This unexpected question appears so abruptly that we must consider it as an intentional reminder by Cervantes: a reminder of Sancho's sole concern with respect to the relationship of the majordomo to La Trifaldi, namely to seek the reality which his senses have warned him is there and for which he must keep his eyes open. His lack of freedom to sleep because of the Duke's warning is therefore more serious than the apparent risibility of an obese peasant desirous of sleep: it is Sancho's turn to be awake, aware, and apprehending.

That he is indeed alert is revealed immediately in his reply to Don Quixote, for one question which Sancho does not choose to answer (because he must dictate it to his secretary, Sancho being illiterate) is Don Quixote's query concerning the majordomo. Significantly, he does close his letter with the hope that "may God free your Grace from those evil-minded enchanters and see me through with my government, safe and sound." The linking of enchantment to his own safety conveys his comprehension of who the "spies" really are: the Duke's employees, that is, those who now surround him and leave him, paradoxically, isolated. It is in this figurative isolation that Sancho Panza acquires sufficient self-knowledge to realize that governorships are not for him and that freedom is indeed the precious gift Don Quixote describes it to be in their first conversation following the lengthy adventure at the ducal estate (II, 58). It is surely intentional that the speech on freedom closes the twenty-seven chapters which had begun with the belief that at last Don Quixote and Sancho Panza would attain recognition as knight and governor, respectively.

In the alienated world of his *ínsula*, Sancho has not only acquired self-knowledge and a greater understanding of the potentialities which life does and does not hold open to him; he has learned as well that the governors may in fact be the governed, that the power may lie with the idle rich who pay lesser ranks to watch, spy, control and inhibit those who presume to govern. Such an atmosphere proved to be intolerable for Sancho. In his insulation, Sancho reached the realization of where his place in life might be.

VII   THE CRISIS OF ISOLATION

Despite the political elements in much of the foregoing (the principal sources for which are well-known treatises of the Renaissance such as Machiavelli's *Prince* and Castiglione's *Courtier*), Cervantes was not writing a political document. *Don Quixote* is, after all, an imaginative work of art, which is not to say that there are no didactic elements contained in the novel, but rather that politics was not the central concern of the author. How, then, are we to deal with the constraints placed upon freedom?

Cervantes does indeed place limits upon the freedom allowed the individual. We have seen the salutary effects in Sancho's case: in being protected against himself, that is, against his purely physical desire to eat and sleep, Sancho was made to see not only the realities of certain illusory aspects of this world, but his own limitations as well. This, too, is the lesson of the freeing of the galley slaves (another reason why it cannot be analyzed as a libertarian expression), of the "liberation" of Andrés and, in a somewhat more subtle way, of the opening of the lion's cage. It may even, to some extent, add another dimension to that other cage in which Don Quixote is returned to his home at the conclusion of Part I. In point of fact, Don Quixote's return in the cage *and to his home* is one of the most pathetic moments of his life, for he is returned to seclusion, a far more bitter experience than the desolation he experiences when Sancho leaves him to assume the governorship. From the moment Don Quixote sets foot in the cage, his submission is symptomatic of his evident sense of alienation despite otherwise familiar surroundings.

Alienation in one form or another is the great malady of modern, which is to say, post-Renaissance, man. Although its diagnosis may properly belong to the nineteenth and twentieth centuries, its existence as a phenomenon was no less real in Cervantes' time. The older, ordered, hierarchical concept of the world was crumbling, and the efforts of theorists and artists to insist upon a great chain of being serves to emphasize the disintegration of the concept more than to suggest its dominance. The antecedents of modern technology—the printing press, the ships to sail around a global world suspended around a sun amid an ever stranger universe, and yes, the windmill!— gave man the appearance of mastery while, slowly, the realization of loss of control provided signs of servitude and uncertainty. The Spanish crown had barely acquired the empire upon which the sun never set when political incompetence produced debacle upon bravado (the Armada followed by only a generation the glories of Lepanto) and fiscal ignorance resulted in inflation and injustice. While Spanish kings attempted to preserve and glorify the Catholic faith throughout the old world and a newly discovered world, the Reformation spawned a Counter-Reformation, and one's very beliefs were put in doubt.

One may debate, as many have, whether Cervantes' faith was steadfast, hesitant, anti-clerical, or steadily progressing from one point to another as he approached greater maturity. What cannot be disputed is that he lived in, observed, and thought and wrote about the individuals caught in the dilemma outlined here. The relationship is well described by Lowenthal:

> The breakdown of the feudal order forced man to fall back upon himself; he had to learn how to cope with countless problems and decisions that were once taken care of by worldly and spiritual hierarchies. But together with the anxieties generated by this new autonomy he sensed a great promise, for in the period of the formation of the national state and the development of a mercantile economy his own future seemed to have infinite possibilities.[23]

And with specific reference to Spain and Cervantes:

> The Spain of Cervantes' novels is a highly mobile and competitive society. Man has become the measure of a world which is losing its theological determinants. . . . He rejects much of his society, particularly those deformations of character that are the result of competition and insecurity, but he does so in the name of a man-made ideal (p xiv).

The dualistic view of life, with its "infinite possibilities" and its "insecurity," is the basis for the dramatic tension within the individual. The critical moments in that life frequently occur, as we have seen, during periods of some form of aloneness. I conclude the present section with a look at another of the *Exemplary Tales* of Cervantes, *La fuerza de la sangre* ("The Power of Blood").[24]

Don Quixote in several crucial moments of his life; Graduate Glass in his crystal confinement; Campuzano in the hospital; Preciosa (*La gitanilla*) among the gypsies; Soldino (*Persiles*) in his cave; Sancho on his island: these are only a few of the many examples—some of which are also readily analyzed from other perspectives, as we have seen—of situations of isolation which lead to a crisis in one's circumstances and subsequently to self-knowledge. Despite the great number of such instances throughout Cervantes' works, including his best-known creations, I venture to say that none is more dramatic than *La fuerza de la sangre*. What is more, this novel contains within its relatively few pages all the elements we have thus far encountered in more elaboratd works.

The tale begins at night on a deserted (*solo*) road. Leocadia, a young lady, is returning from a walk together with her family. The group is met by a quintet of young men led by Rodolfo, the latter described by Cervantes as around twenty-two years old, wealthy, of illustrious blood and with *too much freedom*. In a writer who is known for his yearning for liberty and freedom, we might find these last words perplexing had we not seen earlier that Cervantes recognizes the necessity of tempering freedom with appropriate restraint. Unbridled freedom lurking on an isolated road and hidden from scrutiny (the young men's faces are covered) is what greets Leocadia and her family on a summer's night.

The manner of introducing characters and revealing names is of substantial significance in Cervantes' art of presenting individuals. We should note, therefore, that it requires an extended number of words, sentences and lines between the point at which the young lady is first presented (opening sentence) and the point at which we learn that her name is Leocadia (eighth sentence, Cervantes employing a variation of a favorite formula: "for that was her name").[25] In contrast, Rodolfo is named only one sentence after his existence is related, a rapidity in identification which is comparatively rare in Cervantes' prose.[26]

The quick pace of the tale as a whole has been noted by Casalduero (*Sentido de las Novelas*, p. 152), but this analysis is on a plane entirely distinct from mine. El Saffar also perceives the concise style but passes over the "too much freedom" without comment, inasmuch as she is more concerned here with style, structure, and symbolism: Rodolfo "is depicted with such precision and intensity that his youthfulness, his freedom, his lascivity [*sic*], his selfishness, and his impetuosity can be captured in the single deed of rape which ignites the story in a moment in which beauty and the desire for its possession are compressed in the smallest space of time."[27]

The libertine Rodolfo places Leocadia in emotional isolation even before the abduction is concluded and well before the rape is begun. What had been, moments earlier, a spot for pleasure is now converted into frightful desolation: everything was "covered by the solitude of the place and by the hushed silence [*callado silencio*] of the night." Having blindfolded Leocadia despite her being in a faint, Rodolfo rapes her in the darkness.[28] Regaining consciousness, Leocadia does not know where she is: she is not only in isolation but in absolute darkness. She has lost her bearings and does not know whether she is "in the limbo of my innocence or the hell of my guilt."

This dichotomy does not persist long, for she recalls how she had been abducted as she senses Rodolfo's presence and grasps his hands. Her awareness of the social consequences leads her to go first to one extreme—death, which is preferable to dishonor—and then, in her symbolic isolation, she becomes aware of her own capability to master at least part of her circumstance as she chooses life, in recognition of her own cleverness. Leocadia attempts to rid herself of any illusion (*desengañarse*) with respect to the reality of her abductor. Through the sense of touch, she recognizes that he is human, and realizes (literally translated, "falls into the truth of") her situation. Her momentary desire to seek death, rather than master the circumstances with the wit which is her human patrimony, is overcome in her isolation as she recovers her wits and dominates the situation by defending herself "with her feet, with her hands, with her teeth and with her tongue." Rodolfo at last leaves her to seek advice from his friends.

El Saffar (*Novel to Romance*, p. 128) has observed that *La fuerza de la sangre* is difficult for the twentieth-century reader to accept. Certainly my own students have confirmed this skepticism, more so in recent years with the momentum of the feminist movement. One of the circumstances that tends to leave my students perplexed is the actual rape (consummated while Leocadia is unconscious) in relation to the attempted rape (impeded by Leocadia's wit). Aside from the difficulty in understanding how this woman could ultimately desire a marriage to her abductor, the "liberated" woman of my classes scoffs at Leocadia's inability to *want and enjoy* a sexual relationship. The interpretation I prefer is related to the general topic discussed in the present book. Leocadia's rape is carried out while she is unconscious precisely in order to underscore her total lack of involvement. The scene immediately following presents her still blindfolded, still in the dark but with her wits about her. The point is not whether she enjoys making love—honor questions aside—but whether she is able to dramatize that a woman may, even in her desolation, employ her own intellectual attributes to control her situation. The contrast with her unconscious state (in Spanish *sin sentido*, "without sense") enables us to focus on her conscious self-control. Consequently, although one can scarcely place this tale in a feminist context, what does emerge is Leocadia's own desire to marry Rodolfo. Whether she does so to satisfy the demands of honor or whether she is motivated by the love kindled by her son (the innocent consequence of the rape) are matters outside the scope of my study here. What also comes to the fore is her determination to accept with pride the function of her feminity. Accordingly, it is *she* who identifies the place of her seduction (not in keeping with that part of the honor code which would encourage silence on such matters) and thus brings about the eventual fulfillment of her desire (not merely her social responsibility) to marry the father of her son. I do not mean to suggest that Leocadia is mainly motivated by love, much less by sexual appetite. My use of the word "desire," as distinguished from the exigencies of society, is intended to reflect her own wish to live as a wife and mother. Her *own* concern to live in an honorable state, rather than society's demands that the stain on the family honor be removed, animates her. This is why she prays to God specifying that it is *not* to ask for vengeance but for consolation with which to bear her misfortune with patience. Although it is true that Rodolfo satisfies a variety of appetites—he enjoys sex, benefits from his father's wealth, travels abroad, all the while that Leocadia is made to deal with the consequence of his lasciviousness—it is equally accurate to observe that Leocadia's self-control throughout various stages and kinds of aloneness ultimately directs the course of events. Cervantes' explanation that the events took place prior to the Council of Trent's pronouncements concerning weddings is more than a way of avoiding censorship. His insistence on telling us that in those days all that was required was the will of the parties concerned underscores that it indeed has been the will of Leocadia, as well as that of Rodolfo, that has led to the denouement, an ending which emphasizes happiness, contentment and jubilation above all else.

There is, of course, much more to this tale. A complete analysis is, as my readers now know, not the object of this book so long as my selected episodes remain in their proper context. The scene in *La fuerza de la sangre* is a concise model of where we have come in four chapters and where we may go from here, for it presents questions of names, of sexuality, and of isolation. In this last respect, the experience of being alone with oneself in absolute darkness in order to emerge therefrom with greater self-knowledge and purpose characterizes what in the works of Cervantes is a fundamental process along the path to individuation.

VIII THIS IS I

In an insightful passage placed within her broader analysis of Cervantes' tale *Las dos doncellas* ("The Two Maidens"), Ruth El Saffar observes: "In the effort to rediscover peace and union with self and society that marks the struggle of all of Cervantes' later characters, the character must come to see himself in perspective, beyond the blind passions that motivated his initial actions. . . . The individual struggle of each character to gain a true perspective on himself through which he can be relieved of his suffering and alienation is part of the collective effort of all the characters to reestablish the bonds of union that passion and selfishness have broken."[29]

Don Quixote, of course, remains the character who best exemplifies this process. (If the flaws of passion and selfishness do not appear to describe him appropriately, we should not forget that in his very nobility of purpose he was motivated as well by a zeal so unbridled that his excesses form the basis of much that is risible in the novel; moreover, his repeated yearning for fame and his conviction that his exploits would be recorded for posterity can scarcely be said to veil his egocentricity.) As we have observed from a number of perspectives, Don Quixote has from the beginning claimed to know who he is and who he may be if he chooses. There is in this assertion less self-knowledge than general comprehension of human potential and expression of volition. It is not until the processes which we have been

111

observing have run their course that he is able to state unequivocally who he is. Let us take one more look at this basic recognition.

"I have good news for you, kind sirs," said Don Quixote the moment he saw them [the characters present at his deathbed]. "I am no longer Don Quixote de la Mancha but Alonso Quijano, whose mode of life won for him the name of 'Good.'" This assertion from the final chapter of the novel requires scrutiny beyond that which we have given it in previous chapters. We shall also observe that Putnam's translation reveals sharp insight.

The original Spanish for the final portion quoted above reads: "... *ya yo no soy don Quijote de la Mancha, sino Alonso Quijano, a quien mis costumbres me dieron renombre de 'Bueno.'*" Starkie interprets rather than translates the concluding clause as "the man whom the world formerly called the Good, owing to his virtuous life." Aside from the unfounded interpolation of the word "formerly," which would force us to interpret the entire path of the novel as a moral detour, Starkie's logical but free translation of *costumbres* as "virtuous life"misses the central point implicit in the equally free (but, in my view, accurately perceived) rendition by Putnam. My purpose here is not to judge translations but rather to put into relief the significance of the original by stressing Putnam's discerning intuition, given the point of view I have been espousing in the present study.[30] A grammatical analysis easily clarifies the sense of the original. The subject of the clause in question is *mis costumbres*, which we may translate as "my comportment" or, as Putnam put it, "[my] mode of life."[31] The verb "gave" accordingly agrees with this subject and it is here that Putnam's insight is revealed in his interpretive rendition: "won for him." We have come full circle, for the dying protagonist, in the revelation of his true name, shows himself to be truly a child of his own works. Not only does he know who he is and who he has been because he chose to be; he is conscious of what he is because of his *costumbres*, which is to say, because of how he has behaved.

He has not simply regressed to his pre-quixotic state. And, as if he anticipated a misinterpretation, he clarifies: "I was Don Quixote de la Mancha, and now I am, as I have said, Alonso Quijano the Good." Neither regression nor self-abnegation: he *was* Don Quixote and he *is* Alonso Quijano. The processes of individuation have removed him from the anonymity of the famous opening line of the novel (*un hidalgo*) and the ambiguity of his name. "I am, as I have said, Alonso Quijano the Good."

Hamlet, as we have noted, was able to say, "This is I, Hamlet the Dane." The epithet, as most annotated texts clarify, is an assertion of rank. Don Quixote had also appended his place of origin to his name in the manner of the stories he had read. As in so many instances in Cervantes' writings, to speak of parody is undoubtedly accurate but scarcely complete. We should not overlook that *la mancha* means "stain" or "blemish," and that this connotation is reinforced by the preposition *de* ("of"). In contrast to Hamlet, who manages an assertion of his name and rank, Cervantes' protagonist is able to announce his having developed, become, changed and grown because of his deeds or his *costumbres*, for his "mode of life won for him the name of 'Good.'" His change is not one of rank or privilege; his metamorphosis is not only from anonymity to singularity; the process of individuation has been as well a moral development. He is no longer associated with a blemish but rather he has earned the very word "good" as part of his name. He is not a Hamlet who can only hold on to the trappings of rank, nor a Lear who steps outside himself to see the nature of man. Don Quixote has stepped *inside* himself, as it were, to find his own individual strengths and weaknesses. This is the significance of his and other Cervantine characters' experience with isolation. And he has found himself—not "man," but a man, one man, for there is no other quite like him (one aspect of the extensive debate about the spurious Don Quixote, protagonist of the book by Avellaneda). He is, quite simply, who he knows he is: Alonso Quijano, whose mode of life won for him the name of "Good."

That Cervantes was conscious of the significance of the word *mancha* as applied to his protagonist is revealed toward the end of Part I when Don Quixote is "enchanted" and placed in a cage. In a mock-heroic prophecy, the barber predicts the completion of his adventure when "the frenzied *león manchado* lies down with the white *paloma tobosina*" (I, 46). There is no need to clarify *paloma tobosina*, which quite simply makes an adjective of the town El Toboso and makes of Dulcinea a white Tobosine dove. Moreover, it is not necessary to consult dictionaries of symbolism to relate a white dove to virginal purity. Opposing this emblematic representation is the depiction of Don Quixote as a *león manchado*, literally a stained lion. (To argue that this means no more than "spotted" is to miss the antithesis set up by Cervantes with respect to the white dove.) Most editors attempt to "correct" Cervantes by explaining that the proper way to say "Manchegan" is *manchego*. Not only is this another instance of

113

explaining away rather than illuminating, but it dulls the point of the imagery: the stained lion is in a frenzy (because of his frustrations) and harmony will be restored when the lion lies down with dove. That it is a dove rather than the proverbial lamb serves to emphasize the ethereal, as opposed to the worldly, peace that Don Quixote ultimately seeks.

As if to reinforce this meaning of *manchado*, Cervantes presents the episode of the errant goat, a female runaway whom the goatherd has named Manchada. This brief episode serves to introduce the goatherd's story of an errant girl. Don Quixote, who had observed the affair of the fugitive Manchada, asks the goatherd to relate his story "because I see that this case has a sort of air about it that smacks of a knightly adventure" (I, 50). Since the goatherd has not yet begun his story and the only thing he has related is the account of Manchada, it stands to reason that Don Quixote's sense of recognition is based on what he has heard thus far. Accordingly, it does not require literary exegesis to see that Don Quixote's remark links his own affairs to that of an errant Manchada. From Cervantes' point of view, of course, this association serves as well to introduce the goatherd's tale, that of the wayward Leandra, whose fate it is to end her days in a convent. Don Quixote objects to the involuntary nature of this confinement but attributes to his own alleged enchantment his inability to help Leandra. It is significant that he cannot aid Leandra, who has lost her honor, whereas moments later, he has no compunction about coming to the aid of what he imagines to be a lady who is being carried along against her will: the Virgin Mary, specifically described as the *Virgen sin mancilla*, the stainless Virgin. The relationship of *de la Mancha* as an indication of origin to that of stain (as contrasted with the goodness that Don Quixote ultimately may proclaim) is, consequently, reinforced by these rapid episodes toward the close of Part I.

As this book was in its final stages there came to my attention yet another study on the episode of the Cave of Montesinos.[32] With respect to the matters discussed in the present chapter, Hughes is one of the few to have perceived that "the descent is prompted . . . by an inner urge to be alone. . . ."[33] The thoughts expressed in this chapter have, I trust, attempted to explain not only the need for such an urge, but also the effects of that solitary experience, in that instance as well as in others. Hughes further makes a significant observation on Don Quixote's insistence that the abyss was not hell: "Such references to a pleasing experience cannot easily be accommodated to Don Quixote's

114

knowledge of his spiritual demise."[34] The experience in his isolation did not, of course, impart any such knowledge, as we have seen. If the experience helped to destroy artificial reference points upon which so many of Don Quixote's illusions were dependent, *including the disenchantment of Dulcinea*, the emergence from the Cave of Montesinos represents the emergence of the individual in yet another sense. If, as many agree, the separation of Don Quixote from his library is a liberation from the constraints of the literature of the past which originally had propelled him to seek his own personification of their ideals; if, as many also agree, the characters' ability to discuss in Part II the history written about them in Part I represents yet another liberation from a fiction, then the Montesinos experience may be seen as one more step in the process. In this way the references to a pleasing experience may easily be accommodated to the protagonist's emergence from isolation, for he has been spiritually renewed precisely because of the cathartic disillusionment of the experience.

Some years ago a French scholar observed that "Don Quixote has surrendered to Amadís the individual's fundamental prerogative: he no longer chooses the objects of his own desire—Amadís must choose for him."[35] The reader of the present study will perceive a difference in views. However, the divergence lies not so much in the point of view as in the point of departure. If we consider the protagonist during his knightly phase, particularly the first part, there can be little dispute with the cited observation. On the other hand, if we see the grand scale, particularly as we approach the eventual denouement, we note that the very process of individuation which we have been discussing leads us to a contrary conclusion. And Don Quixote himself directs us to such a conclusion. The basis for Girard's observation is also Don Quixote's own, namely, that one must imitate Amadís if one is to attain perfection as a knight errant. However, we must take into account as well the final chapter. Immediately following the assertion that he is "no longer Don Quixote de la Mancha but Alonso Quijano, whose mode of life won for him the name of 'Good,'" the protagonist exclaims: "I am the enemy of Amadís of Gaul and all his innumerable progeny; . . . I am in my right senses now and I abominate them." We could dismiss this as no more than a confirmation of his having abandoned a chivalric ideal, of which Amadís is the prototype. On the other hand, given Girard's thesis that Amadís embodies the surrender of the individual's prerogative, Don Quixote's assertion at this point of his career that he is no less than Amadís' enemy underscores in a most dramatic fashion the process of individuation that has been at work.

That same process may be seen from yet another angle if we go back two chapters prior to the final one. In II, 72, during the discussion about the spurious Don Quixote in Avellaneda's version, reference is made to the latter as "Don Quixote the bad" in contrast to Cervantes' "Don Quixote the good." Our protagonist replies: "I don't know whether I am good; but I am able to say that I am not the bad one." To a large extent this discussion is concerned with the life-literature theme and is outside the scope of the present study. It is important to note, however, that coming this close to the final chapter's revelation, the comments made in II, 72 cannot be divorced from those in II, 74, and Cervantes assuredly was not oblivious of the apparent paradox. That it is only apparently paradoxical and that the two comments are indeed linked becomes clear when we consider that the protagonist's problem in Chapter 72 is that he is uncertain about the character known as Don Quixote: it is of Don Quixote that he speaks when he says that he does not know whether he is "good." To be sure, he can state unequivocally that he is not "bad." His concern reflects an understanding that although Don Quixote has not erred morally—hence he is definitely not bad—he may not have accomplished anything sufficiently remarkable to have earned the sobriquet of "good." The truly notable achievement is the process we have been observing—that of individuation—and it is not Don Quixote but Alonso Quijano who may unhesitatingly declare, "I am, as I have said, Alonso Quijano the Good."

The life-literature motif, which is present in the novel from its opening chapter in the first part through the denouement, assumes an added twist when the real book (by Avellaneda) and its spurious protagonist become a source of irritation (and reaction) for Cervantes himself. The relationship of this debate within our novel to the matters we are discussing is contained not only in the question of who is the "good" and who the "bad" Don Quixote, but as well in the previously quoted insistence of our hero that "there is no other I in the world." For Don Quixote to accept the notion that there is after all another Don Quixote in this world would amount to a rejection of the individuation process we have been following. From yet another perspective, therefore, the protagonist must declare his aloneness—his uniqueness, if you will—and so he is now prepared to return to his home and his bed, where he may confidently state who he has been able to be, and who he is.

ISOLATION AND DESOLATION

IX THE OTHER SIDE OF THE COIN

On a number of occasions in the course of this book the reader may find references to Don Quixote's life which describe the apparently antithetical movements of isolation and emergence, seclusion and sally. If being alone has a restorative effect, the nature of life is such that the opposite may result. I have dealt more with Don Quixote's physical and psychological isolation for the obvious reason that he is best known for his sallies, literally his coming forth. It is necessary to bear in mind, however, that his life, which is to say that portion of his life worthy of Cervantes' pen, is made up of a series of movements involving his *coming out* of seclusion, whether these be the well-known sallies or the more symbolic emerging from a cave, an inn, a ducal estate, or his own room. These movements are only apparently antithetical because they correspond to the paradoxical character of life itself. Even a passing familiarity with Don Quixote allows this to be accepted readily. As for Sancho, surely the very concept of the *ínsula*—exotic counterpart of El Dorado—confirms his need for emergence from the confines of his birthplace. This "other side of the coin of isolation" also serves to explain why so many scenes of parting are so poignant. On a different level, it also explains why so many of the characters—major and minor—are involved in some form of quest.

It is not necessary to wander into discussions of literary classifications. Let us agree that *Don Quixote* is part of the literature of the quest. Without straying from our purpose of examining the process of individuation, however, we need to see the quest not in its archetypal context, but as the very human need to find one another. Let us therefore move away from heroes seeking the Grail (or a Don Quixote pursuing a Dulcinea), and approach instead some instances of fleeing from seclusion. By seclusion I have in mind not a pejorative sense of confinement, but any cloistered or sheltered existence which, for almost as many reasons as there are such situations in Cervantes' works, requires the individual's emergence in both senses: emergence from the physical as well as the psychological shell. An interesting example may be found in the short story *The Illustrious Kitchenmaid* (La ilustre fregona).[36] A brief summary of the plot follows:

Don Diego de Carriazo, son of a wealthy gentleman of Burgos, "prompted solely by his roguish spirit, without having had any cause to complain of bad treatment at home, but simply for his own whim and pleasure . . . set out for the wide world" (p. 175). The young man was around thirteen when he decided to "unhook himself" from his parents' home.[37] Young Carriazo, during three years in Madrid, Toledo, and Seville, found special pleasure at the tunneries of Zahara, the land's end of the roguish fraternity.[38] There he left "half of his soul, and all his heartfelt longings he entrusted to those parched sands, which in his eyes were fresher and greener than the Elysian fields" (p. 177). Returning from this first sally, he found no excitement in life at home: "The hunting expedition that his father organized for him did not entertain him, nor did the many elegant feasts, which were fashionable in that city, give him much pleasure. Every amusement, in fact, bored him, and even the important ones that were offered to him he rated far below his former celebrations in the tunny fisheries" (p. 178).

Carriazo now forms a close friendship with a young gentleman of similar age and background, Don Tomás de Avendaño, to whom he describes "in detail the life of the 'big net,' admitting that all his gloom arose from his longing to return to it once more" (p. 178). As we might expect, the two young men set out together, the principal part of the plot revolving around their experiences at an inn where Costanza, the "illustrious kitchenmaid," arouses the love of Avendaño. The denouement reveals that Costanza is the illegitimate daughter of Carriazo's father, marriages are agreed upon between various couples, and the story reaches a happy ending. For our purposes here, we need to concentrate upon the two young men.

We need not detain ourselves with a comparison between this tale and *Don Quixote*. The structural parallel is evident but the psychological ambience is quite distinct. Once more, for example, Cervantes presents a series of name changes but the method and motivation are consistent with the requirements of this particular set of circumstances. To begin with, our two young men have specific names. What is more, although Avendaño's given name differs from that of his father's, Don Diego is the name which Carriazo senior and junior share. On this point Casalduero has observed that the distinction serves to focus on the repetition, so that "if in the Christian world the human condition is inherited and sin is transmitted, that inheritance and transmission do not occur in a fatalistic material world, but in the spiritual world of liberty" (*Sentido de las Novelas*, pp. 199-200). In this context, Casalduero reminds us that at the end we are told that young Carriazo went on to have three children who, "without taking after the pattern of their father or remembering that there are tunny fisheries in the world, are all today studying at Salamanca" (Starkie translation, p. 231). It is not necessary to accept or reject Casalduero's ethical interpretation in order to see in it the insightful comprehension that we are being presented with a process of individuation.

We have here, of course, a variation of the *cada uno es hijo de sus obras* theme, and this is reinforced even further by the otherwise enigmatic ending of the tale. During the central portion of the plot, young Carriazo had wagered the tail of his ass, whereupon he had become the butt of all the children in the area who would cry when they saw him, "Let's have the tail! Let's have the tail!" As the story comes to its otherwise happy conclusion, following the remark that Carriazo's children did not follow his pattern of life (any more than the young Carriazo had emulated his own father), Cervantes ends by telling us that Carriazo "hardly sees a water carrier's ass without recalling his experience, fearing that, when he least expects it, he may come across in some satiric squib or other: 'Give us the tail, Asturian; Asturian, give us the tail!'" (p. 231). These final words of the story, following the reference to his children's individuation, serve to remind us of his own process of individuation earlier. These two remarks at the end, together with the opening paragraph of the tale (the reference to the same name for father and son), frame the story within an experience of individuation. It is, of course, necessary to bear in mind the individual's motivation. As El Saffar observes, we are not dealing with alienation (as, for example, in the case of Graduate Glass):

> There is no indication that Diego de Carriazo and Tomás de Avendaño doubt their identity or that they truly reject their background. . . . Their flight to the underworld of *pícaros* is shown to be motivated not so much by feelings of hostility toward their family or society as by their high-spirited desire for adventure and freedom. *La ilustre fregona* begins with Carriazo's return to his family in Burgos after three years with the tuna fisheries in southern Spain. The return reveals that the young man is willing to maintain ties with his family and that his family has not rejected him. . . . [Avendaño and Carriazo] do not want to break entirely with their past as they journey to their adventures with the tuna fishermen.[39]

El Saffar subsequently mentions "the character's relative satisfaction with his family and social situation."[40] She is correct, and we must bear in mind that the process of individuation we are observing in this story is indeed unlike that of some others we have examined. On the other hand, we should not confuse the social circumstances with the psychological ones. Boredom with the customary entertainments and their youthful quest for *different* stimuli are the motivating factors in the young men's compulsion to establish an identity of their own. Accordingly, it is correct to note that "Avendaño and Carriazo had escaped from the plan of life that their fathers had established for them,"[41] but we need to distinguish social rebellion—and all agree that such is not a factor here—from psychological individuation. El Saffar discerns this distinction but does not follow up on it. At any rate, she is once more correct when she observes "a strong sense of the social context of the main male characters [which] is introduced before they emerge as characters outside that context. The extreme deference all the characters show in the presence of their fathers suggests that they become characters in their own right only away from home."[42] This last statement, with clear references to the emergence of character, is far more definitive of the process than the qualifications expressed in the lengthier passage from El Saffar quoted earlier. Quite apart from the purely social context, the characters in this story leave the shelter of their home in order to seek not isolation (in a cave or behind a mask of insanity), but what Casalduero has called "life open to all influences and all winds" (*Sentido de las Novelas*, p. 192).

Name changes, as mentioned above, are significant in this story, but the purpose is not unlike that which we have noted in other circumstances. In his first sally, Carriazo apparently assumed the name of Urdiales, but since this portion of the tale is prior to the main events, nothing is made of it. We are, of course, reminded once more how self-baptism is related to role-playing. Accordingly, during the main portion of the story, Avendaño is known as Tomás Pedro and Carriazo as Lope the Asturian. What is perhaps of most interest is the author's repeated reference to them in this fashion throughout this longest portion of the narrative, thus helping to establish that the narrator himself has accepted the transformation. More directly related to the purpose of the present section of this book, however, is that these name changes reflect the characters' having separated themselves—albeit temporarily—from the names which tied them to their secure but purely inherited origins.

It is of considerable interest, therefore, that the main plot springs from the intrusion upon someone's seclusion. The "illustrious kitchenmaid" Costanza would never have been born, had her widowed mother not "retired to a village belonging to her. There, in seclusion and with great virtue, she was spending a tranquil and quiet life. . . .[Carriazo, Sr. arrived at her estate and] mounted the stairs, without meeting a soul, up to the apartment in which she was taking the siesta, lying asleep on black cushions. She was extremely beautiful, and the silence, the loneliness of the place, and the opportunity aroused [his] guilty desires . . ." (p. 226). As a result of this seduction in the cloister of her home, the lady became pregnant and in order to "escape the prying eyes of my native country . . . I made a vow of pilgrimage to Our Lady of Guadalupe. It must have been her will that my labor should befall me in your house [= the inn where the subsequent events take place]" (p. 219). We should also note that Costanza's mother remains nameless, her wish being "not to call her anything except the Lady Pilgrim" (p. 218).

The foregoing is scarcely astonishing. We need not even cite Cervantes' biography nor the traditional conception of travel as character-building (even in a pejorative context) in order to understand the importance to the personality of seeking to emerge from one's shell. The example of *The Illustrious Kitchenmaid* does, of course, reaffirm such a concept without, as El Saffar's observations emphasize, upsetting any established traditions. The example of this tale serves not only to show that the process of individuation varies with the individual and with the circumstances—in short, that we should more properly speak in the plural of *processes*—but more importantly, places into relief the modernity of Cervantes' approach in the situations discussed earlier, which is to say his appreciation of the role that being alone may play in the process of self-recognition. One conclusion that may easily be drawn is that, as in so many other ways, Cervantes views the problem of the individual from not one, nor even two, but a variety of perspectives. Beyond this, however, we must raise the question, does there exist a relationship between the character and the particular process of individuation which Cervantes applies, or are we simply observing a spectrum of possible approaches?

Bearing in mind that we are dealing not with the methodology of a clinician but with the imaginative creations of a literary artist, we must avoid the temptation to seek formulaic answers to questions that would in this light become impertinent. What is relevant to our investigation, however, is the general variety we have observed thus far. Graduate Glass and Don Quixote share the appearance of insanity and display some form of withdrawal. That they are different we have already noted. That difference reflects as well that Don Quixote *looks back* upon a life of nothingness and sets out to give meaning to his existence, whereas the young Rodaja (who will not disclose his origin until he has earned the privilege) *looks forward* to his variegated experiences. Not only are their sallies dissimilar, therefore, but their experiences in isolation reflect these differences. In the case just examined, Carriazo and Avendaño reflect not only "another" difference, but a diametrical opposition. They know who they are (which they accept, and to which they return), and they know who they *might* have been (replicas of their fathers). What they respond to is the lack of vitality (boredom) inherent in that acceptance. This is why their reaction does not avail itself of isolation. Instead, they not only abandon the cloister but seek their experiences in what is a symbol of unplanned living: an inn. In short, our reply to our own question is that Cervantes is consciously relating the characters, the circumstances, and the processes.

Chapter 5

Psychodrama

I DEVIATION, INSANITY, OR INDIVIDUALITY?

Although inquiry into the nature of art and drama antedates Aristotle —certainly Plato has a good deal to say about it in numerous passages of his dialogues—it is usually to Aristotle's *Poetics* that we turn for the beginnings of a theory of dramatic art. As Fyfe concisely puts it, Aristotle believes that it "is not the 'particulars' of sense . . . that Art represents, but 'universal' truths . . . , the inner interpretation of the mind."[1] With regard to emotions, "we must face them as facts and use Art as their medicine. . . . To afford this pleasurable relief is the object of poetic drama. Poets must be recalled from exile to serve as medical officers."[2]

The above is easily recognized as the germ of the principle of catharsis, which purges the character of the spectator. Within this familiar context, a point of particular relevance to what follows is made by Aristotle (*Poetics*, 6.24): "Character is that which reveals choice, shows what sort of thing a man chooses or avoids in circumstances where the choice is not obvious. . . ." As Fyfe explains in the footnote to this sentence (pp. 28-29), choice or "*proairesis* is a technical term in Aristotle's ethics, corresponding to our use of the term 'Will,' the deliberate adoption of any course of conduct or line of action. It is a man's will or choice in this sense that determines the goodness or badness of his character. If character is to be revealed in drama, a man must be shown in the exercise of his will, choosing between one line of conduct and another, and he must be placed in

123

circumstances in which the choice is not obvious, i.e. circumstances in which everybody's choice would not be the same."

Mandel cites what he calls "the characteristic modern doctrine that 'tragedy is at bottom man's most vehement protest against meaninglessness. . . .'"[3] Mandel then comments:

> If the requirement of piety . . . is ageless, the other thesis, namely that of the beauty of human character and the dignity of man, can be traced back no further than to the Romantic age, when two conditions particularly favorable to this view obtained: the weakening of orthodox faith, leading men to a search elsewhere for consolations, and the revival of fervor as a virtue rather than a defect. This fervor, unable to satisfy itself in adulation of the Virgin Mary or divine mercy, turned to the creature man. Thus was born the apotheosis of Dante, Shakespeare and even Cervantes, and the new perception of tragedy as a vindication of nobility.[4]

Although a hasty reading of the above suggests an anachronistic confusion of Romanticism, Dante, Shakespeare and Cervantes, the passage merits attention. I cannot, of course, agree that the concept of the beauty of human character and the dignity of man can be traced back no further than to the Romantic age. It may be true that the Romantics saw and espoused this vision with more enthusiasm than, say, an audience of the Middle Ages. Nonetheless, what Mandel sees in Cervantes—to limit myself to the object of the present study—is correct and we can indeed go back in time beyond the Romantic period, back at least to Cervantes himself, if by expressions such as "dignity of man" we can divest ourselves of the Romantic excesses and still see worthiness in the common man. (I am assuming that Mandel's frame of reference is outside the philosophical treatises of Pico della Mirandola and others.)

But by speaking of common people we run into an obstacle at the other end of the chronological debate: Aristotle and his contemporaries spoke of tragedy and its healing effects only if the play dealt with heroes in high places; the problems of the common man could not arouse pity and fear: only low comedy. By the time that Cervantes wrote about humanity, however, he "moved the art [of the novel] away from high life and the beautiful people to all life and to all people. . . . [Cervantes] looked to ordinary life rather than to high life for his substance. In this—only in this—he surpassed the greatest of secular writers, Shakespeare. . . . The common man is there in Shakespeare, . . . but he is comic relief out of a lower order. . . . In this Cervantes was more nearly modern."[5]

124

It is not, then, on what Wouk calls the "high life" that we should focus; nor (if one accepts the classical definition), on tragedy. It is common knowledge that Cervantes had an affinity for dealing with characters in his works who, in one way or another, deviated from what would be considered normal behavior, assuming that there ever has been a way of determining what kind of behavior is "normal" and what kind is "deviant." The attempts to explain this penchant have ranged from alleged identifications of historical models, through influences from literary antecedents, to the desire to be free of censorship because potentially dangerous ideas spoken by a madman can be explained away as proof that the author considered them nonsensical. I have no desire to enter this debate—which must also include the artistic creativity of the author, a point which cannot be overstated—other than to make note of the obvious: in a variety of ways, a number of characters who populate Cervantes' works seem to be victims of some mental disturbance, the most common of which would today be called cases of neurosis, of alienation, or of schizophrenia.[6]

Whether or not Cervantes saw them as clinical cases we shall probably never know. It can hardly be doubted, however, that he recognized in his creations certain qualities which caused them difficulty in finding an acceptable place in society. Although, as I indicated earlier, one needs to qualify Otis Green's treatment of the four humors, I do agree with many of his observations and conclusions. Especially relevant to the present discussion is his affirmation that prior to Cervantes, "no one had ever before had the idea of utilizing the derangements and the lucid intervals of a monomaniac as a means of probing—in a work of fiction—into the nature of the universe, of man, and of society, and even into the latent possibilities of art and art forms."[7] What I propose to show is that having recognized the problem, Cervantes set about to rehabilitate his characters in the manner suggested by Aristotle—whether or not he personally had read the *Poetics*[8]—namely that the theater offered therapeutic solutions, and that without the necessity of restoring classical tragedy, he shared Aristotle's view that "we must face [emotions] as facts and use Art as their medicine" by calling upon the dramatists "to serve as medical officers."

Before examining the solutions, we should appraise the problems. Or should I say problem? For, although the specific deviations differ, there is nonetheless a certain communality of social difficulties. I choose these last two words with care, for I see them as problems encountered by people in society, not as diseases which are to be ridiculed or "cured" by the physicians of the particular era: "In medical practice, when we speak of physical disturbances, we mean either signs (for example, a fever) or symptoms (for example, pain). We speak of mental symptoms, on the other hand, when we refer to a patient's *communications about himself, others, and the world about him*. . . . [It is] apparent that the statement that 'X is a mental symptom' involves rendering a judgment. The judgment entails, moreover, a covert comparison or matching of the patient's ideas, concepts, or beliefs with those of the observer and the society in which they live."[9]

That Cervantes understood the arbitrary nature of such a judgment—"Whose agent is the psychiatrist?"[10]—is revealed in the well-known tale of the "loco de Sevilla" in *Don Quijote*. That he understood psychological problems in a context of communication as outlined above should be equally clear.[11] Moreover, as I hope to show shortly, Cervantes recognized as well the social context in which such problems developed. The "loco de Sevilla" example, as well as many others of greater importance in his works, can demonstrate his insight and I suspect he would agree with Szasz that much modern thinking is fallacious or, as I would phrase it, inverted: "Mental illness—as a deformity of the personality, so to speak—is then regarded as the *cause* of the human disharmony. It is implicit in this view that social intercourse between people is regarded as something *inherently harmonious*, its disturbance being due solely to the presence of 'mental illness' in many people."[12] Bearing in mind the importance of harmony to thinkers and artists of Cervantes' time, it follows that Cervantes could not fail to perceive the discordant note sounded by the psychologically troubled individual. Like Szasz, however, he would not place the blame on the illness of the personality; more likely he would recognize that the stability of the world order was itself in danger and that the individual's confusion, if not the result of, was at least related to the great doubts which had beset all of society in its religion, its cosmography and, soon to follow, its socio-political beliefs.

Lyons sums up what he considers Alfred Adler's fundamental contribution: "Psychology deals with people; but equally important, it can only deal with people as they appear to other people. For this reason the data of psychology do not consist simply of people as mere targets for the context of a science but primarily as objects in social perception. Psychology deals with persons as they appear to persons;

with persons as they act in the unique realm which constitutes the ken of other persons who are also engaged in action."[13]

One of the most accessible ways for an individual to see people as they appear to other people (including himself in either role as actor or observer) is the theater. This is one of Adler's definitions of empathy: "Drama is the artistic expression of empathy. . . . In the theatre particularly we can hardly avoid identifying ourselves with the players, or prevent ourselves from acting the most varied roles within ourselves."[14] It comes as no surprise, then, to learn that "Adler believed that the psychologist can actually learn from the great writers. 'Our veneration for the poets can hardly reach a higher degree than in our admiration for their perfect understanding of human nature. Some day soon it will be realized that the artist is the leader of mankind on the path to the absolute truth.' And he adds that he has learned primarily from fairy tales, the Bible, Shakespeare, and Goethe."[15]

He might have learned as well from Cervantes who, intuitively, understood the benefits of what today we may term psychodrama, although Cervantes could scarcely be credited with a systematic, much less scientific, conception of the process. What he did comprehend, as his art reveals and as we have examined to some extent in the previous chapters, was the need of the human personality to seek its place in society. That process—individuation—includes the recognition of a universal commonplace: all the world is a stage and all the men and women are *necessarily* players.

II   TOWARDS A THEATER FOR THE ABSURD

We know something about the protagonist of *Don Quixote* that applies to his personality prior to as well as during his chivalresque period. Mark Van Doren spotted it long before it is confirmed in the novel: "It is that he was first and last an actor, a skillful and conscious actor."[16] Speaking of Don Quixote's readiness to accept the idea that it was enchanters who had done away with his library, Van Doren asks, "Why may it not be supposed that Don Quixote, always, like a good actor, alert to clues, saw at once the advantage of such a dodge, and determined to use it whenever it should come in handy? . . . The trick would last him as long as he cared to use it—of course, with variations."[17] The confirmation of Van Doren's insight comes during the adventure of the *Cortes de la Muerte*, when Don Quixote reveals his love for the theater since he was a youth, a revelation which includes some other pertinent remarks:

> ... when I first saw this wagon, I thought that some great adventure must be awaiting me, but I perceive now that one must actually touch with his hands what appears to the eye if he is to avoid being deceived. God go with you, my good people; be off to your festival; and if I can serve you in any way, I will gladly do so, for as a lad I was very fond of masks and in my youth my eyes were fixed upon the stage. (II, 11).

Aside from the detail about his lifelong affinity for the stage, this passage merits a closer look. I do not need to tell readers of these pages that the appearance-reality motif is a major theme of the book and the age. Beyond that, it should be pointed out that Don Quixote's first thought "that some great adventure must be awaiting me" is not negated by the following clause. Undoubtedly he is referring to the illusion produced by stagecraft; but his truism concerning the need to touch (i.e., use one's senses) before believing appearances, assumes fundamental significance when we bear in mind that it is the theater which inspires this realization and that what it leads to is a word loaded with significance: *desengaño*.

Otis Green devotes an entire chapter of some three dozen pages to the concept of *desengaño*, of which one third are reserved for Cervantes (for the most part *Don Quixote*) alone. No mention is made of this use of the word *desengaño* by Don Quixote; moreover, in his subsequent chapter on death, the section concerned with *Las Cortes de la Muerte* deals primarily with earlier works, the episode in *Don Quixote* being merely summarized and then dismissed as showing that this tradition "was active in the rural districts of Spain around the year 1615."[18] Green is correct of course when he discusses the "inkling of the change which the author plans to carry out in the chapters having to do with Don Quijote's final return from the world of illusion and falsehood."[19] I should like, however, to deal somewhat more deliberately with this episode.

As I suggested above, the fact that Don Quixote has learned the deceptive nature of appearances does not contradict his words that he believed this to be a great adventure. It is in fact a grand adventure because (1) it reveals as fact that he is a lifelong follower of the stage; (2) it is indeed part of his gradual awareness of greater truths than those presented by worldly appearances; (3) the senses with which God has endowed man can lead to *desengaño*; (4) it leads to a key discussion at the beginning of the next chapter; (5) it ties in with the *Danza de la Muerte* theme, whose importance to my topic will be clarified below. (The fact that it ends in a typical misadventure only serves to underscore by contrast some of the aforementioned points: Rocinante, incapable of ratiocination, has no capacity to understand theatrics and his animal reaction is only to be expected. The farcical ending puts in relief the "grandness" of Don Quijote's *desengaño*.)

This adventure gives rise to what many dismiss as the mere repetition of a commonplace, namely the "all-the-world's-a-stage" *topos*. We should not forget, however, that we are dealing with "the great reservoir of Renaissance commonplaces, the *Quijote*, where commonplaces are set up and reduced to rubble, though sometimes sympathetically."[20]

III   THE DANCE OF DEATH

The *topos* of the "Dance of Death" has been admirably studied in a number of works and its thorough analysis lies outside the focus of my study. A concise exposition of the theme is found in Huizinga's classic work, from which I cite the following excerpts:

> The treatises on the contempt of the world had, long since, evoked all the horrors of decomposition, but it is only towards the end of the fourteenth century that pictorial art, in its turn, seizes upon this motif. To render the horrible details of decomposition, a realistic force of expression was required, to which painting and sculpture only attained towards 1400. At the same time, the motif spread from ecclesiastical to popular literature. Until far into the sixteenth century, tombs are adorned with hideous images of a naked corpse with clenched hand and rigid feet, gaping mouth and bowels crawling with worms. The imagination of those times relished these horrors, without ever looking one stage further, to see how corruption perishes in its turn, and flowers grow where it lay.[21]

Huizinga then traces the development of the word "macabre," indicating that a "line of the poet Jean Le Fevre, 'Je fis de Macabré la danse,' which may be dated 1376, remains the birth-certificate of the word for us." He adds:

> Towards 1400 the conception of death in art and literature took a spectral and fantastic shape. A new and vivid shudder was added to the great primitive horror of death. The macabre vision arose from deep psychological strata of fear; religious thought at once reduced it to a means

129

of moral exhortations. . . . The idea of the death-dance is the central point of a whole group of connected conceptions. The priority belongs to the motif of the three dead and three living men, which is found in French literature from the thirteenth century onward. Three young noblemen suddenly meet three hideous dead men, who tell them of their past grandeur and warn them of their own near end. Art soon took hold of this suggestive theme.. . . The theme of the three dead and three living men connects the horrible motif of putrefaction with that of the death-dance (pp. 144-45).

Finally, Huizinga points out that the pictorial image to which these art forms restricted the conception of death, limited such thoughts to the physical aspects of death and dying:

> Thus the cruder conceptions of death, and these only, impressed themselves continually on the minds. The macabre vision does not represent the emotions of tenderness or of consolation. The elegiac note is wanting altogether. At bottom the macabre sentiment is self-seeking and earthly. It is hardly the absence of the departed dear ones that is deplored; it is the fear of one's own death, and this only seen as the worst of evils (p. 150).

Green, in the section of his book cited above, indicates that as we approach the period with which I am here concerned, the intent of most writers is "to encourage meditation upon death as an exercise in self-knowledge and humility, both as a common need of all Christians and as a first step on the *Via Purgativa* of the mystics; as a means of startling and frightening the sinner, thus causing him to turn from his folly; and finally as a reminder of the eternal blessedness to which death is the one and only gate" (p. 110).

We are now prepared to return to *Don Quixote*. In II, 11, the chapter begins by describing Don Quixote as "deeply dejected" because of the recent experience of seeing "Dulcinea" in her enchanted guise as invented by Sancho. The latter advises his master that "sorrows are made not for beasts but for men, but if men feel them too much they become beasts. Your Grace ought to . . . wake up and cheer up." The original Spanish for the last part is "*avive y despierte*" which literally means "revive and awaken." Rosenblat (p. 240) has noted that these words are the same as those used in the opening lines of the oft-quoted *Coplas* of Jorge Manrique: "*avive el seso y despierte*," and he views Sancho's use of these words as a clear reminiscence of Manrique's verses. It is not necessary for me to leap some dozen chapters to the Montesinos episode in an attempt to link Manrique's poem and its famous lines about the three lives to Don Quixote's realization of the significance of this triad. The carefully planned sequence of events continues smoothly if we allow Cervantes to guide us.

Shortly after Sancho's words—and I agree that the reference to Manrique is clear—Don Quixote and Sancho come upon the company of strolling players who are presenting in various towns *Las Cortes de la Muerte*. We are clearly faced with a favorite device of Cervantes: the convergence of themes. The allusion to Manrique brings to mind the other traditional themes present in the *Coplas*: the *ubi sunt*, the vanity of worldly goods and glory, their transitory nature and the use of Death as a personage. The *Cortes de la Muerte* are a direct representation of many of these same matters, particularly the inexorability of death and the equalizing nature of death. These same eternal truths are contained in the Dance of Death.

Following a typical misadventure between Don Quixote and some of the actors, Don Quixote introduces another theme (not original with either Cervantes or Shakespeare), namely that all the world is a stage. All this happens, says Don Quixote, "in the comedy we call life, where some play the part of emperors, others that of pontiffs—in short, all the characters that a drama may have—but when it is all over, that is to say, when life is done, death takes from each the garb that differentiates him, and all at last are equal in the grave." To this Sancho responds: "It is a fine comparison . . . though not so new but that I have heard of it many times before. It reminds me of that other one, about the game of chess. So long as the game lasts, each piece has its special qualities, but when it is over they are all mixed and jumbled together and put into a bag, which is to the chess pieces what the grave is to life." Don Quixote's response is "Every day, Sancho . . . , you are becoming less stupid and more sensible" (II, 12).

What is important here, it seems to me, is not the utterance of two commonplaces in succession. Even Sancho has heard them both many times before. Bearing in mind Cervantes' fondness for combining topics, we should focus on the linking of the "all-the-world's-a-stage" theme with the "life is chess" equation. Both of these are readily associated with the *ubi sunt* (the players and the chess pieces disappear when their roles have been played out), the inexorability and evenhandedness of death (all the players disappear when the last act is over and all the chess pieces are returned to their resting place) and the Dance of Death (the players and the chess pieces go through the motions assigned to them and eventually fall off the boards).

There now follows the adventure of the Knight of the Mirrors and his squire (Sansón Carrasco and Sancho's friend Tomé Cecial). What links this encounter to the foregoing is first that the knight and squire

131

duplication comes on the heels of an allusion to the game of chess, the knight and squire (rook) in opposition, each knight with his own queen (Dulcinea and Casildea) and, as we later learn, Sansón's plan to play the role of knight came about as the result of his conference with the curate, analogous to the bishop of the game. Secondly, the repeated references to the refusal on the part of the Knight of the Mirrors to lift his visor and reveal his face, followed by the ultimate revelation that he "looks like" Sansón (Don Quixote insists that the resemblance is the result of enchantment), as well as the newcomer's assertion that he had already conquered someone called Don Quixote de la Mancha and his reply, when pressed, that "you are as like the knight I overcame as one egg is like another" (II, 14), reinforce the notion that we are all playing roles and that when the performance is over, we shall appear equal.

It is after this adventure that Don Quixote encounters another knight, the more modern version of the *Caballero*, Don Diego de Miranda, otherwise referred to as the Knight of the Green-Colored Greatcoat, followed in turn by the adventure of the lions, both episodes upon which I have already commented. One adventure remains between these and the climactic Montesinos experience. It is the wedding of Camacho, during which a number of points are made that sustain the themes described above. It is Sancho who makes the most direct connection when he observes that "there's no trusting that one with no flesh on her bones [Death] who eats lamb as well as mutton, for I've heard our curate say that she treads both the tall towers of kings and the humble cottages of the poor." As most editors point out, this is a translation from Horace's fourth ode (*Pallida mors aequo pulsat pede pauperum tabernas, / Regumque turres*), which Cervantes first quotes in the Prologue to Part I. Hence the theme has been with us even before the first chapter.

Don Quixote picks up the wisdom of Sancho's remark and tries to put his squire down a notch at the same time as he adds, "But what I cannot make out is this: the fear of God, they tell us, is the beginning of wisdom, yet you are more afraid of a lizard then you are of Him." But Cervantes allows Sancho to have the last word: "Your Grace would do well to judge your own deeds of chivalry and not go meddling with the fears or bravery of other people. I'm as God-fearing a man as any neighbor's son; . . . all the rest is idle talk and we'll have to answer for it in the life to come" (II, 20).

This talk of the inexorability of death is framed by the observation about swordsmanship in II, 19 to the effect that "brute strength is overcome by skill," and Basilio's cleverness in II, 21, which the bystanders are tempted to call a miracle, but which Camacho simply terms "no miracle . . . but a trick."[22] The emphasis on cleverness, trickery or strategy, is the prelude to the Montesinos adventure which, in turn, is followed by the adventure of Master Pedro's puppet show. It is the second time now that Don Quixote is presented with a theatrical spectacle, this time performed by marionettes.

IV   A THEATER FOR THE ABSURD

"It tells how Señor Don Gaiferos freed his wife, Melisendra, who was held captive by the Moors in Spain. . . . Here your Worships may see Don Gaiferos playing at backgammon, as in the song: 'At backgammon playing is Don Gaiferos, / Melisendra's already forgotten now'" (II, 26).[23]

The reader will recall that the gist of the plot performed by the puppets revolves around the abduction of Melisendra by the Moors, Don Quixote's leaving his place in the audience to fight the Moors, help the knight Gaiferos and rescue Melisendra, in the course of which Don Quixote draws his sword and "in less time than it takes to say two Credos he had knocked the entire theater to the ground and had slashed to bits all its fixtures and its puppets, King Marsilio being badly wounded while the Emperor Charlemagne had both his head and his crown split in two." This causes Master Pedro to moan some lines from a *romance* ("Yesterday I was lord of Spain, / And today I do not have a tower left / That I can call my own"), following which he bemoans his fate: "Not half an hour ago, nay, not half a minute ago, I was lord of kings and emperors; my stables were filled with countless horses and my trunks and bags with any number of gala costumes; and now I am but a poor beggar, ruined and destitute."

There can be no mistaking the "all-the-world's-a-stage" theme together with all the other commonplaces about death described above. Kings, emperors, knights and damsels have performed the dance of death. It is also no accident that the episode begins with the depiction of Gaiferos playing at backgammon. The thirteenth-century Spanish King Alfonso X, known as *el sabio* or "the learned," published in 1283 the *Libros de ajedrez, dados y tablas* (Books of Chess, Dice and Backgammon). As King Alfonso points out, backgammon differs from chess and dice, yet combines aspects of the two, for the player must use his intelligence (as in chess) together with his luck (as in dice).[24] In a way, then, backgammon is more analogous to life than is chess, for although both games end in the clearing of the board (that is, egalitarian and inexorable death), backgammon includes the element of chance. At least one critic has observed a connection between the puppet episode and previous episodes:

> The irreverent treatment of Gaiferos and Melisendra echoes the chronicler's mock-heroic view of Don Quijote and Dulcinea, and certain coincidences of detail seem designed to make the connection explicit. Melisendra, captive in the Moorish palace, must be rescued by Gaiferos, just as Dulcinea, prisoner of a wizard's spell, Don Quijote believes, must be rescued from the Cave of Montesinos by Don Quijote—or rather, disenchanted by Sancho, who is just as unwilling to flagellate himself as Gaiferos is to leave his chess game. Melisendra's leap onto the croup of Gaiferos' horse, where she sat [astride it like a man], invites comparison with the earlier episode in which the country lass (Dulcinea, according to Sancho) falls from her mount and takes a running leap into the saddle, where [she remained astride it like a man (II, 10)].[25]

Although I obviously agree that these several adventures are connected, my own focus is on other aspects. (It is interesting to note in passing that Haley makes the slip of describing Gaiferos' game not as backgammon but as chess.) Without detracting from Haley's analysis— which simply deals with other perspectives that are not in contradistinction to mine—I should like to concentrate on the interrelationship among the various themes I have been discussing, namely, the death theme and its various manifestations and the games which relate to it.

Just as Cervantes saw fit to have the pseudo-author call Don Quixote's cave adventure apocryphal while relegating a similar task to the "translator" when making the same judgment of Sancho's wise statements, so does Cervantes have Don Quixote and Sancho discuss chess while relegating to puppets (or past figures of *romances*) the slightly less intellectual backgammon. In short, the central episode of the Cave of Montesinos, which not only answers the *ubi sunt* question, is itself a dance of death, with Don Quixote the spectator. The adventure—aside from being part of a larger and well thought out literary work—is itself framed by the hints that it contains a secret language, that it will present the real-life dilemma of skill (*industria*) versus fortune (*ventura*), and that it will lead the protagonist on the road to the "third life."

What is this third life? According to Jorge Manrique, it is the only eternal one; and it is attained in one of two ways: religious people achieve it through prayer and tears, and famous knights through travail and affliction in the struggle against the Moors. One way, then, is that of the saint, an interpretation of Don Quixote expounded by Chambers.[26] While I do not care to reject this evaluation, particularly as it applies to Don Quixote's gradual awareness of the true and eternal values, I cannot go so far as to say that the protagonist of this greatest of all parodies is destined for sainthood. More consistent with his character is the twofold nature of Don Quixote's apparently irrational action of intervening in a puppet show: first, we once more note that when it is not a question of flesh and blood women, our hero does not hesitate to take part in the action. Secondly, his attempted heroism is directed against Moors, one of the ways in which the true and eternal life is gained by knights. In this respect—and not in the sense of storybook heroes—he truly believes in his mission of chivalry. The vista—or, if you will, vision—of the Cave of Montesinos has opened his eyes to this truth of eternal values. The Cave adventure was his experience of the dance of death. The remainder of the novel— including the lengthy stay at the ducal palace—presents Don Quixote's gradual and ever clearer view of these truths.

To pause for a moment and sum up: the adventure of the Cave of Montesinos, in addition to the erotic and cryptic analogies referred to earlier, as well as the inversion of the *locus amoenus* and Golden Age *topoi*, caused Don Quixote to view the "second life," in effect a dance of death, for he was forced to see the inexorability of even a second death, a death which was graphically represented by the decay of heroes and heroines, in short, a death awaiting us all eventually, no matter what our worldly accomplishments. In this sense I agree that the Montesinos episode is an Orphic experience, as William of Conches (1080-1145) explicated the work of Boethius: "Then Orpheus descended to the underworld in order to bring back his wife, just as the wise man must descend to a knowledge of earthly things in order to see that there is nothing of value in them before he can free himself from human desire."[27] In the same vein I agree that "it was really Bernard Silvestris [twelfth century] in his commentary on the *Aeneid* who offered the most influential explanation of the descent to the

135

underworld. . . . Bernard had said that there were four ways of descending to hell. 'One is by the way of nature, another of virtue, a third of vice, a fourth by artifice. . . .' The descent by way of virtue is the way of the wise man who descends through his consideration of worldly things, not in order to cling to them but rather by knowing them to reject them in favor of 'invisibilia.'"[28] In short, while I do not believe that the Cave represents Hell in the sense that it is the place where sinners spend eternity as a punishment, it does seem to me to represent a prelude to death, intermediate between this life and the eternal one. Whether one gains the eternal "third life" in Heaven or ends up in total decay and nothingness is the problem presented to Don Quixote in the Cave as he witnesses people of all stations in life go through their dance of death.

Cervantes' contribution to the "descent-into-the-underworld" or Orpheus theme is that what is found there (the response to the *ubi sunt* question) is the panoply of men and women in the full revelation of their mortality. As noted earlier, Dante pointed the way. But Cervantes adds his peculiar twist. The underworld is indeed a world figuratively below ours, hence a descent, because it represents life there as boring, monotonous, anti-heroic and grotesque, despite its serving as evidence that people who had achieved worldly renown do indeed attain a second form of life. The irony provided by Cervantes, then, is that knights, squires, ladies, damsels and the rest are the pieces on the chessboard of life that end up in the inverted *locus* which is anything but pleasant, and it is there that they must go through their grotesque dance of death. Shakespeare, too, had a perception of the greater tragedy that befalls the things we treasure most when the latter face the inevitable decay: "*corruptio optimi pessima*: the corruption of the best becomes the worst; or, as Shakespeare puts the same sentiment, 'sweetest things turn sourest by their deeds; / lilies that fester smell far worse than weeds.'"[29]

The realization or discovery of these truths is found by Don Quixote, as I have noted, in the crypt where hidden meanings lie. For the cousin, the meanings are mere encyclopedic details for his disorganized scholarship (or he can interpret them in erotic ways). Sancho cannot believe the adventure because, as is indicated later in the ducal palace, he is the deceiver deceived. His own mischief in "enchanting" Dulcinea prevents him from sharing and believing in the discovery. We now know why Don Quixote found it all so pleasant. Not only has he seen the pleasance with his mind's eye, but the prior emphasis on skill versus fortune and the subsequent beginning of the next adventure which converts the deadly game of chess to the similar game in which one must pit one's skill against fortune, explains to him that he can still do something about his ultimate destiny. It is in this context, I believe, that we must view Don Quixote's famous line in II, 66: "there is no such thing as luck in this world, and whatever happens, whether it be good or bad, does not occur by chance but through a special providence of Heaven; hence the saying that each man is the architect of his own fortune."

V ALL THE WORLD IS A STAGE

Shakespeare's Jaques (*As You Like It*, II.vii) observes that "one man in his time plays many parts." It turns out, however, that the description of these "parts" is in actuality a *chronological* development, beginning with infancy ("mewling and puking in the nurses arms"), through youth, manhood, middle age, senility and death ("sans teeth, sans eyes, sans taste, sans everything"). The final line is equivalent to Don Quixote's conclusion that "when it is all over, that is to say, when life is done, death takes from each the garb that differentiates him, and all at last are equal in the grave."

The relationship to the theme of the egalitarian nature of the *Danza de la Muerte* seems clear. Yet, when we ponder the equality of death, a corollary suggests itself: the inequality of life. In contrast to Shakespeare's more limiting statement that one man plays many parts in a *chronological* sense, Cervantes emphasizes the *variety* of roles, which present to the spectator "all the varied aspects of human life; and I may add that there is nothing that shows us more clearly, by similitude, what we are and what we ought to be than do plays and players" (II, 12). Don Quixote goes on to describe the range of roles played by the actors: kings, emperors, pontiffs, knights, ladies, as well as "numerous other characters" such as the bawd, the cheat, the merchant, the soldier, the fool ("who is not so foolish as he appears"), and the foolish lover. Cervantes emphasizes not only that the theater mirrors reality, nor only that it presents the illusion of reality, but that it as well depicts the reality of illusion.[30]

This inversion of the commonplace, namely the emphasis on the theater as a mirror of what opportunities life may hold for us, appears elsewhere in Cervantes. In *El Licenciado Vidriera* we are told that "anyone who paid court to an actress was the slave of a whole mass of ladies at the same time—a queen, a nymph, a goddess, a kitchenmaid, a shepherdess—and very often it also fell to his lot to serve a page and a lackey too; for all these roles and many more are normally played by actresses." A similar commentary is made by the title character in Act III of Cervantes' drama, *Pedro de Urdemalas*, following the suggestion that he turn actor: "I can be a patriarch, / a pontiff and a student, / emperor and monarch: / for the career of an actor / embraces all states." Pedro goes on to list some other roles he must be prepared to play, such as gallant, old man, young man, jealous lover, all done with such skill that he turns completely into the figure he is representing.

The pessimistic aspect of these statements is revealed in another portion of the same act when reference is made to the unanticipated accidents of life (fortune). The optimism, on the other hand, is reflected in the readiness of the individual to assume a variety of roles. For this reason I see the greater grasp of the possibilities inherent in the nature of the individual as perceived by Cervantes than as articulated by Shakespeare.

As was the case earlier in our discussion of the nature of backgammon, the theater presents not only the equalizing aspect of death as the final act closes, but the opportunities inherent in life through skill. Far more than a game of backgammon, moreover, the stage represents not only an individual's ability to maneuver, but the wide range of possibilities open to him, once given an experiential discovery of his own capabilities and limitations. In this sense, I see Shakespeare stressing the singularity of an individual whereas Cervantes emphasizes the plurality or multiplicity of potentialities which life may accord to the individual with self-knowledge. This explains one further difference in the two statements on the analogy of life to the stage. Unlike Shakespeare's simpler statement which primarily elaborates the stages of life and the ultimate egalitarian nature of death, Cervantes has Don Quixote comment that nothing shows more clearly "what we are *and what we ought to be* than do plays and players" (italics mine). Leaving to one side the Horatian principle that literature ought to provide pleasure and profit, this observation reinforces the notion that an individual can first perceive what he is and from there infer what else he can be. Admittedly, the sentence here seems somewhat more restrictive than Don Quixote's earlier assertion that he knows who he is and who he may be if he chooses, but it is consistent if we interpret "ought to be" not as an exemplary model but as the consequence of first having discovered "what we are," so that we may be able to act accordingly, that is, with a greater awareness of our potentialities.

It should be noted that the passage quoted above from *Pedro de Urdemalas* is not simply a gratuitous observation taken from some play which may support the issue under consideration here, for the context of the play itself is central to our concerns in this and in previous chapters. As a critic has recently observed, "the problem of identity motivates the main plot of Cervantes' *Pedro de Urdemalas* and forms the basis of the play's analogous structure. Cervantes parallels Pedro's search for a specific role in society with the gypsy-princess Belica's search for society's recognition of the role she intuitively claims. . . . Pedro's metamorphoses become elements of the mutability of man, seen in the context of a changing society. Cervantes' conscious reliance on the theater as a backdrop to the innate theatricality in man allows for the same type of multiperspectivism found in *La Numancia* and the Argel plays. . . . The play ends when the search for identity ends; Pedro, ironically, finds his place in the most protean of professions, acting, and Belica assumes her role of princess when society verifies her previous assertions of nobility."[31]

A further variation on the theme of the stage as revelatory of the possibilities inherent in a lifetime is presented by Cervantes in his last novel, the *Persiles* (Book III, Chapter 2): Auristela and Constanza "took up lodging in an inn where a company of well-known actors was staying and who, that very night, were to present a rehearsal at the Corregidor's house in order to secure permission to perform in public. . . . [A poet who accompanied the actors was so taken by Auristela that he at once] considered her to be more than well-suited to be an actress. . . . He was pleased by her figure, delighted by her spirit, and in one instant he mentally dressed her in the short coat of a man; he then [mentally] undressed her and dressed her as a nymph, and almost simultaneously dressed her in the majesty of a queen, without omitting a single comical or serious costume with which to dress her, and in all of them he could imagine her as serious, happy, discreet, acute, and especially virtuous. . . ."

VI PSYCHODRAMA

I shall deal rather rapidly with one important example in *Don Quixote*: the lengthy adventure of Luscinda, Cardenio, Dorotea, and

Fernando. It will be recalled that the original plan to return Don Quixote to his home and to his "senses" was devised as a pure theatrical farce: the priest would impersonate a damsel in distress—he actually dons a lady's costume—and the barber would disguise himself as "her" squire. It is not long before the "dramatist" revises his plot for reasons of decorum, and the two men are to change roles. (One notes again the facility with which roles are exchanged.) As the cast begins to take shape, a young boy turns out to be a beautiful young woman in disguise (Dorotea) and so it is decided that *she* will play the role of the damsel in distress. The very word employed by Cervantes—*representar*—makes the play-acting interpretation inescapable.

As many commentators have noted, Dorotea is really acting out her own dilemma. Less obvious, perhaps, is Madariaga's illuminating observation: "The tone in which [the monstrous giant] is conceived is the same wherewith the 'discreet' young woman neatly interprets the comedy contrived by the Curate and the Barber in order to bring Don Quixote back home. A well-meaning comedy, to be sure, but still somewhat uncouth and awkward, lacking the last touch of *art* which puts the bloom of *reality* over the face of *imitation*. That last touch Dorotea gives it when she joins in the plot. . . ."[32] I need not summarize this well-known adventure, but there are two points to be emphasized: first, everyone is encouraged to act out his role—Sancho's skepticism because he saw Fernando and Dorotea embracing only serves to underscore what the unimaginative may focus on in an artistic environment, whether it be a glimpse of the stagehands or a moment of privacy between the actors. In short, Don Quixote is welcomed to join the others in role-playing and this is one reason he so readily accepts the "enchantment" in the cage.

Secondly, it will be recalled that the climactic scenes and denouement took place at the inn, which is to say, in a house. This detail assumes increased significance when it is transferred to the adventure of the Cave of Montesinos. In a passage taken from *Memories, Dreams, Reflections*, Esther Harding recounts that "Jung tells a dream of his own in which he found an unknown lower floor in his house and under it a cellar, and beneath that a cave containing the remains of primitive and archaic man."[33] Harding continues:

> The variations on the theme of house are endless. For instance, instead of being a personal abode, the house may be a collective building, perhaps a

theater. This is the place where the typical stories of man's life are shown, that is, the mythologems are presented to consciousness. And in the dream the dreamer may discover that he has to play a part in such a theater, and not infrequently arrives at the theater only to discover to his consternation that he does not know what play is to be presented or what his role is to be. ... And so the "object," theater, leads into the "situation" of ordeal, namely, the necessity to act as best one can.[34]

The descent into the "cave" becomes of course an adventure in a house: "a sumptuous royal palace or castle" (II, 23). For some time now Cervantes has been preparing his readers for a theatrical experience. Let me go back once more to what we know of the protagonist's early life: I have already alluded to his fondness for acting; we are also told that he was fond of hunting. Now while psychologists may wish to tell us that the hunt is a substitute for warfare—and I have no quarrel with this imagery—it is also a fact that the hunt is an acting out of a well-understood drama. In short, we have a second clue to Don Quixote's readiness to play a role.

Moreover, when I suggested earlier that Green was too hasty in his dismissal of II, 11 as showing no more than that the tradition of the *Cortes de la Muerte* was "active in the rural districts of Spain around the year 1615," I had in mind as well that the activity need not be limited to this one sub-genre, but that the ready acceptance by Don Quixote of the troupe *as actors* demonstrates that traveling *theatrical* companies were an active phenomenon in those days. Thus the adventure at the inn in Part I is in accord with a custom of the times: one could expect troupes of *comediantes* to appear at an inn, or run into them on the road between performances.

A further clue is, I believe, present in the adventure which begins immediately following the introduction of the "all-the-world's-a-stage" *topos*: it is the confrontation with Sansón Carrasco who is himself acting out a series of roles, this time as the "Knight of the Mirrors."[35] Now if the theater is a mirror of life, does it not follow that a mirror does not do what one expects of it, namely that it does not allow one to see oneself? A mirror reveals the reverse, not the "self" that one is seeking. Cervantes, conscious of this weakness in the Ciceronian analogy, presents a knight dressed in so many mirrors that the plurality of perspectives—particularly following upon the discussion of the world as a stage—suggests first that the theater *is* capable of presenting the variegated facets of life, and secondly that these facets are restricted only by the spectator's limited (but not unitarian)

141

perspectives and his capacity to apprehend them. In a word, the stage may after all reflect reality, at least within a human context. The principle of *deleitar enseñando* may thus be better expressed as *enseñar deleitando*.

I am on somewhat less secure ground with my next point, but my case rests not so much on my imagination as on my conviction that a major writer—whose stock in trade, after all, is the use of words— chooses his words with a purpose. As Don Quixote begins his description of the cave prior to his noticing the castle, his choice of terms for comparison is significant. To indicate its size he suggests "a concave recess capable of containing a large cart with its mules. A small light filters into it through distant chinks or crevices in the surface of the earth." Of all the possible yardsticks, why a cart? I suggest that the cart is a clear echo of the recent experience with the cart that bore the actors for the *Cortes de la Muerte*. The theatrical ambience is further enhanced by the description of the sources of light (and entry), as well as the words preceding the entire narration, as though we were about to be told to take our seats: "Let no one arise . . . but both of you listen most attentively to what I have to say." Finally, viewing the Montesinos experience as a theatrical one would offer another explanation for the time discrepancy (Sancho and the guide, waiting outside the "theater" and dealing in chronological time, a half hour; Don Quixote, in the theater, living artistic time, three days and nights).

If life is a dream, then a dream—which is to say, the workings of the imagination—may also be life, as Durán has observed.[36] The well-known dispute about the veracity of the cave experience thus becomes a moot point: physical experience, dream, invention—it is all beside the point, which is that in any event it is a *psychological experience* undergone by the protagonist. It is an experience in which the characters he has tried to emulate reenact their poetic lives and really become antipoetic.

As we have seen earlier, Don Quixote does indeed apprehend the grotesque elements. The lovers of the chivalric legends are taking metaphor and converting it into reality: Durandarte has lost his heart to Belerma and she is literally holding his heart in her hands. As for Dulcinea, she is unattainable without worldly goods (money) and her unladylike behavior frees Don Quixote from the need to pursue the girl she once represented. (I am obviously in disagreement with most observers on this point, who believe the disenchantment to be the primary motivating force for Don Quixote through his ultimate physical defeat and until his "recovery" at his death. There are numerous examples of his refusal to leap to her defense, as well as of his recognition that his true mission is the attainment of what Dulcinea had once *represented*, not Dulcinea herself.) The key statements, I believe, are Don Quixote's own analysis and Durandarte's famous muttering.

Don Quixote tells us that his experience in the cave has taught him that "all the pleasures of this life pass away like a shadow or a dream or wither like the flower of the field." Although Rodríguez Marín suggests the Book of Job as a possible source, I see better parallels in Psalms 102.11 and 103.15, as well as Isaiah 40.6-8. These are the eternal truths, which, as Don Quixote himself says, he understands *now*. He does not have to make up for five decades of nothingness by knightly exploits which fade as the "flower of the field," as exemplified by the slow death of the "flower and mirror of the brave and enamored knights of his age," Durandarte, who had mumbled, "patience and shuffle." The virtue of patience is an idea with a history all its own. Suffice it to say that this is the lesson learned by Don Quixote: "No one can insult Señor Don Quixote without his being able to avenge himself, unless he chooses to ward off the blow with the shield of his patience, which appears to me to be great and strong" (II, 59). And it has been learned by watching, with his mind's eye, the performance of characters with whom he can identify. The cave experience is a psychodrama, a theater of the interior, so to speak, and thus Don Quixote emerges from it with his eyes closed.

Clearly there are additional theatrical elements in the "Curioso impertinente" episode, in the entire adventure at the ducal palace, in Sancho's governorship, in Sansón Carrasco's attempt to find his role in life, and in many more. In fact, I believe the entire novel can be viewed as a theatrical experience for each of the major characters, as well as for some of the minor ones. The curtain rises on "a gentleman" residing in "a place" and after 126 chapters or many "scenes," he achieves self-awareness (recognition) through the catharsis of his experiences. Moreover, the description of his first sally, recited by the character himself, is not only the parody it is usually classified as with respect to its grandiloquent style; it is also the typical beginning of a drama of the times with respect to its purpose: the "here we are" type of speech to make up for the lack of scenery, as well as references to the sun to indicate time. Nor should we overlook Cervantes' theatricalism in the "intermission" between Chapters 8 and 9 of Part I. The suspension of the action with swords raised has all the drama of the stage in it and the intervening discussion about author, translator, and producer is not unlike that in which an audience might engage between acts. Moreover, the technique which is carefully constructed during Sancho's governorship, namely the alternation of chapters between Don Quixote's and Sancho's separate yet parallel misadventures is a good reflection of the theatrical technique of alternating scenes in a play. A similar but less perfected parallelism of the plot and the related sub-plot occurs in Part I, once again during Sancho's absence, and in fact prepares the way for a play within a play, as my brief discussion of the Micomicón episode above suggests. That many of these adventures of the drama of life seem to be occurring on the open road while always having some significant link to a house—castle, inn, palace, hut, etc.—should not be overlooked in the stage metaphor. The image of the house, discussed briefly above, should be related as well to the individual's emergence and reentry. The stage analogy of exits and entrances should be linked to the individual's alternation of these movements. In Don Quixote's case, his self-confinement in his library, his periods of isolation such as in Sierra Morena and the Cave of Montesinos, must be seen in a pattern of alternating emergences in what most translators felicitously render as his "sallies." The individuation process, as we see more and more, is composed of a number of overlapping concepts.

VII   THE DANCE OF LIFE

I have already described some aspects of the individuation process in *The Dogs' Colloquy* in Chapter 1. What I wish to inject here is that Campuzano's treatment is in response to his failure to find a useful position as a man. Instead, he allowed his animal instincts to get the better of him and thus his "cure" consists of going to the theater (hospital) in order to be a spectator (or auditor) of another Dance of Life, spoken by animals. (It is noteworthy to recall that in the drama of animals, the dogs, too, play roles and display emotions which they [as in the case of all actors] must be trained by apprenticeship and observation to portray.) As in the case of Don Quixote, Campuzano

144

insists that it occurred while he was "wide awake and with all my five senses . . . I heard, listened, noted, and finally wrote down."[37]

The key to all this lies, I believe, in the dialogue format of *The Dogs' Colloquy*, a script ("I put it in the form of a colloquy to avoid the 'Scipio said,' 'Berganza replied'") approximating theater. Cervantes, in the previously cited prologue to his *comedias* and *entremeses*, reminds us that *comedias* or plays "were colloquies like eclogues, between two or three shepherds and a shepherdess" in the infancy of the theater prior to the development of the genre into its mature form as full-length drama.

The lesson of the Dance of Life is what the knocked-down Campuzano perceives through his window as he writes down his own account of the drama of the dogs. Campuzano is cured and, unlike Tomás Rueda, turns to intellectual rather than military glories. Don Quixote in a glass palace, Graduate Glass through the glass which encases him, and Campuzano through the window of his hospital: all are given an opportunity to be spectators of life as a chance to seek empathy and acceptable status through the salutary effects of psychodrama.

Green deals briefly with the didactic nature of theatrical representation and suggests that its purpose was to learn perfection: "It is an extension of the Socratic (and Christian) 'Know thyself.'"[38] In a footnote on the same page, Green suggests, "Truth was as near as the nearest parish church." I doubt that the awakening Renaissance mind was that comfortable with ready-made truths.

I would venture to say that what distinguishes the *comedias* of Lope de Vega (drama for the stage) from the novels of Cervantes (drama within a book) is precisely that the *comedias* could represent the idealistic and unattainable by vicarious participation, whereas Cervantes, whose reputation for idealism is even today still overemphasized—consider the use of the word "quixotic" even among scholars—is the one who presents the frustrations and the possibilities that accompany real lives. To put it another way, Lope dramatizes Spain's dream and illusion whereas Cervantes penetrates life's drama and allusions. The examples given above are a reflection of the sixteenth- and seventeenth-century dilemma, hence the questions posed earlier concerning the rendering of judgments on "patients" whose ideas do not coincide with the accepted norms. Cervantes was not giving these probing minds models of perfection; rather he was allowing them the temporary safeguard of insanity while they could observe the range of possibilities inherent in the drama of life, following which they were enabled to find their own "place in the sun."

It is, in the final analysis, the drama of life with which Cervantes wishes to deal. The classical formula for tragedy may have required death as the appropriate ending. In the works of Cervantes, death is only the occasional ending, the context rather than the genre being the determining factor. (Even the *Comedia's* conventional ending with marriage as symbolic of harmony and order is not a formal requisite for Cervantes' world view.) Death *per se* is after all not a tragic concept, for it is common to all mortals of whatever station. (In this respect, the only true tragedy about death begins, naturally enough, in Genesis, when mankind assumed its mortality; but even there death is not the final curtain, for the denouement must await the Day of Judgment.) What Cervantes perceives about life, on the other hand, is not only the multiplicity of roles to play but the one truly inevitable aspect of life: not the cessation (a point in time) but the passage (a process in time). This is the structure of life over which we have no control, hence the episodic nature of our lives.

VIII EPILOGUE

Certainly the "all-the-world-is-a-stage" *topos* by far antedates Cervantes. Curtius traces the concept back to Plato; when he moves forward to Cervantes, Curtius refers to the commonplace that when the play is over and the costumes are removed, the actors reveal their equality. With regard to Sancho's reply that it is a fine comparison but not so new that he has not heard it many times before, Curtius concludes: "Thus does Cervantes make fun of a literary cliché. Witty—indirect—mockery of fashionable ornament: That is the first form in which the theatrical metaphor meets us in the Spain of the seventeenth century. . . ."[39] However, Curtius not only oversimplifies but misses the mark as well. To state that a metaphor is a commonplace, even when it comes from the mouth of a peasant, simply reinforces how accepted the comparison had become. That in itself is hardly "mockery of a fashionable ornament." The metaphor is still with us three centuries later. I make this point not to single out Curtius' hurried observation but rather to close this chapter by putting Cervantes' contribution in relief. Certainly one cannot atttribute to Cervantes the origin of the "life-is-a-theater" *topos*, not even its inversion (i.e., that the theater mirrors life), all of which is commonly accepted metaphor. In fashioning his narrative, Cervantes' episodic structure reveals at once the inexorable step-by-step, scene-by-scene, act-by-act (in both senses of the words "step," "scene," and "act") progress of time; the eventual end of physical life as the players reach their climactic moments and find their potentialities; and conversely, the desperate effort of the individual to live one scene at a time, to put off the march of time, as it were, while all along realizing the interconnection of the scenes to form the grand play of life.

Cervantes does not mock the theatrical metaphor. He takes it from the hands of the dramatists and composes a new art form: a thousand-page history of an individual's attempt to find his *persona*. In the hands of an artist like Cervantes, this process of individuation through dramatization (psychodrama) may also be compressed into short stories which even he preferred to call novels. In similar fashion was he able to present such actions on the stage itself in his short *entremeses*. The episodic is, in the long run, the thread of life, and it is this transporting of the *topos* to its most nearly literal level—the participation in dramatic episodes as a spectator as well as actor—that is Cervantes' contribution. What is missing from the commonplace that all the world is a stage and *all* the men and women merely players is that these same men and women must, by definition, as well form part of the audience. In the world of art, it was simple to separate actors from spectators. In the world of life, the confusion is constant. The twentieth-century theater has, as we know, experimented in numerous ways with the joining of actor to spectator, ranging from seating arrangements to at least one play in which I was forced to run back and forth throughout the performance. (Curiously, it was a modern staging of *Orlando Furioso*, a work which originally was a source for *Don Quixote*.) In this perception of actor-spectator relationship, Cervantes was three centuries ahead of his time.[40]

Chapter 6

Postlude

If my opening chapter served to orient the reader with respect to the paths I would and would not follow, then it was appropriate to call it an introduction. It would be presumptuous, however, to refer to my final chapter as a conclusion, for the subject is far from closed. An interpretive study can scarcely lay claim to having arrived at conclusions, at ideas which are conclusive, at judgments which confine rather than liberate the creative efforts of the artist under consideration. If the present book were to be viewed as having settled Cervantes' view and treatment of the individual, I would be not only startled but disappointed. For I have not set out to prove but rather to probe.

A postlude, as the word suggests, is simply what follows the playing of roles, the playing of games, the play itself. It may even serve as an interlude, in which case it may be considered a prelude for what follows. If it does this, then the chapters which make up this book have served their purpose, for not only are my ideas subject to scrutiny but it is my hope that they will serve as an invitation for additional perspectives on the process of individuation in the works of Cervantes. I have used the word "process" throughout this volume, for I wished to stress an evolving and dynamic continuum rather than focus upon calculated and contrived moments. Such moments exist; we have come to know them through the use of labels commonly applied in literary criticism: recognition, reversal, inversion, and the like. To make them acceptable artistically, however, the writer must weave a fabric of experiences which provide a context for the critical moments. It is this process which makes up the stuff of the literature and it is this stuff and this process which engage the reader. For this reason, the word "process" must not be seen in a scientific or clinical context. We cannot speak of "the process" of individuation if by this we meant a supposedly systematic approach which we would presumably dub the Cervantine process.

A quick example will serve to illustrate the caveat. We have seen from a number of viewpoints how Don Quixote acquires the prerequisite self-knowledge in order to unveil his true self. In this process, then, he has had to confront the illusions of reality: his very real illusions with respect to sexual prowess, heroic exploits (his own as well as those of his literary predecessors, in turn illusions of another reality, for books are real), and his understanding of the various potential roles that the game of life afforded him. How very different is the process which serves to individuate the characters of the "Curioso impertinente" interpolated in the first part of *Don Quixote*. In this tale, it will be recalled, a happily married newlywed persists in subjecting his bride to so many tests of her fidelity that eventually she breaks down and deprives him as well as herself of love and honor. In the bargain, the friendship which had existed between Anselmo and Lotario is destroyed. The process of individuation here is quite unlike any we have described in this volume. The author has presented the two men as such steadfast friends that we are given to understand that this was in fact how they were known: "the two friends." The author similarly portrays Camila as a woman of apparently indestructible virtue. However, the process by which are created new personalities from those presented by the author at the beginning is the evolving definition *by the characters* of traits in themselves and in each other. In short, had the same process been applied to Don Quixote, the protagonist would not have revealed himself as Alonso Quijano the Good, but as the personification of his continuous self-definition: the embodiment of the knights-errant of his library. (It is essential to understand the distinction between psychological make-up and the process of individuation. Anselmo and Alonso Quijano are psychologically opposed: the former subjects his illusion to tests of extremity whereas the latter fears the test of the most elementary reality, e.g., whether his armor will withstand the blow of a sword. This may help to explain why the process of individuation is distinct in the two cases. What I wish to point out, however, is the simpler fact: they *are* distinct processes.)

To be sure, we could never have expected Cervantes to provide us with a systematic approach to individuation. If the famous opening sentence of *Don Quixote* with its intentional imprecision did not make that abundantly clear, then surely we were alerted by his subsequent warning that the accuracy of the name was of little importance so long as we did not stray from the truth. And if the truth is relative, then we must ask, in relation to what? We must go back once more to Ortega: "I am I and my circumstance," a statement which is simultaneously absolute and relative. Cervantes was able to have his hero say, "There is no other I in the world," which in its own way is at once absolute and relative. In both statements, the first part is absolute but dependent upon the individual's position in relation to his circumstance or his world to give it significance. That relationship and how it emerges is a constant source of curiosity for Cervantes.

Notes

Preface

1. Herman Wouk, "You, Me, and the Novel," *Saturday Review / World*, 29 June 1974, p. 9.
2. Raymond Southall, "The Novel and the Isolated Individual," in *Literature, the Individual and Society* (London: Lawrence & Wishart, 1977), p. 17.
3. Thomas Wolfe, *The Hills Beyond* (cited by Joan Berg Victor, *To Be Alone* [New York: Crown Publishers, 1974], p. 27).
4. Mark Van Doren, *Don Quixote's Profession* (New York: Columbia Univ. Press, 1958), p. 3.
5. *Ibid.*
6. Jorge Luis Borges, *Other Inquisitions*, trans. Ruth L. C. Simms (Austin: Univ. of Texas Press, 1964), p. 53. (Emphasis mine.)
7. Jorge Luis Borges, *Discusión* (Buenos Aires: Emecé Editores, 1957), p. 46. (The translation and the emphasis are mine.)
8. Unless otherwise noted, translations of *Don Quixote* are based on Samuel Putnam's version (New York: Viking, 1949). I say "based" on it because, although I regard it as the best rendering of the original without the constraints of anti-quated English on the one hand or forced vernacular on the other, I have nonetheless felt free to amend it when I felt it appropriate to do so. In the present instance, for example, the original refers to *sus cosas*, quite plainly "his things." Putnam refers to "his appurtenances" and J. M. Cohen (Harmondsworth: Penguin, 1950) translates "his possessions." Precisely because of the irony and Cervantes' sensitivity to style, the simple word "things" is there in contrast with the protagonist's belief in his own grandiloquence. I shall also have occasion to cite Walter Starkie's translation (New York: New American Library, 1964), which in the present instance evades the matter altogether. With respect to the *Novelas ejemplares*, I have similarly drawn on the translation by C. A. Jones, *Exemplary Stories* (Harmondsworth: Penguin, 1972), and, as noted in the appropriate places, the translation by Walter Starkie (New York: New American Library, 1963).
9. *Discusión, loc. cit.* (Translation mine.)
10. Ruth S. El Saffar, *Novel to Romance: A Study of Cervantes's "Novelas Ejemplares"* (Baltimore: Johns Hopkins Univ. Press, 1974), p. 3.
11. *Ibid.*, p. 6.
12. *Ibid.*, p. 8.
13. *Ibid.*, p. 9.

THE INDIVIDUATED SELF

Chapter 1

1. The reader is reminded of Ortega's famous *"Yo soy yo y mi circunstancia"* and his observation that one must *"buscar el sentido de lo que nos rodea"* ("I am I and my circumstance" and we must "seek the meaning of what surrounds us"). *See* José Ortega y Gasset, *Meditaciones del Quijote* (Madrid: Revista de Occidente, 1966), pp. 51-52.

2. A similar process led to the contrary epithet, *hi de puta,* "son of a whore." My point is not to give an oversimplified lesson in linguistics but to show that whose son (or whose child) one was, i.e., *hijo de . . .* , was of no small importance.

3. I do not believe that we must await the age of Balzac, as Swart suggests, in order to distinguish between the *concepts* of individualism as an expression of potential anarchism, and individuality as a search for personal identity and self-realization. The use of the vocabulary is, of course, another matter. *See* K. W. Swart, "'Individualism' in the Mid-Nineteenth Century (1826-1860)," *Journal of the History of Ideas,* 23 (1962), 84.

4. *"Faust* and the Birth of Time," in *The Energies of Art,* Vintage Books (New York: Random House, 1962), pp. 47-48. The reader is reminded of the quotation from Herman Wouk in my preface: Cervantes "looked to ordinary life rather than to high life for his substance. In this—only in this—he surpassed the greatest of secular writers, Shakespeare."

5. With regard to the picaresque novel, one of whose major characteristics is the autobiographical format, particularly in the narrow sense of the depiction of life as seen through the eyes of a lowly and socially unimportant protagonist, it may be of interest to note the possibilities for viewing the nature of the character's tone. Writing about the first such novel, *Lazarillo de Tormes* (1554), Howard Mancing, in "The Deceptiveness of *Lazarillo de Tormes,"* PMLA, 90 (1975), 427, concludes: "The extraordinary 'Prólogo' to *Lazarillo de Tormes* is a dense fusion of disparate elements—the bravado of the opening words . . . , mild erudition . . . , suspicious humility . . . , and outright pride . . .—which on balance probably produces a negative reaction in most readers." Mancing's footnote to this sentence refers us to the view of Stephen Gilman, "The Death of Lazarillo de Tormes," *PMLA,* 81 (1966), 150, who "finds the Prologue shocking in its arrogance and bombast."

6. Cf. Leicester Bradner, "From Petrarch to Shakespeare," in *The Renaissance* (New York: Harper & Row, 1962), p. 107: "The conflicts and uncertainties of the sixteenth century have introduced into literature a new way of writing tragedy, a way which perhaps owes something to the ironic attitude of More and Erasmus, but which had to wait for Cervantes before it could receive the creative myth-making power which could make it immortal and add one more figure to that great society of imagined persons who are so much more memorable than the real persons of history."

7. Erich Neumann, *The Origins and History of Consciousness,* trans. R. F. C. Hull (Princeton: Princeton Univ. Press, 1970), p. 105.

8. Theodore Spencer, *Shakespeare and the Nature of Man* (New York: Macmillan, 1966). The view is repeated throughout the book and is most succinctly stated on p. 146: "The bad characters . . . are incorrigible individualists and egoists."

9. *Ibid.,* p. 212.

10. This concept is repeated elsewhere in Shakespeare. *See,* for example, Act IV of *Henry V:* "I think the king is but a man, as I am: . . . his ceremonies laid by, in his nakedness he appears but a man. . . ."

11. Spencer (p. 133) explains his expression "emotional eunuch" as follows: "Lust is something that as a man of the world he has always heard about, and so he attributes it to everybody, even himself, since he wants to be like other people." (One wonders how he can be simultaneously an unscrupulous individualist and someone who wants to be like other people.) Spencer concludes that Iago's attack on Othello is "based on a sexual jealousy about which he really knows nothing." The fact that Iago is married need not, of

course, alter his views on love and sex. As for asexualism in Don Quixote, *see* my Chapter 2.

12. Sallust [Gaius Sallustius Crispus, 86-34 B.C.], trans. J. C. Rolfe, Loeb Classical Library (Cambridge: Harvard Univ. Press, 1931), p. 445. The reference, according to Rolfe's footnote, is to Appius Claudius Caecus, consul in 307 B.C., the earliest Roman writer known to us.

13. Periandro's statement appears to reflect a contradiction when he subsequently maintains that "it is not possible for anyone to construct his fortune, although they say that each man is its architect, from beginning to end" (Book IV, Chapter 1). The contradiction is more problematic than absolute, however, and is related to another *topos* of the age, namely, the question of the power of the stars versus man's ability to determine his own actions and consequent fortune. In addition to the fact that there was a distinction between worldly fortune (the vicissitudes of life) and divine providence, it was also held that the stars have the power to influence but not to determine man's destiny. Calderón's *La vida es sueño* is probably the best known of the many *literary* works that deal with this theme. In the same vein we must accept Cervantes' dual view: ultimately one's destiny is in the hands of God, but it is God who has given man certain abilities, talents, intelligence, and wisdom, distributed unequally and therefore in man's hands to fashion within the limitations of his God-given abilities. This is why self-knowledge is fundamental to individuation.

14. Aristotle, *The Nichomachean Ethics*, trans. H. Rackham, Loeb Classical Library (Cambridge: Harvard Univ. Press, 1934), 3:3.15.

15. Richard L. Predmore, *The World of Don Quixote* (Cambridge: Harvard Univ. Press, 1967), p. 23.

16. Quoted by Barzun, "*Faust* and the Birth of Time," p. 29.

17. Erich Auerbach, *Mimesis: The Representation of Reality in Western Literature*, trans. W. R. Trask (Princeton: Princeton Univ. Press, 1968), pp. 293-94.

18. Harry Levin, "The Quixotic Principle: Cervantes and Other Novelists," in *The Interpretation of Narrative: Theory and Practice*, ed. M. W. Bloomfield (Cambridge: Harvard Univ. Press, 1970), p. 65.

19. The translation is my own, inasmuch as Putnam, Cohen and Starkie all refer to no one else in the world with such a name. The original Spanish reads: "*no hay otro yo en el mundo.*"

20. A. J. Ayer, *The Central Questions of Philosophy* (New York: Holt, Rinehart & Winston, 1974), p. 11.

21. Aubrey F. G. Bell, *Cervantes*, Collier Books (New York: Crowell-Collier, 1961), pp. 135-37.

22. Frederick R. Karl, "Don Quixote as Archetypal Artist and *Don Quixote* as Archetypal Novel," in *The Adversary Literature* (New York: Farrar, Straus & Giroux, 1974), p. 66. (The *Buscón* was published in 1626 but written around the time of *Don Quixote*, Part I.)

23. Henry Bamford Parkes, *The Divine Order: Western Culture in the Middle Ages and the Renaissance* (New York; Alfred A. Knopf, 1969), p. 19.

24. María de las Mercedes Outumuro, "Sentido y perspectiva del personaje autonomo," *Cuadernos Hispanoamericanos*, 72 (1967), 169.

25. Martín de Riquer, *Aproximación al Quijote* (Barcelona: Editorial Teide, 1967), p. 117.

26. I say "has been described" because the discussion of the theater as subsuming the various possibilities inherent in this life precedes the Master Pedro episode. *See* my article, "'La superchería está descubierta': Don Quijote and Ginés de Pasamonte," *Philological Quarterly*, to be published shortly. What follows is a slightly varied version of that article, reprinted here with the permission of the Univ. of Iowa Press, publishers

of *PQ*. In that article the reader may find a more detailed explanation of my reasoning for Don Quixote's recognition of Pedro as Ginés.

27. *Op. cit.*, p. 59.

28. Cervantes has Cid Hamete say that "whoever has read the first part of this story will very well remember Ginés de Pasamonte, who was one of the galley slaves that Don Quixote freed. . . ." It would appear that Cervantes has a reason to ensure that the reader recall everything that happened in I, 22.

29. Philip E. Slater, *The Pursuit of Loneliness* (Boston: Beacon Press, 1971), p. 23. The word "other" in the quotation refers to the contrast with secure mechanisms in one's home community.

30. Although I disagree with several aspects of Madariaga's interpretation (particularly that which culminates in his final chapter, "The Decline of Don Quixote"), his is probably still the best study of the mutual influence of knight and squire. *See* the chapters entitled "Don Quixote's Influence on Sancho" and "Sancho's Influence on Don Quixote," in Salvador de Madariaga, *Don Quixote: An Introductory Essay in Psychology* (London: Oxford Univ. Press, 1961), pp. 136-56.

31. Joaquín Casalduero, *Sentido y forma de las Novelas Ejemplares*, (Madrid: Gredos, 1962), p. 147. Hereafter this work will be referred to as *Sentido de las Novelas*.

32. To be accurate, just as Cervantes actually knew a Don Diego de Miranda, so did he know a Don Diego de Valdivia, as Rodríguez Marín reminds us in the first volume of his edition of the *Novelas Ejemplares*, Clásicos Castellanos (Madrid: Espasa-Calpe, 1957), p. 16. One need not read too much into the use of the same first name—a common one at that—but the fact that Cervantes' memory conjured up a Don Diego who played the role of a *caballero* while not wishing to fight, and a Don Diego who is a soldier and urges a budding licentiate to fight (the original Diego de Valdivia was a licentiate!), should not be dismissed out of hand. I am not suggesting that we explain away Cervantes' art by identifying real life models, as some critics have done; I am, however, suggesting as fruitful the study of the transformation of people who may have lodged themselves in an author's memory and who may subsequently reappear as entirely new creations—in fact, at times the antitheses of their originals—because of the artistic handling of the lives observed throughout the author's own lifetime.

33. This is clarified in my Chapter 2.

34. George Gilder, *Naked Nomads* (New York: Quadrangle, 1974), pp. 24-26. In a review of this book, Larry McMurtry reduces it to the problems of "the single male, who is by all odds, the most vulnerable, endangered male of all. . . . [Single men] fight a constant battle against depression and neurosis, and often lose." The connection between this observation and Cervantes' fondness for dealing with (apparently, at least) neurotic and psychotic types could stand further investigation, particularly since Mr. McMurtry erroneously believes that "the male as victim entered our literature, after all, with Hemingway." Unless we insist on limiting "our" literature to American literature, it should be clear that not only did Hemingway not rise spontaneously out of the Western Hemisphere and not only did he have a strong affinity for Spanish culture which is reflected in his writings, but even Americans have been reading *Don Quixote* for generations and considering it part of the Western, if not worldwide, heritage of us all. (*See* the review in *The New York Times Book Review*, 5 Jan. 1975, p. 6.)

35. I am scarcely the first to note Cervantes' use of the duality of human nature, Don Quixote and Sancho being the best known example of two persons whose contrasting characters complement each other. It is worth noting here, however, that whereas in *The Glass Graduate* the protagonist was able to combine in himself the roles of licentiate and ensign, here in *The Deceitful Marriage* Cervantes finds it useful to split the roles. Added to the previous information supplied by Rodríguez Marín (*see* note 32 above) that the captain in the novel was modeled on a real-life licentiate, the fabric of Cervantes' novelistic cloth assumes an intriguing aspect.

154

NOTES

36. Amezúa, in his critical edition of *The Deceitful Marriage* and *The Dogs' Colloquy*, elaborates upon this use of the term "cousin," giving examples from other novelists, moralists and some sarcastic lines by the satirical poet Góngora. See Agustín G. de Amezúa y Mayo, ed., *El casamiento engañoso y El coloquio de los perros*, by Cervantes (Madrid: Bailly-Bailliere, 1912), pp. 391-92.

37. Amezúa, *Cervantes: Creador de la novela corta española*, II (Madrid: C.S.I.C., 1948), 385. The translation is my own.

38. *Sentido y forma de las Novelas*, p. 245. As I shall show below, my own view shares some of Casalduero's views with regard to Campuzano's having become an author. However, I have difficulty seeing tragedy here, even in the sense that there may be an autobiographical element in the wounded-soldier-turned-author analogy, for we must not forget how Cervantes received his wounds and how Campuzano became debilitated. Moreover, there is some inconsistency in Casalduero's subsequent assertion that in Campuzano's case there is no allusion to the spirit nor to sex. The allusions to sex are far from subtle and Casalduero puts it better only a few lines later: "The sexual relationship itself is divested of any spiritual meaning, positive or negative; it only leads to syphilis" (p. 247). Translations from Casalduero's works are my own.

39. Alexis de Tocqueville, *Democracy in America*, ed. J. P. Mayer, trans. George Lawrence, Anchor Books (Garden City: Doubleday & Co., 1969), p. 506.

40. *Ibid.*, p. 508.

41. José Ortega y Gasset, *The Modern Theme*, trans. James Cleugh, Harper Torchbooks (New York: Harper & Brothers, 1961), p. 105.

42. Mia I. Gerhardt, *"Don Quijote": La vie et les livres* (Amsterdam: Noord Hollandsche Uitgevers Maatschappij, 1955). *See also* E. C. Riley, *Cervantes's Theory of the Novel* (Oxford: Clarendon Press, 1962).

43. Bruce W. Wardropper, "Cervantes' Theory of the Drama," *Modern Philology*, 52 (1955), 219 n.

44. The fact that the *Amadís* has since been shown not to be the first is immaterial if Cervantes believed it to be the first.

45. Cf. Russell Fraser, *The Dark Ages and the Age of Gold* (Princeton: Princeton Univ. Press, 1973), p. 30: "Originality is the proud possession of Thomas Nashe, who [in 1592] boasts that 'the vein which I have . . . is of my own begetting, and calls no man father in England but myself.'"

Chapter 2

1. Angel Rosenblat, *La lengua del "Quijote"* (Madrid: Gredos, 1971), pp. 243-354; Américo Castro, *Hacia Cervantes* (Madrid: Taurus, 1957), p. 292. A condensed version of the fundamatal tenets of this chapter (and with all quotations left in Spanish) is scheduled to appear in a future issue of *Hispanófila*. I wish to express my appreciation to Professor A. V. Ebersole, editor of that journal, for permission to include that material in this book.

2. Juan Bautista Avalle-Arce, "Conocimiento y vida en Cervantes," in *Deslindes Cervantinos* (Madrid: Edhigar, 1961), pp. 61-62.

3. Constantino Láscaris Comneno, "El nombre de don Quijote," *Anales Cervantinos*, 2 (1952), 364. Frederick A. Busi, who cites Comneno in "'Waiting for Godot': A Modern 'Don Quixote'?" *Hispania*, 57 (1974), 879, prefers to believe that the suffix *-ote* "was patterned after the knight errant, Lanzarote [Launcelot]" This is quite likely; my only dispute would be with one who insisted this to be the only meaning of the name. As my text indicates, Cervantes is asking us to use our imagination. Pierre Groult, in his "¿Quijote nombre significativo?" *Les Lettres Romanes*, 23 (1969), 172, suggests Camilote (Camelot) as another analogue. He adds that it was a simple matter to add a pejorative or

comic suffix such as -ote to a character whose real name was Quijano or Quijada. Groult fails to see the irony in his use of the words "real name" followed by the word "or." See also the interesting footnote to Henryk Ziomek's "Parallel Ingredients in Don Quixote and Dom Casmurro," Revista de Estudios Hispánicos, 2 (1968), 229-30. which traces the etymology of the name to "the Latin word, cuxa, meaning 'muscle,' which in turn became cuixot in Catalan and later cuxot in early Castilian, both of which meant 'shin-guard' or 'cuisse.'" The word "cuisse," however, means "thigh" and the Oxford English Dictionary traces it to the Latin coxa, meaning "hip." The dictionary also defines "cuisse" in the singular as a "thigh-piece" and in the plural as "armour for protecting the front part of the thigh." I cannot accept Spitzer's reply to Yakov Malkiel's establishment of the etymology of quijote from cuissot. Spitzer agrees but says Malkiel "confuses historical linguistics with the study of a work of art when he writes: 'The etymology of this word naturally aroused the curiosity of Cervantes.'" I would respond that the delightful ambiguity intrigued Cervantes, who himself would consider the separation of linguistic sensibility and art as an artificial dichotomy. See Leo Spitzer, "Linguistic Perspectivism in the Don Quijote," in Linguistics and Literary History (Princeton: Princeton Univ. Press, 1967), p. 77. See also Edward W. Said, Beginnings: Intention and Method (New York: Basic Books, 1975), p. 70, who observes that "when Spitzer speaks of philological evidence, he differentiates that from philosophical evidence. This may seem unclear to a scholar not of Spitzer's generation, so we can say that differentiation is sometimes the specialized function of a received tradition. . . ." The observation is exact, and precisely because Cervantes is clearly of a different and much earlier generation we may—in fact, must—say that he cannot have received the philological tradition of a Spitzer. It is appropriate and valid for Spitzer to perceive and make the distinction, but it is anachronistic to apply the dichotomy to Cervantes and to what Malkiel aptly calls the curiosity of Cervantes.

4. For further observations on Don Quixote's names, see Avalle-Arce, op. cit., pp. 61-62. On the same pages will be found a summary of the name changes in Cervantes' short story, El Licenciado Vidriera. For a brief treatment of the same phenomenon in Cervantes' novel Persiles y Sigismunda, see Avalle-Arce's pp. 69-70. See also Francisco García Lorca, "El Licenciado Vidriera y sus nombres," Revista Hispánica Moderna, 31 (1965), 159-68. Yet another aspect of names concerns Cervantes' use of more than half a dozen words to describe the animals on which ride the three peasant lasses in II, 10. See Howard Mancing, "Dulcinea's Ass: A Note on Don Quijote, Part II, Chapter 10," Hispanic Review, 40 (1972), 73-77, and Carroll B. Johnson, "A Second Look at Dulcinea's Ass," Hispanic Review, 43 (1975), 191-98. See note 23 below.

5. T. Anthony Perry, "Ideal Love and Human Reality in Montemayor's La Diana," PMLA, 84 (1969), p. 227. Another of the many examples can be found in the Prologue to Part I of Don Quixote, in which Cervantes refers to the giant "Golías or Goliat." In his Clásicos Castellanos edition of Don Quixote (Madrid: Espasa-Calpe, 1913), I, 18, Francisco Rodríguez Marín attempts to "correct" Cervantes by telling us what was usually said in Cervantes' time, in the face of what Cervantes himself has written: "Golías, y no Goliat, solía decirse en tiempo de Cervantes."

6. Cf. Northrop Frye, Anatomy of Criticism (Princeton: Princeton Univ. Press, 1971), p. 189, in which Frye refers to "Adonis's traditional thigh-wound being as close to castration symbolically as it is anatomically."

7. Miguel de Unamuno, Our Lord Don Quixote, trans. Anthony Kerrigan, Bollingen Series, 85 (Princeton: Princeton Univ. Press, 1967), pp. 27-28.

8. Cf. Kaiser's comments on Hotspur (a significant name as well) in Shakespeare's Henry IV, part one: "Hotspur, who tends to compare everything to horses . . . seems even to prefer his horse to his wife. There is an ironic ambiguity in his response to Lady Percy's question, 'What is it that carries you away?' for he answers, 'Why, my horse, my love, my horse!'" Kaiser goes on to quote Hotspur's confession: "'Love? I love thee not'" and

observes: "Though he makes a pretense to love, his real love is war." *See* Walter Kaiser, *Praisers of Folly* (Cambridge: Harvard Univ. Press, 1963), pp. 226-27.

9. Otto Olivera, "Don Quijote, el caballero de la angustia," *Hispania*, 44 (1961), 441.

10. Michael P. Predmore, "Madariaga's Debt to Unamuno's 'Vida de don Quijote y Sancho,'" *Hispania*, 47 (1964), 288-94. *See also* Donald D. Palmer, "Unamuno, Freud and the Case of Alonso Quijano," *Hispania*, 54 (1971), 243-49, especially p. 244, which notes Unamuno's use, in 1905, of the word "sublimates" when discussing Don Quixote's response to his frustrated love.

11. Américo Castro, p. 205, calls them epilogues for this reason.

12. Levin, *Quixotic Principle*, p. 56.

13. "*Faust* and the Birth of Time," p. 40. I include the final sentence because it concludes Barzun's paragraph. It, of course, would require some stretching to apply to Don Quixote as readily as to Faust, but it could indeed be argued that Don Quixote's status as a nonentity ("powerlessness") at the beginning of the novel is the result ("punishment") of his empty life of nearly five decades.

14. Margaret Church, *Don Quixote: The Knight of La Mancha* (New York: New York Univ. Press, 1971), p. 120.

15. Otis H. Green, *Spain and the Western Tradition*, IV (Madison: Univ. of Wisconsin Press, 1966), 121.

16. I am referring to Don Quixote's apprehension of Dulcinea's real significance after his adventure in the Cave of Montesinos.

17. Joaquín Casalduero, *Sentido y forma del Quijote* (Madrid: Ediciones Insula, 1949), p. 303.

18. Joseph Campbell, *The Hero With a Thousand Faces*, 2nd ed. (Princeton: Princeton Univ. Press, 1968), p. 121.

19. *Ibid.*, p. 116.

20. It is I who need say no more with regard to the parallel between Don Quixote's cave experience and Sancho's ditch experience (II, 45), in view of the detailed analysis provided by Casalduero in his *Sentido y forma del Quijote*, pp. 332-35. On the other hand, Harry Levin, in his "The Example of Cervantes" in *Contexts of Criticism* (Cambridge: Harvard Univ. Press, 1957), p. 85, does not say quite enough when he describes Sancho's experience as a "fall into a mere hole so utterly different from Don Quixote's exploration of the Cave of Montesinos: 'There saw he goodly and pleasant visions and here, I believe, I shall see nothing but snakes and toads.' The pleasant visions are abstract and remote; the snakes and toads are concrete and immediate; the variance is all in the point of view." I believe my text shows why Levin here does not go far enough with regard to the "point of view." He is correct, of course, when he refers to Don Quixote's point of view as a set of pleasant visions which are abstract and remote, but the pleasantness of Don Quixote's visions is even more abstract and remote than I believe Levin realized: the abstract pleasantness is not idealistic (and so opposed to Sancho's concrete realism), but revelatory.

21. Campbell, p. 218.

22. Leland H. Chambers, "Irony in the Final Chapter of the *Quijote*," *Romanic Review*, 61 (1970), 21-22. Although it is of no great consequence, accuracy requires it to be noted that on one occasion in this chapter, Sansón Carrasco does refer to the protagonist as Don Quixote.

23. Rodríguez Marín, in his critical edition of 1948, remarks that in the *editio princeps* as well as in the first editions of Lisbon, the name is as quoted in my text, Quijana. In others, he says, the name is Quijada. No comment is made on the second reference by the neighbor, which in all cases is Quijana. In I, 49, Don Quixote claims descent from the Quijada family. A number of observers see in this a real life model for Cervantes' protagonist. The evidence I have seen suggests this is very likely. It does not shed light on the process we are considering here, however, unless we can find a reason to explain

Cervantes' insistence on Quijano ten years later. Aside from my own interpretation in this chapter, may we speculate that Cervantes himself has been carried away by his own artistic transformation? On this matter, *see* Richard L. Predmore, *Cervantes* (New York: Dodd, Mead, 1973), pp. 123-35.

24. Harry Sieber, "Literary Time in the 'Cueva de Montesinos,'" *MLN*, 86 (1971), 272.

25. Alejandro Ramírez, "The Concept of Ignorance in *Don Quixote*," *Philological Quarterly*, 45 (1966), 477.

26. Patrick Cullen, "Imitation and Metamorphosis: The Golden-Age Eclogue in Spenser, Milton, and Marvell," *PMLA*, 84 (1969), 1562.

27. Ernst Robert Curtius, *European Literature and the Latin Middle Ages*, trans. Willard R. Trask, Bollingen Series, 36 (Princeton: Princeton Univ. Press, 1973), pp. 195-202.

28. David Evett, "'Paradice's Only Map': The *Topos* of the *Locus Amoenus* and the Structure of Marvell's *Upon Appleton House*," *PMLA*, 85 (1970), 507.

29. S. K. Heninger, Jr., "The Renaissance Perversion of Pastoral," *Journal of the History of Ideas*, 22 (1961), 255.

30. Harry Levin, *The Myth of the Golden Age in the Renaissance* (New York: Oxford Univ. Press, 1972), p. xv.

31. Angel Sánchez Rivero, "Las ventas del 'Quijote,'" in *El concepto contemporáneo de España*, ed. Angel del Río and M. J. Benardete (Buenos Aires: Editorial Losada, 1946), sees in this paradox the duality of fantasy (castle) and bodily hunger (hut), a duality which he views as the literary cause of the birth of Sancho Panza (pp. 662-63).

32. *See* Vernon A. Chamberlin and Jack Weiner, "Color Symbolism: A Key to a Possible New Interpretation of Cervantes' 'Caballero del Verde Gabán,'" *RomN*, 10 (1969), 342-47. The two salient points of this study are that Pérez Pastor's *Documentos cervantinos hasta ahora inéditos* reveal that "Cervantes actually knew a man who bore the same name which he gives to his character. Moreover, the conduct of the real-life Diego de Miranda and his relationship to the Cervantes family were such that our author would have every justification for characterizing him primarily by means of erotic green" (p. 344). Assuming Chamberlin and Weiner to be correct, I should like to add a postscript which reinforces what I have been saying about Cervantes' style. During a discussion with Don Diego about the ambition of the latter's son to be a poet, Don Quixote happens to mention that a poet may criticize vices "without, however, designating any particular individual. On the other hand, there are poets who for the sake of uttering something malicious would run the risk of being banished to the shores of Pontus" (II, 16). If Chamberlin and Weiner are correct, Cervantes is doing in this episode precisely what he is apparently advising against. Most of Cervantes' works reveal such a device as typical of his style. Furthermore, as numerous editors have pointed out, the example of the banished poets seems a clear allusion to Ovid, presumably for his *Art of Love*. This in turn has a double significance: it adds force to the eroticism symbolized by Don Diego's green, thus serving as a rebuke to the real Don Diego unearthed by Pérez Pastor; secondly, as another example of the stylistic device just mentioned, Cervantes is laying further groundwork to alert the reader to erotic (or anti-erotic) responses to Don Diego on the part of Don Quixote as well as preparing for Ovid's importance in II, 22 without so much as mentioning him in II, 16 except by indirection.

33. Vernon A. Chamberlin, "Symbolic Green: A Time-Honored Characterizing Device in Spanish Literature," *Hispania*, 51 (1968), 29-37. Chamberlin points out that the "national dictionaries of Spain, France, Italy, and Portugal all confirm the fact that the color green has a special and important connotative value—amorous desire—in Latin countries that does not exist in today's English-speaking world, though at one time it was clearly present in English literature" (p. 29). He adds: "During the Renaissance, with its increased zest for living life to the fullest, the symbolic use of erotic green appears to have intensified" and gives among his examples the Spaniard Don Adriano de Armado in

NOTES

Love's Labor Lost, who affirmed that "green is indeed the color of lovers" (p. 30). It is surely no coincidence, then, that of the eighteen colors used by Cervantes to describe clothing in *Don Quixote*, the most frequent is green. *See* E. Lewis Hoffman, "Cloth and Clothing in the *Quijote*," *Kentucky Foreign Language Quarterly*, 10 (1963), 82. An explanation for why green not only meant spring, renewal and rebirth, but connoted as well erotic values, is found in Levin's previously cited *The Myth of the Golden Age in the Renaissance*, p. 86: "To give a lass 'a green gown' was to tumble her in the grass. The may-games, with their morris-dances and hobby-horses, could be not only rough but frankly carnal. . . . Nationally celebrated, May Day was the most gladsome festival of the seasons, a veritable *sacre du printemps*. More intimately, it was an annual reminder that the best time for love was passing all too quickly. . . ."

Cervantes employs the eroticism connoted by green in the *Persiles*, Book III, Chapters 19-21. The travelers come upon a woman seated on a rich saddle (but on a mule), all dressed in green, her face covered by a green veil. She is immediately referred to as the lady in green ("la [dama] de lo verde"). At first, the episode appears extraneous to the main plot; it does, however, serve to introduce a discourse between the two protagonists on the nature of love. More importantly, we meet her again when it turns out that a young lass by the name of Isabela Castrucho, who is feigning madness because she really is lovesick, is the same lady in green (Cervantes repeats the phrase). The erotic imagery is compounded by the name of her lover's father, Juan Bautista Marulo. The combination Juan Bautista (John the Baptist) is common in Spanish; what is significant is that Cervantes refers to him as simply Juan Bautista three times, as Juan Bautista Marulo seven times, and as Marulo only twice, these two instances surrounding a reference to St. John's Day, a traditional day of lovemaking in Latin countries, similar to the May Day mentioned above.

That such connotations have a long history can be verified by a reading of Eleanor Irwin, *Colour Terms in Greek Poetry* (Toronto: Hakkert, 1974), pp. 31-78, which constitute Chapter 2, "*Chloros*," and examine this word and its various cognates, the meanings of which range from the simple description of pale, greenish-yellow objects through metaphorical connotations of virility, swelling of youth, the supple limbs of lovers, and the general associations of moisture, tears, dew, etc., with life and loving. The bibliography provided by the author confirms that the book includes the scholarship of those who have specialized in color imagery over the years and thus represents a modern updating of this aspect for those particularly interested in the examination of color symbolism.

34. The most comprehensive study of the episode of the Cave of Montesinos is undoubtedly the 177-page analysis by Helena Percas de Ponseti, included in her *Cervantes y su concepto del arte* (Madrid: Gredos, 1975). My point of departure differs because of a difference in purpose, as our corresponding titles reflect. Moreover, my use of this episode is more restrictive because of a more particularized examination.

35. *Spain and the Western Tradition*, IV, 68. Cf. Cervantes' drama *El cerco de Numancia*, Act 3, in which Scipio, having been challenged to hand-to-hand combat by the besieged citizens of Numancia, turns his back on them and compares them to a caged beast whom only a madman would let loose when he can simply outwait them while they starve. Scipio himself finds it necessary to disclaim any suspicion of cowardice, but one of the citizens, hurling a long series of insulting epithets after the departing Scipio, uses the word "coward" five times within fourteen lines of verse.

36. The reversal of the order between I, 13 and II, 22 has been noted by Leland H. Chambers, "Structure and the Search for Truth in the *Quijote*: Notes Toward a Comprehensive View," *HR*, 35 (1967), 319. Chambers does not mention that Don Quixote had already inverted the order in II, 17. I mention it to emphasize that Don Quixote's attitude is a gradual and carefully planned evolution, a point reinforced by his own interpretation of the lion adventure: "I don't need to do any more [with regard to

159

the lions], away with enchantments, and may God aid reason, truth and the true chivalry" (II, 17). Don Quixote's mind has been at work, as I have tried to show, and his reasoning is leading him ever closer to the "true chivalry," as he describes in II, 8: "Chivalry is a religion in itself, and there are sainted knights in glory." There exists as well the possibility of an even earlier reversal, as early as I, 26 during Don Quixote's "penance" when he fashions a rosary, says a "round million of Hail Marys" and composes verses to Dulcinea. Although Cervantes does not specify the order in which Don Quixote prayed and wrote poems to Dulcinea, the order in which he describes them is to speak first of the rosary and Hail Marys, then of the verses to his lady. This should be taken into account when one tries to follow Don Quixote's gradual awakening to eternal truths, which, as I have repeatedly insisted, is more gradual and begins far earlier than most scholars believe. In point of fact, Cervantes had already allowed Don Quixote to consider the implications of the order as far back as I, 13: The traveler Vivaldo complains that knights-errant, when they are about to begin an adventure, "never at that moment think of commending themselves to God as every good Christian is obliged to do . . . but, rather, commend themselves to their ladies with as much fervor and devotion as if their ladies were their God." Don Quixote begins his response by defending his storybook knights on the simple grounds of "the usage and custom of chivalry," but concludes by pointing out that one should not assume that knights fail to commend themselves to God, "for there is a time and place for that in the course of the undertaking."

37. Rafael Osuna,"¿Dos finales en un capítulo (II, 24) del Quijote?" *Romance Notes*, 13 (1971), 318.

38. I am following Cohen's translation here, for the Putnam rendition of *gayado* as "striped," while not incorrect, fails to add the polychromatic nature of the stripes contained in the Spanish word. Starkie translates it as "manycolored." *See also* Rodríguez Marín's critical edition of 1948, vol. 5, p. 148, in which he quotes the famous Covarrubias dictionary of 1611 to the effect that *gayado* is applied to the mixture of different, vivid colors which blend together (*la mezcla de diferentes colores alegres que matizan unas con otras*).

39. Herbert A. Kenyon, "Color Symbolism in Early Spanish Ballads," *Romanic Review*, 6 (1915), 327.

40. I have followed Putnam here although his translation is not so exact as Cohen's or Starkie's, both of which do not disturb the original description that Sancho filled his saddlebags, which were then accompanied by those of the cousin. The original reads that he *proveyó sus alforjas, a las cuales acompañaron las del primo*. I prefer the Putnam rendition not because it adds weight to my own thesis but because logic suggests that since the cousin arrived with his saddlebags already filled, it was Sancho's newly packed bags which now accompanied those of the cousin and not the reverse. In any event, my central point is not affected by either the original or the translations, which is that the arrival of the cousin with filled saddlebags prompted Sancho to fill his own.

41. As most editors explain, this was an Italian historian who died in the mid-sixteenth century, one of whose works was entitled *On the Invention of Things*. Those who see in such works no more than the accumulation of useless facts might be interested to know that a recent (1974/1975) edition of Brentano's catalogue not only included *Eureka! An Illustrated History of Inventions from the Wheel to the Computer*, but as well *The Book of Firsts*, which is described as containing answers to questions such as "Who won the first beauty contest?" and "How about the first toothbrush?"

42. The fact that modern translators—not to mention scholarly interpreters—view the same words in differing ways is one more confirmation of Cervantes' success in juggling appearance and reality, as well as leaving the reader in confusion with respect to whether words, passages and episodes are to be interpreted literally, or as they serve possible symbolic function. Perhaps the best known example (because it is less subtle than some others) is the characters' conflicting interpretations of the barber's basin as Mambrino's

helmet, with the ultimate conclusion that it is a combination of both (*baciyelmo*), while all along Cervantes plays with the words himself. For analyses of this aspect of Cervantes' linguistic playfulness, *see* the previously cited *La lengua del "Quijote"* by Rosenblat and, with particular relevance to the reality-and-appearance conflict as a result of such linguistic devices, the cited book by Richard Predmore, *The World of Don Quixote*.

43. J. E. Cirlot, *A Dictionary of Symbols*, translated from the Spanish by Jack Sage (New York: Philosophical Library, 1962), p. 31. Cirlot's source is George W. Ferguson, *Signs and Symbols in Christian Art* (New York, 1954).

44. The reference is to Cervantes' contemporary, the Spanish mystic San Juan de la Cruz (1542-91) and his poem, "*Noche oscura del alma*" ("Dark Night of the Soul").

45. Quoted by Cirlot from Ania Teillard, *Il Simbolismo dei Sogni* (Milan, 1951).

46. Cirlot, p. 55. The work referred to is H. P. Blavatsky, *The Secret Doctrine* (London, 1888). Don Cameron Allen, "Symbolic Color in the Literature of the English Renaissance," *Philological Quarterly*, 15 (1936), observes that "one finds [black] used very often to signify a love that lives beyond death" and that black "is also the color of the disappointed or forsaken lover as well as of the lover constant in death" (p. 83). He further adds that black "is also used by the men of this time to indicate chastity" (p. 84). While one must be careful not to confuse an Anglo-Saxon culture's symbolic code with that of a Latin culture, Allen's comments provide two useful points: first, that a color may come to mean its opposite and must therefore be analyzed in context; second, that the color black, even in contrary senses, was related to matters of love in Renaissance England.

47. Since the last indication in the text, all quotations from *Don Quixote*, unless otherwise identified, have been from II, 22. The quotation to which this note refers is from II, 23, as will be all subsequent ones that remain unidentified.

48. Eric Partridge, *Shakespeare's Bawdy*, rev. ed. (New York: E. P. Dutton, 1969), p. 117, says of this illness that the "Elizabethan dramatists emblemized it as a sign of a girl's love-sickness, or of vague desire, for a man." He cites *Romeo and Juliet*, III, 5, "where Juliet is taxed with green sickness." Cf. Viola's description of her sister's concealed (hence unrequited) love: "She pin'd in thought; / And with a green and yellow melancholy, / She sat like Patience on a monument, / Smiling at her grief" (*Twelfth Night*, II, 4). Cf. also *2 Henry IV*, IV, 3, in which John of Lancaster is accused by Falstaff of having "a kind of male green-sickness."

49. Another favorite device of Cervantes. *See The Glass Graduate*, p. 134: ". . . it was in [poets'] power to be rich, if they knew how to take advantage of the opportunity which they had at their disposal all the time; namely their ladies, who were all extremely rich, for their hair was gold, their brow burnished silver, their eyes green emeralds, their teeth ivory, their lips coral and their throats clear crystal, while their tears were liquid pearls."

50. Russell Fraser, *The Dark Ages and the Age of Gold* (Princeton: Princeton Univ. Press, 1973), p. 215.

51. See the translation by Rolfe Humphries of Ovid's *The Art of Love* (Bloomington: Indiana Univ. Press, 1957), p. 138: "Oh, [poems] are praised, to be sure; but the girls want something more costly. / Even illiterates please, if they have money to burn. / Ours is a Golden Age, and gold can purchase you honors, / All the 'Golden Mean' means is, gold in the end."

52. Harry Sieber, "Literary Time in the 'Cueva de Montesinos,'" *MLN* 86 (1971), 269, n. 6. The quotation is taken from E. C. Riley, *Cervantes's Theory of the Novel* (Oxford: Clarendon Press, 1962), p. 187.

161

Chapter 3

1. Aristotle, *Poetics*, trans. W. Hamilton Fyfe, The Leob Classical Library (Cambridge: Harvard Univ. Press, 1973), p. 41. Fyfe, in a footnote, adds that the reversal in *Oedipus* "is the more effective because it is immediately coincident with the discovery of the truth."

2. Francis Fergusson, Introduction to Aristotle's *Poetics* (New York: Hill and Wang, 1961), p. 29.

3. *See*, in this regard, the perceptive study by Armando Zárate, "La poesía y el ojo en 'La Celestina,'" *CA*, 164 (1969), 119-36. *See also* the comment on the dream as the revelation of opposites in Apuleius's *The Golden Ass*, trans. Robert Graves (New York: Farrar, Straus & Giroux, 1951), p. 95: "The dreams that come in daylight are not to be trusted, everyone knows that, and even night-dreams often go by contraries." For a study of the use of sight by Cervantes outside *Don Quixote*, see Margarita Levisi, "La función de lo visual en *La fuerza de la sangre*," *Hispanófila*, 49 (1973), 59-67. It should not be forgotten that sight in the metaphysical sense has a long tradition, religious and secular. *See* especially Dante's gaze into Beatrice's eyes (*Purgatorio*, 31). *See also* note 21 below.

4. Wayne A. Rebhorn, "The Metamorphoses of Moria: Structure and Meaning in *The Praise of Folly*," *PMLA*, 89 (1974), 469.

5. Walter Kaiser, *Praisers of Folly* (Cambridge: Harvard Univ. Press, 1963), p. 294.

6. Otis H. Green, "Imaginative Authority in Spanish Literature," *PMLA*, 84 (1969), 213.

7. Ruth El Saffar, "The Function of the Fictional Narrator in *Don Quijote*," *MLN*, 83 (1968), 169.

8. The reference is to his *Coplas a la muerte de su padre*.

9. Elias L. Rivers, "Lope and Cervantes Once More," *Kentucky Romance Quarterly*, 14 (1967), 116.

10. *Spain and the Western Tradition*, IV, 60. Green's ideas on this aspect are summarized in his book from his article, "Realidad, voluntad y gracia en Cervantes," *Ibérida: Revista de filología*, 3 (1961), 113-28.

11. Otis H. Green, "El *ingenioso* hidalgo," *Hispanic Review*, 25 (1957), 175-93.

12. Curtis Brown Watson, *Shakespeare and the Renaissance Concept of Honor* (Princeton: Princeton Univ. Press, 1960), p. 252.

13. Watson contrasts the Renaissance humanists' understanding with "many a modern critic [for whom Lear] is instead a pathetic figure. Granville-Barker sees Lear as 'an old man on the verge of dotage. His self-knowledge has never been strong, and infirmity of years has made bad discrimination worse. Further, the decay of age renders him all the more liable to attacks of choler, and thereby to the overclouding of reason'" (p. 318; the reference is to Harley Granville-Barker, *Prefaces to Shakespeare* [Princeton: Princeton Univ. Press, 1946], I, 301). Watson's warning should be kept in mind when reading Green's analysis which is so dependent upon the choler-bile relationship.

14. The original is cited from the edition of Víctor Said Armesto, *Clásicos Castellanos* (Madrid: Espasa—Calpe, 1952).

15. Ramón Menéndez Pidal, *Flor nueva de romances viejos* (Madrid: Espasa-Calpe, 1955), p. 135. Father Atilano Sanz, in *El Romancero y el Quijote* (Madrid: Imprenta del Asilo de Huérfanos del S. Corazón de Jesús, 1919), pp. 29-30, refers to the original *romance* when commenting on I, 5, suggesting that the confusion of ballads was

done by Cervantes to show how his mad protagonist confused things. He makes no mention of the partial repetition of the *romance* when he discusses the Montesinos episode.

16. I have preferred to use the Cohen translation. Putnam's translation of the first part of the vow is more accurate, but the evasion of the sexual meaning of the second part not only avoids but voids it ("not to eat bread off a tablecloth, not to embrace his wife").

17. Cf. the final lines of Tourneur's *The Atheist's Tragedy: The Honest Man's Revenge*, composed between 1607 and 1611, as cited in Fredson Bowers, *Elizabethan Revenge Tragedy: 1587-1642* (Princeton: Princeton Univ. Press, 1966), p. 141: "Only to Heaven I attribute the work. / Whose gracious motives made me still forbear / To be mine own Revenger. Now I see / That. *Patience is the honest man's revenge*" (italics in the original; I have modernized the spelling). *See also* two other lines cited by Bowers from the same play(again I have modernized the spelling): "Attend with patience the success of things; / But leave revenge unto the King of kings."

Impatience may also be related to sexuality. *See*, for example, Lucius' account of his affair with Fotis in *The Golden Ass*, ed. cit., p. 37: "The wine went to my head; but it also went to my thighs. I grew restive and, like a fallen soldier displaying a wound, pulled off my nightshirt and gave Fotis visible proof of my impatience." *See also* my Chapter 4, in which I present Don Quixote's patience in a slightly different context.

18. Cervantes claimed this distinction on several occasions. The sentence most often quoted in this respect comes from his *Viaje del Parnaso*: "*Yo soy aquel que en la invención excede a muchos*" ("I am the one who excells many others in inventiveness").

19. Kaiser, p. 292.

20. "The Renaissance Perversion of Pastoral," p. 261.

21. Auerbach (p. 10), on referring to the three-day journey which Abraham made to the place where the sacrifice was to be made, mentions the fact that on the third day, Abraham lifted up his eyes. "Three such days positively demand the symbolic interpretation which they later received," he writes, having in mind the anticipation of Christ's sacrifice and the three days prior to the Resurrection. I would assuredly not argue an analogous interpretation for the Cave episode. However, the fact that Sancho and the cousin insist that Don Quixote's stay was no longer than one hour (earlier it had been limited to half an hour) whereas Don Quixote insists that he was there for three days, does suggest to me that Cervantes wants a metaphoric interpretation to be made.

22. Cervantes does indeed have Cid Hamete claim this. It is significant, therefore, that Cervantes' detailed description of Don Quixote's hour of death (including several retractions) does *not* mention any retraction of the Cave adventure's veracity.

23. Stephen Gilman, "The Death of Lazarillo de Tormes," *PMLA*, 81 (1966), 152. Cf. the observation by Bruce W. Wardropper, "The Strange Case of Lázaro Gonzales Pérez," *MLN*, 92 (1977), 202-12, particularly p. 203. Wardropper emphasizes that we do know Lázaro's name whereas we "never learn the names of the other principals in the 'caso,' the Archpriest of San Salvador and Lázaro's wife. The long string of masters . . . are all characterized by what they do, and not by who they are. The peripheral characters . . . are all nameless. Against this backdrop of anonymity the name of Lázaro stands out with a beckoning prominence."

24. I owe this perspective to Joseph Silverman, who used it in a somewhat different context in "The Scrutiny of Literature and Life in *Don Quixote*," a paper delivered in San Francisco at the 1975 convention of the Modern Language Association.

Chapter 4

1. Robert S. Weiss, *Loneliness: The Experience of Emotional and Social Isolation* (Cambridge: The MIT Press, 1973), p. 4 n. The note refers to a paragraph on the first page of Weiss' book, which complains that "loneliness has received remarkably little professional attention" from psychiatrists, psychologists and sociologists.

2. Nathan S. Kline, M.D., "Feelin' Mighty Low," The *New York Times*, 10 Jan. 1975, p. 35.

3. Weiss, p. 14. The words in quotation marks are taken by Weiss from Clark E. Moustakas, *Loneliness and Love* (Englewood Cliffs: Prentice-Hall, 1972), p. 22. Weiss identifies Moustakas "among those who find redeeming features in loneliness," while he himself points out that the condition described in the passage I quote "is different from the experience described to my colleagues and me in our studies of loneliness in ordinary life."

4. *Ibid.*, p. 149.

5. The reference cited by Weiss is to Erik H. Erickson, *Identity and the Life Cycle*, published as *Psychological Issues* Monograph No. 1 (New York: International Universities Press, 1959), pp. 104-107.

6. Georg Lukacs, *The Theory of the Novel* (Cambridge: The MIT Press, 1971), pp. 103-104.

7. *Cervantes' Christian Romance: A Study of "Persiles y Sigismunda,"* p. 83-84. The repetition not only of caves, but of islands and certain kinds of adventure may be part of another *topos* and may have its most immediate source in Dante.

8. *Ibid.*, pp. 100-101.

9. The best analysis of this aspect of Cervantes' art, as well as of his most likely sources, remains Américo Castro, *El pensamiento de Cervantes*, ed. cit., pp. 23-74. There may exist in the Soldino passage a more immediate reason for the warning: despite Soldino's own denial of having magic powers, he nevertheless exhibits a talent for foretelling the future, something which, if taken literally, would have displeased the ecclesiastical censors. This would be confirmed by Cervantes' use in this passage of the phrase, "he who wrote this history," a disclaimer he rarely makes in the *Persiles*. In the main body of my text, I suggest yet another reason for the warning with respect to the final sentence of the adventure. *See* the following note.

10. If this interpretation is correct, it provides yet another example of Cervantes' ever maturing mastery of his art: two totally different and apparently unrelated statements, one a direct warning, the other a subtle clue to the symbolic nature of the episode, frame the adventure to provide the message and its corroboration.

11. The fact that history's account of Charles' reign as well as the lack of the ascetic life which one would expect of the resident of a monastery detract from the idealized portrait given him by Cervantes (among other writers of his time) hardly matters. What *is* of importance is Cervantes' view, since it is upon that that any significance of the Emperor's being mentioned alongside creations of Cervantes' literary imagination must be based. Aside from the obvious association with the political dominance of the world—it was during the Emperor's reign that Cortés, Pizarro, De Soto, Coronado, Ponce de León, Cabot and, under Charles' auspices, Portugal's Magellan, explored and conquered major portions of the world—Cervantes' personal opportunity for heroism at the Battle of Lepanto in 1571 occurred under the leadership of Don Juan de Austria, the illegitimate son of the Emperor.

12. *Cervantes: Creador de la novela corta española*, I (Madrid: C.S.I.C., 1946), 279. I must take exception to Amezúa's use of what he calls Aristotle's aphorism, which is quoted out of context, and is in fact contrary to Amezúa's viewpoint (and to mine). The passage from Aristotle reads: "The proof that the state is a creation of nature and prior to the individual is that the individual, when isolated, is not self-sufficing; and therefore he

is like a part in relation to the whole. But he who is unable to live in society, or who has no need because he is sufficient for himself, must be either a beast or a god: he is not part of a state." *Politics*, 1.3, trans. Benjamin Jowett, The Modern Library (New York: Random House, 1943). I believe that I share with Amezúa the view of Aristotle that the individual cannot remain in isolation—witness the subsequent qualification by Amezúa—but the quotation from Aristotle in Amezúa's text clearly is not appropriate in support of Cervantes' love of solitude.

13. Passages from *La Galatea* are my own translations from the two-volume Spanish edition in the Clásicos Castellanos series, edited by Juan Bautista Avalle-Arce (Madrid: Espasa-Calpe, 1961). Although *La Galatea* is divided into books, there are no chapter divisions. To facilitate matters for the reader with a knowledge of Spanish, I indicate the volume and page number of the edition cited (as opposed to my practice in *Don Quixote* and *Persiles*, where I cite the book or part and the chapter). Thus, the passage just quoted about the *locus amoenus* is taken from vol. I, p. 18, the statement on solitude from I, 30, and Avalle-Arce's comment appears as a footnote on I, 30.

14. The reader is reminded of my previous comments with respect to the "insanity" of Don Quixote, Graduate Glass, and Ensign Campuzano. Riquer (*Aproximación al Quijote*, pp. 119-20) suggests a subtle demonstration of Don Quixote's sanity in the Sierra Morena episode, an interpretation which he believes is strengthened by the revelation to Sancho in this episode that Dulcinea is really Aldonza Lorenzo, the only time in the entire novel that Don Quixote admits this.

15. So that there will be no need to wonder whether Putnam's translation has added or removed an important nuance, I quote the original, which shows Putnam to be exact: ". . . enviaron a Sancho . . . al lugar que para él había de ser ínsula." I should also point out at this juncture that the farce which is being carried out would ordinarily require quotation marks around the words "governor," "island," etc., but I omit them in my text to avoid a clutter of punctuation marks. The reader should mentally consider them to be there in this context.

16. At the previously mentioned congress of the Asociación Internacional de Hispanistas in 1977, Agustín Redondo presented a penetrating analysis of the *ínsula* episode as an example of the "world upsidedown" structure. That analysis, though quite unlike anything presented in the present book, serves to confirm the parallelism of what otherwise is less clearly seen: the evident inversion of values in Don Quixote's cave experience and the similar transvaluation in Sancho's island experience.

17. The abuse of the title *Don* was becoming widespread in Cervantes' time. *See* John C. Dowling, "A Title of Distinction," *Hispania*, 41 (1958), 449-56.

18. Ernst Cassirer, *The Individual and the Cosmos in Renaissance Philosophy*, trans. Mario Domandi (Philadelphia: Univ. of Pennsylvania Press, 1972), p. 84. The reader with special curiosity about this ethical debate is urged to read the chapter in Cassirer entitled "Freedom and Necessity in the Philosophy of the Renaissance." I could repeat what has been said before with reference to the positions of Augustine, Thomas Aquinas, Luther, Erasmus and others. This would not be to the point of my study, for my purpose is simply to outline the problem and relate it to Cervantes' understanding of individuation.

19. P. J. Proudhon, *General Idea of the Revolution in the Nineteenth Century*, trans. John Beverly Robinson (London: Freedom Press, 1923), cited by Robert Nozick, *Anarchy, State, and Utopia* (New York: Basic Books, 1974), p. 11.

20. *See* Chapter 2 in connection with erotic green and its use to reflect the baser attributes of selected individuals, for the first description of the Duchess most probably conveys something analogous: "Don Quixote looked out over a green meadow. . . . Drawing closer . . . and . . . coming nearer still he perceived among the company a fine lady seated upon a gleaming white palfrey or hackney caparisoned in green and with a silver sidesaddle. The lady was in green also. . . ."

21. Although the disenchantment is credited to Don Quixote in II, 41, all readers will recall that the Clavileño episode revolves primarily around the imagination of Sancho Panza, causing Don Quixote to whisper in his squire's ear at the conclusion of II, 41: "Sancho, if you want us to believe what you saw in Heaven, then you must believe me when I tell you what I saw in the Cave of Montesinos. I need say no more." Sancho's response to "La Trifaldi" in II, 40 serves to underscore his growing awareness of his existence as an individual: "Are [masters] to get all the fame for what they accomplish while we [squires] do all the work? . . . If the historians would only say 'Such and such a knight brought such and such an adventure to a successful conclusion, with the aid of So-and-So, his squire, without whom it would have been impossible. . . .'" Sancho knows how it is however: "But no, they simply write down, 'Don Paralipomenon of the Three Stars accomplished the adventure . . .' without so much as mentioning the squire, who was present all the time, just as if he didn't exist!" In this statement there is clear evidence of a nascent individualism, whose cry in the wilderness is put into relief by Cervantes when he does indeed give credit to the master: "The renowned knight, Don Quixote de la Mancha, merely by undertaking it, has finished and concluded the adventure. . . ."

22. The fact that Sancho invents a bizarre story for the Duchess does not negate my conclusion. He is having his fun and the deceived deceiver is deceiving once more. The Duchess may find it amusing; Sancho has the last laugh.

23. Leo Lowenthal, *Literature and the Image of Man* (Boston: Beacon Press, 1957), p. xiii.

24. This novel is not contained in either of the translations most often cited (those by Starkie and by Jones), nor is it included in the two-volume Spanish set edited by Rodríguez Marín. The translations are therefore my own and are based on the original as published in the cited edition by Valbuena Prat of Cervantes' complete works.

25. The variation of *que así se llamaba* which Cervantes actually uses here provides additional food for thought: *que así quieren que se llamase la hija* ("for that is what they would have her name be"). Although one may dismiss it as a pseudonym for a real personage, it hardly seems necessary for Cervantes to let us know this, if he indeed wanted to inject his own experiences into his artistic creations. I suggest that, given Cervantes' penchant for playing with names, he is toying with the reader and once again beckoning him to note the manner in which names are bestowed. The phrasing here forces us to compare this name with the greater playfulness in the announcement of Rodolfo's name: "for now, disguising his name out of respect, we shall call him Rodolfo."

26. The argument that the concision of this tale produces a concomitant quickening of the constituent elements does not negate the contrast: One sentence separated the presentation of the character from the revelation of his name in Rodolfo's case; seven sentences separate the same elements in Leocadia's case. What is more, Rodolfo's rapid introduction occurs *within* the points which separate Leocadia's presentation from her identification by name.

27. Ruth S. El Saffar, *Novel to Romance*, p. 129. I am at a loss to understand El Saffar's basis for concluding that "Rodolfo individualizes the girl, *gives her a name*" (p. 130; italics mine). That he individualizes her in the sense that she becomes a specific person whose particular beauty arouses his lust (as opposed to remaining in a generic category of young maidens) is readily acceptable, although there is some inconsistency since El Saffar views Rodolfo as an abstraction: "The type represented by Rodolfo emerges in Cervantes's idealistic stories as a familiar category to be used symbolically to introduce not the failures of a particular social class but an abstract force very much related to the creative process. In *La fuerza de la sangre* Rodolfo epitomizes all the tendencies outlined in other characters of this type" (p. 129). A subsequent elaboration that Rodolfo "created Leocadia fictionally by killing her socially [rape = dishonor]," because without him "there would be no story, no Leocadia, apart from the unnamed sixteen-year-old daughter" (p. 132), seems to me a kind of *post hoc, ergo propter hoc* reasoning. In fact,

166

Cervantes tells it the other way around: Rodolfo was going to pass on *but* it was Leocadia's great beauty that aroused in him the desire to seduce her. With respect to giving her a name, again it is Cervantes, and not an autonomous character who tells us what "they" would have her name be.

28. The blindfold in addition to the swoon and the darkness reinforce not only desolation and—at least temporarily—ignorance, but the imagery of sight and blindness, light and darkness, which pervades this tale. (We shall recall the Clavileño and Montesinos episodes in *Don Quixote*.) For analysis of this device in the exemplary tale, see Margarita Levisi, "La función de lo visual en *La fuerza de la sangre,*" *Hispanófila*, 49 (1973), 59-67. Levisi also has counted the frequency of the words for "look," "see," "eyes," "light" and "light of the eyes," and observes that the frequency in the other exemplary novels is minimal in comparison.

29. *Novel to Romance*, p. 114.

30. The Jones translation approaches Putnam's but does not go far enough: ". . . called for my way of life the Good." Smollet's impressionistic rendition cannot be considered seriously: ". . . surnamed the Good, on account of my life and conversation."

31. Although *costumbre* means "custom" or "habit," its use in the plural stresses behavior. The dictionary of the Royal Spanish Academy gives for the plural, "Sum of the qualities or tendencies and habits which make up the distinctive character of a nation or person" (*Conjunto de cualidades o inclinaciones y usos que forman el carácter distintivo de una nación o persona*). The *Diccionario de autoridades* stresses the moral aspect of the plural (*Moralmente se toma por inclinación y calidad que reside en algún sujeto: y así se dice, es persona de buenas o malas costumbres*). [The modernized orthography is mine.]

32. Gethin Hughes, "The Cave of Montesinos: Don Quixote's Interpretation and Dulcinea's Disenchantment," *Bulletin of Hispanic Studies*, 54 (1977), 107-13.

33. *Ibid.*, p. 107.

34. *Ibid.*, p. 109. (Emphasis in the original.)

35. René Girard, *Deceit, Desire, and the Novel: Self and Other in Literary Structure*, trans. Yvonne Freccero (Baltimore: The Johns Hopkins Univ. Press, 1976), p. 1.

36. My translations are taken from Walter Starkie's collection (New York: New American Library, 1963), but once again with variations of my own.

37. Starkie's rendition of *se desgarró* (literally to remove the anchor or bolt) as "played hooky" is misleading.

38. Starkie's accurate translation of "land's end" for Cervantes' use of the Latin *finibusterrae* helps us to focus on the point made by Cervantes in contrast to the comforts of home, or even simply to the concept of home as the beginning point rather than the *finibus* of the Latin expression. Rodríguez Marín, in his *Clásicos Castellanos* edition (I, 225), correctly explicates the expression as being used here in its meaning of *non plus ultra*, but points out that on other occasions (as in *Rinconete and Cortadillo*) it may mean the gallows. This added connotation also serves to reinforce the contrast with the seclusion of home.

39. *Novel to Romance*, p. 87.

40. *Ibid.*, p. 90.

41. *Ibid.*, p. 93.

42. *Ibid.*, p. 100.

Chapter 5

1. W. Hamilton Fyfe, ed. and trans., Aristotle, *Poetics*, Loeb Classical Library (Cambridge: Harvard Univ. Press, 1932), p. xvi.

2. *Ibid.*, p. xvii.

3. Oscar Mandel, *A Definition of Tragedy* (New York: New York Univ. Press, 1961), p. 47. Mandel's quotation is taken from H. Weisinger, *Tragedy and the Paradox of the Fortunate Fall* (East Lansing: Michigan State Univ. Press, 1953), p. 230.

4. Mandel, p. 47.

5. Wouk, p. 9.

6. Manuel Torre, "Cervantes, precursor del psicoanálisis," *El Nacional* (Mexico), 14 Sept. 1941; Mariano Górriz, "Cervantes psicólogo y psiquiatra," *Revista de la Universidad* [de Panamá], 27 (1947), 81-102; F. Sánchez Escribano, "Sobre un incidente posiblemente freudiano en el *Quijote* (I, 15)," *Anales Cervantinos*, 9 (1962), 261-62; Edward J. Schuster, "Schizophrenia and the Flight from Reality in Golden Age Spanish Literature," *Kentucky Foreign Language Quarterly*, 13 (1966), 103-11; "Datos sobre los síntomas de esquizofrenia experimental a base del 'hechizo' en *El Licenciado Vidriera* (1613)," *Folia Humanística*, 5 (1967), 927-38; Alan R. Messick, "Tomás Rodaja: A Clinical Case?" *RomN*, 11 (1970), 632-28; Nora I. Kirchner, *Don Quijote de la Mancha: A Study in Classical Paranoia*, unpubl. diss. (Illinois State Univ.).

7. *Spain and the Western Tradition*, vol. 4, p. 279.

8. Bruce W. Wardropper, "Cervantes' Theory of the Drama," p. 221, assures us that Cervantes "undoubtedly approached dramatic criticism, as did Torres Naharro, Juan de la Cueva, and Lope de Vega, from a well-assimilated background of the classical precepts." Forcione's work has confirmed this, although it is likely that Cervantes' acquaintance with the *Poetics* is through the Renaissance interpretations rather than by his reading of the original.

9. Thomas S. Szasz, "The Myth of Mental Illness," *The American Psychologist*, 15 (1960), 114. (Italics by Szasz.)

10. *Ibid.*

11. As Szasz makes clear (p. 117), his arguments do not "imply that the social and psychological occurrences also do not exist. Like the personal and social troubles which people had in the Middle Ages, they are real enough. It is the labels we give them that concerns us and, having labelled them, what we do about them."

12. Szasz, p. 114. (Italics by Szasz.)

13. Joseph Lyons, "Heidegger, Adler, and the Paradox of Fame," *Journal of Individual Psychology*, 17 (1961), 159.

14. Alfred Adler, *Understanding Human Nature* (Greenwich, Conn.: Fawcett, 1927), pp. 59-60.

15. Paul Rom and Heinz L. Ansbacher, "An Adlerian Case or a Character by Sartre?" *Journal of Individual Psychology*, 21 (1965), 36.

16. *Don Quixote's Profession*, p. 8.

17. *Ibid.*, p. 19.

18. *Spain and the Western Tradition*, IV, 120. The chapter on *desengaño* covers pp. 43-76; the portion on Cervantes is found on pp. 60-73. For those not familiar with the *Cortes de la Muerte* ("Parliament of Death"), Green's summary of the earliest manifestation of this theatrical genre in 1557 is the most concise: "It is a play in twenty-three scenes and has much in common with the *Dance of Death*, except that, in the *Cortes*, Death presents himself in a gentle and friendly light, and the representatives of the various social classes . . ., in making their complaints to Death, present their views exactly as Spanish subjects did when the king held his *cortes*" (p. 114).

19. *Ibid.*, p. 67. The reference is to II, 8 and the discussion concerning worldly and saintly fame. I would, however, disagree that this is the "first" inkling of such a change.

20. *See* note 26 to Chapter 2.

21. J. Huizinga, *The Waning of the Middle Ages* (Garden City: Doubleday Anchor, 1954), pp. 140-41.

22. Both Putnam and Cohen use the word "trick." Starkie is closer to the original, I think, when he renders it "stratagem." The Spanish is *industria*, which is closer to

cleverness, plot or stratagem than to trick. *See* Casalduero's commentary on these two points in *Sentido y forma del Quijote*, pp. 260-65.

23. The original refers to the game as *tablas*. Cohen also refers to backgammon, as does Starkie, who refers in a footnote to the game of *tablas* as "a very ancient game resembling our backgammon." Putnam's footnote is slightly more ambiguous: "The table games included chess, draughts (checkers), backgammon, and dice. . . . It would appear that the game that [Gaiferos] is playing is . . . backgammon."

24. *Antología de Alfonso X el Sabio*, ed. Antonio G. Solalinde, Colección Austral, 2nd ed. (Buenos Aires: Espasa-Calpe, 1943), p. 220. In an interesting article by John O'Neill, "Backgammon Comes Back," *Aramco World Magazine* 24 (1973), it is noted that legend has it that an Iranian king "once called in his wise men and ordered them to invent a game which, like life itself, depended on an uncertain balance of skill and chance. It should also, he said, sum up human existence in the world of finite time" (p. 30). Although O'Neill points out that in fact the game is even older, the nature of the game, "with its mix of skill and chance," is what stands out as its characteristic and thus its use by Cervantes at this juncture is of significance.

25. George Haley, "The Narrator in *Don Quijote*: Maese Pedro's Puppet Show," *MLN*, 80 (1965), 162-63.

26. "Structure and the Search for Truth in the *Quijote*," *HR*, 35 (1967), 309-26.

27. Quoted and translated by John Block Friedman, *Orpheus in the Middle Ages* (Cambridge: Harvard Univ. Press, 1970), p. 107.

28. *Ibid.*, pp. 142-43. It is interesting to note a parallel between Orpheus and Don Quixote concerning women, a parallel which is strengthened by Don Quixote's vow after his treatment by Dulcinea in the Cave. Friedman (pp. 122-23) quotes Giovanni del Virgilio's explanation (c. 1325) of Ovid's *Metamorphoses* to the effect that the devil killed Eurydice "because the devil drew her from the good path." (Montesinos explains that Dulcinea, along with the others, is held enchanted in the Cave by Merlin, son of the devil.) Giovanni goes on to say that "Orpheus renounced Hell, that is, temptation, and reconciling himself to God began to spurn women, giving his soul instead to God, and began . . . to act in a manly way, on which account he was dead to the world. . . ."

29. Robert C. Elliott, *The Shape of Utopia: Studies in a Literary Genre* (Chicago: Univ. of Chicago Press, 1970), p. x. The Shakespeare lines come from his Sonnet 94.

30. I owe the phrase "reality of illusion" to Anthony Zahareas, who used it to describe some other aspects of Cervantes' art in a seminar at the 1975 MLA convention in San Francisco. Cf. the similar concept expressed by Fielding in the preface to his *Voyage to Lisbon*: ". . . the great, original poets are not 'so properly said to turn reality into fiction, as fiction into reality.'" (Cited by Maurice Johnson, *Fielding's Art of Fiction* (Philadelphia: Univ. of Pennsylvania Press, 1961), p. 14.

31. Edward H. Friedman, "Dramatic Structure in Cervantes and Lope: The Two 'Pedro de Urdemalas' Plays," *Hispania*, 60 (1977), 486-87.

32. Salvador de Madariaga, *Don Quixote: An Introductory Essay in Psychology*, rev. ed. (London: Oxford Univ. Press, 1961), p. 83. (Italics mine.)

33. M. Esther Harding, *The "I" and the "Not-I,"* (Princeton: Princeton Univ. Press, 1973), p. 171.

34. *Ibid.*, pp. 172-73.

35. Cervantes further toys with the multiplicity by referring to Sansón as the "Knight of the Wood" and the "Knight of the Forest."

36. Manuel Durán, *La ambigüedad en el Quijote* (Xalapa: Universidad Veracruzana, 1960), pp. 224-25.

37. It is important to note that only *after* having observed the action does he write it down. It is not a literary document ("false" fiction) but a true history of the scene he overheard.

38. *Spain and the Western Tradition*, III, 427-28. In another study, Green views Graduate Glass as a "sort of Don Quijote in reverse," because he seeks his fame in letters and ends up with a career in arms. This is of course accurate, and I agree as well that the central and most important theme of this novel (as well as of *Don Quixote* and countless other works of many authors and many ages) is the "nature of the world and of man." But Green's contention that the story shows that society will not let a man fulfill himself and that we therefore have a "semi-tragic ending" is not borne out by my own analysis as my text shows. What Thomas ends up doing may very well be the antithesis of what he had earlier sought, and this challenge is to me what constitutes the maturation and individuation process. Who is to say that finding one's future in something other than one's adolescent aspirations is even semi-tragic? A truly pessimistic view would allow the story to leave Thomas in his glass shell, to abandon him without the benefits of his experiential learning, whose negative aspects (like the Montesinos grotesqueness) enabled him to find the part best suited for his individual capabilities (and which does not rule out a further reversal at a subsequent stage; witness Cervantes' own change from heroism at Lepanto to immortality in the world of letters). *See* Otis H. Green, "*El Licenciado Vidriera*: Its Relation to the *Viaje del Parnaso* and the *Examen de ingenios* of Huarte," in *Linguistic and Literary Studies in Honor of Helmut A. Hatzfeld*, ed. Alessandro S. Crisafulli (Washington: Catholic Univ. of America Press, 1964), pp. 213-20.

39. Curtius, *European Literature and the Latin Middle Ages*, p. 141.

40. It may be of interest to note another twentieth-century dramatic performance, one presented at the University of Texas recently under the direction of Paul C. Smith. An oral presentation of *Don Quixote*, with roles primarily portrayed by human actors, did nevertheless relegate two episodes to puppets: one, the puppets of Master Pedro (for obvious reasons); the other, the Cave of Montesinos. Although the underlying reason was the attempt to represent various levels of reality, the choice of this particular episode to be an adventure of a theatrical sort suggests a reading not far removed from the interpretation I have presented in this chapter.

170

Bibliography

Adler, Alfred. *Understanding Human Nature.* Greenwich, Conn.: Fawcett, 1927.

Allen, Don Cameron. "Symbolic Color in the Literature of the English Renaissance." *Philological Quarterly,* 15 (1936), 81-92.

Amezúa, Agustín G. *Cervantes: Creador de la novela corta española.* 2 vols. Madrid: C.S.I.C., 1946-48.

Apuleius. *The Golden Ass.* Translated by Robert Graves. New York: Farrar, Straus & Giroux, 1951.

Aristotle. *The Nichomachean Ethics.* Translated by H. Rackham. Loeb Classical Library. Cambridge: Harvard Univ. Press, 1934.

————. *Poetics.* Translated by W. Hamilton Fyfe. Loeb Classical Library. Cambridge: Harvard Univ. Press, 1973.

————. *Politics.* Translated by Benjamin Jowett. Modern Library. New York: Random House, 1943.

Auerbach, Erich. *Mimesis: The Representation of Reality in Western Literature.* Translated by W. R. Trask. Princeton: Princeton Univ. Press, 1968.

Avalle-Arce, Juan Bautista. *Deslindes cervantinos.* Madrid: Edhigar, 1961.

Ayer, A[lfred] J. *The Central Questions of Philosophy.* New York: Holt, Rinehart & Winston, 1974.

Barzun, Jacques. *The Energies of Art.* Vintage Books. New York: Random House, 1962.

Bell, Aubrey F. G. *Cervantes*. Collier Books. New York: Crowell-Collier, 1961.

Borges, Jorge Luis. *Discusión*. Buenos Aires: Emecé Editores, 1957.

_____. *Other Inquisitions*. Translated by Ruth L. C. Simms. Austin: Univ. of Texas Press, 1964.

Bowers, Fredson. *Elizabethan Revenge Tragedy: 1587-1642*. Princeton: Princeton Univ. Press, 1966.

Bradner, Leicester. "From Petrarch to Shakespeare." In *The Renaissance*, pp. 97-119. New York: Harper & Row, 1962.

Busi, Frederick A. "'Waiting for Godot': A Modern 'Don Quixote'?" *Hispania*, 57 (1974), 876-85.

Campbell, Joseph. *The Hero With a Thousand Faces*. Second edition. Bollingen Series, 17. Princeton: Princeton Univ. Press, 1968.

Casalduero, Joaquín. *Sentido y forma del Quijote*. Madrid: Insula, 1949.

_____. *Sentido y forma de las Novelas Ejemplares*. Madrid: Gredos, 1962.

Cassirer, Ernst. *The Individual and the Cosmos in Renaissance Philosophy*. Translated by Mario Domandi. Philadelphia: Univ. of Pennsylvania Press, 1972.

Castro, Américo. *Hacia Cervantes*. Madrid: Taurus, 1957.

_____. *El pensamiento de Cervantes*. Revised edition. Barcelona: Editorial Noguer, 1972.

Cervantes Saavedra, Miguel de. *Obras completas*. Edited by Angel Valbuena Prat. Madrid: Aguilar, 1965.

_____. *El ingenioso hidalgo Don Quijote de la Mancha*. Edited by Francisco Rodríguez Marín. 8 vols. Clásicos Castellanso. Madrid: Espasa Calpe, 1911-13.

_____. *El ingenioso hidalgo Don Quijote de la Mancha*. Edited by Francisco Rodríguez Marín. 10 vols. Madrid: Ediciones Atlas, 1947-49.

————. *Novelas ejemplares.* Edited by Francisco Rodríguez Marín. 2 vols. Clásicos Castellanos. Madrid: Espasa-Calpe, 1915-17.

————. *El casamiento engañoso y El coloquio de los perros.* Edited by Agustín G. de Amezúa. Madrid: Bailly-Balliere, 1912.

————. *La Galatea.* Edited by Juan Bautista Avalle-Arce. 2 vols. Clásicos Castellanos. Madrid: Espasa-Calpe, 1961.

————. *Los trabajos de Persiles y Sigismunda.* Edited by Juan Bautista Avalle-Arce. Madrid: Castalia, 1969.

————. *The Ingenious Gentleman Don Quixote de la Mancha.* Translated by Samuel Putnam. 2 vols. New York: Viking Press, 1949.

————. *The Adventures of Don Quixote.* Translated by J. M. Cohen. Harmondsworth: Penguin, 1950.

————. *Don Quixote of La Mancha.* Translated by Walter Starkie. New York: New American Library, 1964.

————. *The Deceitful Marriage and Other Exemplary Novels.* Translated by Walter Starkie. New York: New American Library, 1963.

————. *Exemplary Stories.* Translated by C. A. Jones. Harmondsworth: Penguin, 1972.

Chamberlin, Vernon A. "Symbolic Green: A Time-Honored Characterizing Device in Spanish Literature." *Hispania,* 51 (1968), 29-37.

————. and Weiner, Jack. "Color Symbolism: A Key to a Possible New Interpretation of Cervantes' 'Caballero del Verde Gabán.'" *Romance Notes,* 10 (1969), 342-47.

Chambers, Leland H. "Structure and the Search for Truth in the *Quijote*: Notes Toward a Comprehensive View." *Hispanic Review,* 35 (1967), 309-26.

————. "Irony in the Final Chapter of the *Quijote*." *Romanic Review,* 61 (1970), 14-22.

Church, Margaret. *Don Quixote: The Knight of La Mancha.* New York: New York University Press, 1971.

Cirlot, J. E. *A Dictionary of Symbols*. Translated from the Spanish by Jack Sage. New York: Philosophical Library, 1962.

Cullen, Patrick. "Imitation and Metamorphosis: The Golden-Age Eclogue in Spenser, Milton, and Marvell." *PMLA*, 84 (1969), 1559-70.

Curtius, Ernst Robert. *European Literature and the Latin Middle Ages*. Translated by Willard R. Trask. Bollingen Series, 36. Princeton: Princeton Univ. Press, 1973.

Dowling, John C. "A Title of Distinction." *Hispania*, 41 (1958), 449-56.

Durán, Manuel. *La ambigüedad en el Quijote*. Xalapa: Universidad Veracruzana, 1960.

Elliott, Robert C. *The Shape of Utopia: Studies in a Literary Genre*. Chicago: Univ. of Chicago Press, 1970.

El Saffar, Ruth. "The Function of the Fictional Narrator in *Don Quijote*." *MLN*, 83 (1968), 164-77.

—————. *Novel to Romance: A Study of Cervantes's "Novelas Ejemplares."* Baltimore: Johns Hopkins Univ. Press, 1974.

Evett, David. "'Paradice's Only Map': The *Topos* of the *Locus Amoenus* and the Structure of Marvell's *Upon Appleton House*." *PMLA*, 85 (1970), 504-13.

Fergusson, Francis. Introduction to Aristotle's *Poetics*. New York: Hill and Wang, 1961.

Forcione, Alban K. *Cervantes, Aristotle, and the "Persiles."* Princeton: Princeton Univ. Press, 1970.

—————. *Cervantes' Christian Romance: A Study of "Persiles y Sigismunda."* Princeton: Princeton Univ. Press, 1972.

Fraser, Russell. *The Dark Ages and the Age of Gold*. Princeton: Princeton Univ. Press, 1973.

Friedman, Edward H. "Dramatic Structure in Cervantes and Lope: The Two 'Pedro de Urdemalas' Plays." *Hispania*, 60 (1977), 486-97.

Friedman, John Block. *Orpheus in the Middle Ages*. Cambridge: Harvard Univ. Press, 1970.

Frye, Northrop. *Anatomy of Criticism.* Princeton: Princeton Univ. Press, 1971.

Gilder, George. *Naked Nomads.* New York: Quadrangle, 1974.

Gilman, Stephen. "The Death of Lazarillo de Tormes." *PMLA,* 81 (1966), 149-66.

Green, Otis H. "El *ingenioso* hidalgo." *Hispanic Review,* 25 (1957), 175-93.

————. "Realidad, voluntad y gracia en Cervantes." *Ibérida: Revista de filología,* 3 (1961), 113-28.

————. *Spain and the Western Tradition: The Castilian Mind in Literature from "El Cid" to Calderón.* 4 vols. Madison: Univ. of Wisconsin Press, 1963-66.

————. "*El Licenciado Vidriera*: Its Relation to the *Viaje del Parnaso* and the *Examen de Ingenios* of Huarte." In *Linguistic and Literary Studies in Honor of Helmut A. Hatzfeld,* edited by A. S. Crisafulli, pp. 213-20. Washington, D.C.: Catholic Univ. of America Press, 1964.

————. "*Imaginative Authority in Spanish Literature.*" *PMLA,* 84 (1969), 209-16.

Groult, Pierre. "Quijote, [¿] nombre significativo?" *Les Lettres Romanes,* 23 (1969), 172-74.

Haley, George. "The Narrator in *Don Quijote*: Maese Pedro's Puppet Show." *MLN,* 80 (1965), 145-65.

Harding, M. Esther. *The "I" and the "Not-I."* Bollingen Series, 79. Princeton: Princeton Univ. Press, 1973.

Heninger, S. K. Jr. "The Renaissance Perversion of Pastoral." *Journal of the History of Ideas,* 22 (1961), 254-61.

Hoffman, E. Lewis. "Cloth and Clothing in the *Quijote*." *Kentucky Foreign Language Quarterly,* 10 (1963), 82-98.

Huizinga, J. *The Waning of the Middle Ages.* Garden City: Doubleday Anchor, 1954.

Irwin, Eleanor. *Colour Terms in Greek Poetry.* Toronto: Hakkert, 1974.

Johnson, Carroll B. "A Second Look at Dulcinea's Ass." *Hispanic Review*, 43 (1975), 191-98.

Kaiser, Walter. *Praisers of Folly*. Cambridge: Harvard Univ. Press, 1963.

Karl, Frederick R. "Don Quixote as Archetypal Artist and *Don Quixote* as Archetypal Novel." In *The Adversary Literature*, pp. 55-67. New York: Farrar, Straus & Giroux, 1974.

Kenyon, Herbert A. "Color Symbolism in Early Spanish Ballads." *Romanic Review*, 6 (1915), 327-40.

Kline, Nathan S. "Feelin' Mighty Low." The *New York Times*, 10 Jan. 1975, p. 35.

Levin, Harry. "The Example of Cervantes." In *Contexts of Criticism*, pp. 79-96. Cambridge: Harvard Univ. Press, 1957.

————. "The Quixotic Principle: Cervantes and Other Novelists." In *The Interpretation of Narrative: Theory and Practice*, pp. 45-66, edited by M. W. Bloomfield. Cambridge: Harvard Univ. Press, 1970.

————. *The Myth of the Golden Age in the Renaissance*. New York: Oxford Univ. Press, 1972.

Levisi, Margarita. "La función de lo visual en *La fuerza de la sangre*." *Hispanófila*, 49 (1973), 59-67.

Lowenthal, Leo. *Literature and the Image of Man*. Boston: Beacon Press, 1957.

Lukács, Georg. *The Theory of the Novel*. Cambridge: The MIT Press, 1971.

Lyons, Joseph. "Heidegger, Adler, and the Paradox of Fame." *Journal of Individual Psychology*, 17 (1961), 149-61.

Madariaga, Salvador de. *Don Quixote: An Introductory Essay in Psychology*. London: Oxford Univ. Press, 1961.

Mancing, Howard. "The Deceptiveness of *Lazarillo de Tormes*." *PMLA*, 90 (1975), 426-32.

————. "*Dulcinea's Ass: A Note on Don Quijote*, Part II, Chapter 10." *Hispanic Review*, 40 (1972), 73-77.

BIBLIOGRAPHY

Mandel, Oscar. *A Definition of Tragedy*. New York: New York Univ. Press, 1961.

Menéndez Pidal, Ramón. *Flor nueva de romances viejos*. Madrid: Espasa-Calpe, 1955.

Moustakas, Clark E. *Loneliness and Love*. Englewood Cliffs: Prentice-Hall, 1972.

Neumann, Erich. *The Origins and History of Consciousness*. Translated by R. F. C. Hull. Bollingen Series, 42. Princeton: Princeton Univ. Press, 1970.

Nozick, Robert. *Anarchy, State, and Utopia*. New York: Basic Books, 1974.

Olivera, Otto. "Don Quijote, el caballero de la angustia." *Hispania*, 44 (1961), 441-44.

Ortega y Gasset, José. *Meditaciones del Quijote*. Madrid: Revista de Occidente, 1966.

———. *The Modern Theme*. Translated by James Cleugh. New York: Harper & Brothers, 1961.

Osuna, Rafael. "¿Dos finales en un capítulo (II, 24) del Quijote?" *Romance Notes*, 13 (1971), 318-21.

Outumuro, María de las Mercedes. "Sentido y perspectiva del personaje autónomo." *Cuadernos Hispano-Americanos*, 72 (1967), 158-77.

Ovid. *The Art of Love*. Translated by Rolfe Humphries. Bloomington: Indiana Univ. Press, 1957.

Palmer, Donald D. "Unamuno, Freud and the Case of Alonso Quijano." *Hispania*, 54 (1971), 243-49.

Parkes, Henry Bamford. *The Divine Order: Western Culture in the Middle Ages and the Renaissance*. New York: Alfred A. Knopf, 1969.

Partridge, Eric. *Shakespeare's Bawdy*. Revised edition. New York: E. P. Dutton, 1969.

Perry, T. Anthony. "Ideal Love and Human Reality in Montemayor's *La Diana*." *PMLA*, 84 (1969), 227-34.

177

Ponseti, Helena Percas de. *Cervantes y su concepto del arte: Estudio crítico de algunos aspectos y episodios del "Quijote."* 2 vols. Madrid: Gredos, 1975.

Predmore, Michael P. "Madariaga's Debt to Unamuno's 'Vida de don Quijote y Sancho.'" *Hispania*, 47 (1964), 288-94.

Predmore, Richard L. *The World of Don Quixote.* Cambridge: Harvard Univ. Press, 1967.

————. *Cervantes.* New York: Dodd, Mead, 1973.

Ramírez, Alejandro. "The Concept of Ignorance in *Don Quixote.*" *Philological Quarterly*, 45 (1966), 474-79.

Rebhorn, Wayne A. "The Metamorphoses of Moria: Structure and Meaning in *The Praise of Folly.*" *PMLA*, 89 (1974), 463-76.

Redondo, Agustín. "Estructura y significado del episodio de la Insula Barataria en el *Don Quijote* de Cervantes." Sixth *Congreso* of the Asociación Internacional de Hispanistas, Toronto. 26 Aug. 1977.

Riley, E[dward] C. *Cervantes's Theory of the Novel.* Oxford: Clarendon Press, 1962.

————. "Simbolismo conflictivo en *Don Quijote*, II, cap. 73." Sixth *Congreso* of the Asociación Internacional de Hispanistas, Toronto. 26 Aug. 1977.

Riquer, Martín de. *Aproximación al Quijote.* Barcelona: Editorial Teide, 1967.

Rivers, Elias L. "Lope and Cervantes Once More." *Kentucky Romance Quarterly*, 14 (1967), 112-19.

Rom, Paul, and Ansbacher, Heinz L. "An Adlerian Case or a Character by Sartre?" *Journal of Individual Psychology*, 21 (1965), 35-37.

Rosenblat, Angel. *La lengua del "Quijote."* Madrid: Gredos, 1971.

Said, Edward W. *Beginnings: Intention and Method.* New York: Basic Books, 1975.

Sallust [Gaius Sallustius Crispus]. Translated by J. C. Rolfe. Loeb Classical Library. Cambridge: Harvard Univ. Press, 1931.

BIBLIOGRAPHY

Sánchez Rivero, Angel. "Las ventas del 'Quijote.'" In *El concepto contemporáneo de España*, edited by Angel del Río and M. J. Benardete, pp. 662-72. Buenos Aires: Editorial Losada, 1946.

Sieber, Harry. "Literary Time in the 'Cueva de Montesinos.'" *MLN*, 86 (1971), 268-78.

Silverman, Joseph H. "The Scrutiny of Literature and Life in *Don Quixote*." MLA Convention, San Francisco. 27 Dec. 1975.

Slater, Philip E. *The Pursuit of Loneliness*. Boston: Beacon Press, 1971.

Southall, Raymond. "The Novel and the Isolated Individual." In *Literature, the Individual and Society*, pp. 11-17. London: Lawrence & Wishart, 1977.

Spencer, Theodore. *Shakespeare and the Nature of Man*. Second edition. Collier Books. New York: Macmillan, 1966.

Spitzer, Leo. "Linguistic Perspectivism in the *Don Quijote*." In *Linguistics and Literary History: Essays in Stylistics*, pp. 41-85. Princeton: Princeton Univ. Press, 1967.

Swart, K. W. "'Individualism' in the Mid-Nineteenth Century (1826-1860)." *Journal of the History of Ideas*, 23 (1962), 77-90.

Szasz, Thomas S. "The Myth of Mental Illness." *The American Psychologist*, 15 (1960), 113-18.

Tocqueville, Alexis de. *Democracy in America*. Translated by George Lawrence. Edited by J. P. Mayer. Anchor Books. Garden City: Doubleday, 1969.

Unamuno, Miguel de. *Our Lord Don Quixote*. Translated by Anthony Kerrigan. Bollingen Series, 84. Princeton: Princeton Univ. Press, 1967.

Van Doren, Mark. *Don Quixote's Profession*. New York: Columbia Univ. Press, 1958.

Wardropper, Bruce W. "Cervantes' Theory of the Drama." *Modern Philology*, 52 (1955), 217-21.

—————. "*Don Quixote*: Story or History?" *Modern Philology*, 63 (1965), 1-11.

————. "The Strange Case of Lázaro Gonzales Pérez." MLN, 92 (1977), 202-12.

Watson, Curtis Brown. Shakespeare and the Renaissance Concept of Honor. Princeton: Princeton Univ. Press, 1960.

Weiger, John G. "'La superchería está descubierta': Don Quijote and Ginés de Pasamonte." Philological Quarterly, forthcoming.

————. "Sublime Sublimation in Don Quijote." Hispanófila, forthcoming.

Weiss, Robert S. Loneliness: The Experience of Emotional and Social Isolation. Cambridge: The MIT Press, 1973.

Wouk, Herman. "You, Me, and the Novel." Saturday Review / World, 29 June 1974, pp. 8-13.

Zárate, Armando. "La poesía y el ojo en 'La Celestina.'" Cuadernos Americanos, 164 (1969), 119-36.

Ziomek, Henryk. "Parallel Ingredients in Don Quixote and Dom Casmurro." Revista de Estudios Hispánicos, 2 (1968), 229-40.

INDEX